Cook & Celebrate

FOOD *and the* **AMERICAN** *South*

Cook & Celebrate

A Collection of Southern Holiday &
Party Culinary Traditions

Johnathon Scott Barrett

MERCER UNIVERSITY PRESS
MACON, GEORGIA

MUP/ H1031

© 2022 by Mercer University Press
Published by Mercer University Press
1501 Mercer University Drive
Macon, Georgia 31207

26 25 24 23 22   5 4 3 2 1

Books published by Mercer University Press are printed on acid-free paper that
meets the requirements of the American National Standard for Information
Sciences—Permanence of Paper for Printed Library Materials.

Printed and bound in the United States.

This book is set in Adobe Garamond Pro.

Cover/jacket design by Burt&Burt.

ISBN   978-0-88146-844-1
Cataloging-in-Publication Data is available from the Library of Congress

Contents

To Tom, in appreciation for thirty-plus years of joyful holidays—and more parties than we can count. Cheers to many, many more!

JSB and Cassandra King, Highlands, North Carolina, 2015

Foreword

One thing most Southern cooks will tell you: we can spot an authentic Southern recipe from a mile off. If you like your cornbread sweet enough to serve for dessert, fine. But try bringing super-sweet cornbread to a church supper in the deep South and see what happens, especially if some helpful soul puts the pan near the turnip greens. Check out the trash can afterward, and you're likely to see a lot of pretty, golden-brown cornbread wedges with one bite missing. The consensus of the good church folks is bound to be that if you put that much sugar in your cornbread, you're not from around here.

As soon as I picked up Johnathon's previous cookbooks, *Rise and Shine!* and *Cook & Tell*, I knew that he was the real deal: a seventh-generation Georgian who doesn't know how to separate a story from the food that goes with it. In the South, a recipe without a story is as rare as a summer supper without iced tea. (And yes, I'm putting on airs, calling it *iced* tea instead of what it's called around here, *ice* tea.) Such things surely exist, but I doubt you'll find a single dish on Johnathon's table that doesn't have a story with it. When Johnathon visited the Conroy household for the first time, it goes without saying that he brought us a treat from his kitchen. Handing me a jar of fig preserves—big fat whole figs in a thick brown syrup—he told me he'd grown up knowing how to make them. I asked him if they had a fig tree in the backyard, and we exchanged stories about fighting off the yellow jackets to get to the good ones. I'm not sure you can truly appreciate a fig unless you've dodged a yellow jacket to get to it.

Sometimes the food's just not the same without the story that goes with it. It's sort of like eating field peas without thick slices of tomatoes, still sun-warmed from the vine. You can, but it's not as good. When a Southerner shares a recipe with me, I want to hear the story just as bad as I want to try the recipe. Take Johnathon's Texas caviar recipe, for instance. I can't wait to make it now that I know what the secret ingredient is and where it came from. Who knew said secret ingredient could be traced back to a company in Georgia? And that the same company also makes pear relish, the secret ingredient of my mama's famed chicken salad? Mama made her own relish from the rock-hard pears we grew, but I'm not about to go to that much trouble. Thanks to Johnathon, and the story behind the Texas caviar, I don't have to.

That's the way it is in the South. A recipe leads to a story, which leads to another story and another recipe. Open up the pages of *Cook & Celebrate!* and settle in for a good read and a gracious plenty of mouth-watering recipes. But don't let yourself get too comfortable. You're not going to turn too many pages before you start craving something you see. If you'll excuse me, I need to run to the Piggly Wiggly to get a jar of Braswell's Red Pepper Relish. I'll make sure to get in Yolanda's checkout line so I can tell her about Texas Caviar, and how I read about it in my friend Johnathon's new cookbook. Stories and recipes, I'll tell her. It's the way we cook in the South.

—Cassandra King, author of
Tell Me a Story:
My Life with Pat Conroy

Preface

Cook & Celebrate has been a natural progression starting with *Rise and Shine!* which recounted my life's journey through food. With that book came an extensive speaking tour across the South. Along the way hundreds of folks shared with me their own delicious tales and favored recipes—from those stories emerged the food-filled anthology *Cook & Tell*. On a second promotional junket, time and again it became evident that much of the food people claimed as personal favorites were the dishes served at holidays. It's true that folks in the South need no reason—at all—to have a party. We will throw a shindig at the drop of a hat. Even small get-togethers and "gatherins" were described with spirited recollections of comestibles from yesteryear. This love of festivals and feast-day foods, along with the embracement of appetizing camaraderie, resulted in the pages of *Cook & Celebrate.*

That said, while this book was easy to write in certain terms, it was challenging in others.

The ease came about from my celebration of life through food. How I love a glass (or two) of bourbon, an inspired meal, and great friends—and the three together make for one happy fellow. I can sit and talk, or write, about hundreds, if not thousands, of personal stories with related recipes that have been a special part of this life for almost six decades: fruitcakes and brightly decorated cedar trees, homemade peach ice cream and fireworks, pimento cheese sandwiches eaten on a creek bank, the tickle of champagne bubbles and a kiss at New Year's…the list is endless.

With that access to an extensive storyline inventory came the burden of deciding what to include—and what to omit. The task of outlining *Cook & Celebrate* having started, it quickly became evident that all of what might be covered could not possibly fit into one book; heck, there could be an entire volume on the quintessential Southern foods of Christmas right by itself. So, apologies in advance if a dish (or two or three!) that you firmly believe should have been here in print was not among the mix.

Cook & Celebrate! is divided into two sections. The first includes treasured food and related narratives from our most prominent holidays, such as New Year's, Independence Day, and Christmas. The second portion compiles stories and recipes from a variety of delectable fetes as well as dining-centric customs, like Mary Martha Greene's annual Twelfth Night soiree, where Christmas is extended with a Mardi Gras flair, and another chapter that demonstrates the popularity, and sometimes serious business, of supper clubs.

Thanks for taking the time to read through this collection of culinary reminiscences. May these trips down memory lane help you recall, with love and fondness, those holidays and get-togethers through the years that have made your life special. Cheers to each of you—and best wishes for happy cooking!

Appreciatively yours,
JSB

Cook & Celebrate

Part 1

Holidays

Chapter 1

New Year's Eve and New Year's Day

The most popular and well-recognized tune for New Year's Eve and into New Year's Day would be Guy Lombardo's "Auld Lang Syne," which he and his Royal Canadian Orchestra expertly performed for the world over the course of fifty years. I remember it playing first over the radio when I was a child and then on the big wooden television set, which in itself was a piece of furniture, in our living room. The song, inspired by the national poet of Scotland, Robert Burns, is about old friends who come together for a drink, recall their adventures, and share warm recollections. The last stanza is my favorite:

> And there's a hand my trusty friend,
> And give me a hand o' thine,
> And we'll take a right good-will draught,
> For auld lang syne.

I can't think of a better way to begin the first chapter of this book than with those words from the Bard of Ayrshire. It is my aim with *Cook & Celebrate!* to share the stories, camaraderie, and culinary memories of folks across the South—particularly as they relate to our holidays and celebrations so dear to us. The poem encapsulates all I hope to bring to you in these pages.

New Year's Eve celebrations across our region of the country vary from big cities to small towns; for many it means a casual quiet night at home, resting up from the Christmas holidays. As I've gotten older, I choose that option more often, sometimes spending the evening with a small group of friends, or simply with Tom and our dog, Max, by the fire with a good drink and a simple supper. My favorite is a late-night breakfast with farm-fresh sausage, biscuits with gravy and homemade jelly,

Carey Pickard standing, Christopher Howard seated to his left,
in their historic home with friends, New Year's Eve celebration

My mother's engagement photo, 1949

stone-ground grits, and a fat, cheesy omelet. In prior years I would host larger, more formal gatherings, such as when we rang in the millennium on December 31, 1999. There were ten guests for our black-tie "dîner avec des intimes" as the menu card read, and the multi-course meal included such items as lump crab and shrimp remoulade and a classic bœuf Bourguignon.

Two young fellows who are famous these days for their parties and formal festivities—and who know how to ring in New Year right—are Carey Pickard and Christopher Howard of Macon, Georgia. The husband-and-husband team, both business executives, met through their involvement in Historic Macon Foundation and share a love of architecture, preservation, and neighborhood revitalization. This passion for history is shown in their choice of a home, a stellar example of adaptive re-use. The solidly built brick structure, located downtown, was built in the mid-nineteenth century as the waterworks for the city. It was used later as an antique shop, and my friends purchased it in 2001 to repurpose as their home. The interior is stylishly eclectic and an elegant mix, pairing exposed, painted brick walls and large beamed ceilings with crystal chandeliers, original works of art, and oriental carpets. Candelabras and sconces abound and provide incredible lighting in each room; the entire house photographs beautifully and has been the setting for dozens and dozens of lauded gatherings. I asked them about the secrets of their success in hosting an event and found that we share many of the same thoughts and practices. One is to have a mixture of guests—folks that might not know one another but have similar interests. I find that type of group leads to more interesting conversations, as guests around the table get to know one another, and many times learn just how fractional their degrees of separation are. Too, like Tom and myself, Christopher and Carey seat spouses separately during dinner, which keeps the table fully engaged in banter as opposed to a couple deciding whose turn it is for the school carpool on Monday. The two gentlemen also make certain to have everything planned and in place in advance—as the French say *mise en place*—so that they have time to mix and mingle with their guests. A fully stocked bar is also a standard offering in their home.

For this chapter, Christopher and Carey have graciously provided a stellar menu for one of their New Year's Eve soirees. Their formal dinners are usually five courses, which you'll see here, with a soup, salad, fish course, beef or fowl course, and dessert. The recipes they provided come from *Macon Sets a Fine Table*, a hard-to-find book that's now out of print. Two of the recipes in this chapter come from my collections, and another from another "culinary" couple.

During cocktail time at the Howard-Pickard home, the famed cheese wafers of the late Katherine Willingham Carmichael Oliver are offered. According to Carey, Kitty Oliver was *the* leading lady of Historic Preservation for much of his life. She had been the director of the Middle Georgia Historical Society and was known for her devotion to historic Rose Hill Cemetery and Fort Hawkins, along with the stewardship of her own house, the Raines-Carmichael House, one of Macon's two National Historic Landmarks. Carey shared that he and Chris spent many happy times listening to her stories about life in Macon and enjoyed countless libations on her magnificent porch and think of her often with fondness.

KITTY OLIVER'S CHEESE WAFERS

Ingredients
16 ounces sharp New York cheddar cheese, hand grated, at room temperature
16 tablespoons butter, at room temperature
3 cups all-purpose flour, sifted
1 teaspoon salt
¼ teaspoon cayenne pepper

Directions
1. Preheat oven to 325 degrees.
2. In a large bowl, mix the cheese and butter together; add the sifted flour, salt, and cayenne pepper; stir well to mix. You will have a very stiff dough.
3. Fill a cookie press with the dough and line 3 cookie sheets with waxed paper. Using the press, make 1-inch rounds of the dough on the cookie sheets. Cook for approximately 15 minutes—until slightly brown. Allow to cool completely before serving. May be stored in an airtight container for 1 week.
Makes approximately three dozen wafers

Our Macon hosts like to start their New Year's Eve dinner with oyster stew, which is a tradition of mine as well. You'll read a good bit about oysters and other seafood in this edition, as the delicious bounty of the sea off our shores is a favorite food for celebrations.

The recipe is from my mom, Joyce Nipper Barrett. If you have read my other two cookbooks, you know her from those writings. Mom learned how to cook during the Great Depression and into the days of World War II, working beside her mother (who was called "Ninnie" by her grandchildren) in the family home in the tiny hamlet of Clinchfield, Georgia, located about halfway between Perry and Hawkinsville. The fare prepared in the Nipper kitchen was produce and livestock grown on the family place, and my mom continued a tradition of using farm-to-table food up until she cooked her last meal. My sister's classmates claimed that Mrs. Barrett was the prettiest of all the mothers; it was often remarked that she looked like the movie actress Joan Bennett. She was also a sport of a lady, and although she had a huge heart, she did not suffer fools well, not at all. She had a hearty laugh and showed her love through cooking— she so enjoyed preparing favorite dishes for family and friends. How I miss her and my dad, every single day.

Mama's oyster stew is really—and I'm not exaggerating—excellent, and one in which you can very much taste the brine of the sea. Just make sure to follow the directions on the cooking time, as once you overcook an oyster, well, there's no reparation.

MAMA'S OYSTER STEW

Ingredients
8 tablespoons butter, divided
¼ cup celery, diced
¼ cup plus 1 tablespoon (5 tablespoons) green onion, diced, white parts only
1 quart oysters, drained, liquid reserved
1 quart whole milk
2 cups heavy cream
¼ teaspoon kosher or sea salt (or to taste)
¼ teaspoon white or black pepper
½ teaspoon Texas Pete hot sauce
Paprika and fresh, minced parsley for garnish

Directions
1. In a large pot, melt 4 tablespoons of butter over medium heat.
2. Add the celery and cook for 1 to 2 minutes, stirring constantly.
3. Stir in the onions and cook another 2 minutes or so, until the celery and onions are soft.
4. Add the remaining butter and pour in 1½ cups of the reserved oyster juice. Stir to mix.
5. Continuing on medium heat, stir in the milk and cream. Allow the liquid and vegetables to come to a slight simmer. Reduce the heat to low. Allow the stew base to cook for 12 to 15 minutes—the tastes will marry, and the liquid thicken. Stir often.
6. Taste the stew at this point to see how much salt it needs. Because different oysters and their juices are brinier than others, you may not need ¼ teaspoon of salt, or you may need more. Adjust to your taste.
7. Add the black or white pepper and the Texas Pete. Stir.
8. Finally, add in the oysters and stir. The oysters will cook quickly; smaller varieties will be done in 2 minutes or so; larger ones will take up to 4 minutes. The oysters are done when their outside edges *begin* to curl and "wave." Do not let the delicate oysters overcook, or they will be rubbery. Remember, the oysters will continue to cook even as you ladle them into your bowls.
9. Serve immediately. Garnish each bowl with a sprinkle of paprika and freshly minced parsley.

Serves 6 to 8 as a main course

The next course for New Year's Eve dinner with Chris and Carey would be a dressed-up spinach and watercress salad from Elizabeth Dunwody Sams, a friend of Carey's grandmother. Betty Sams was admired greatly for her talents in the garden and kitchen—and for her preservation efforts. Carey tells me that Betty saved one of Macon's greatest structures, the 1830 Cowles House, which is considered one of the finest Greek Revival homes in existence. The stately and impressive mansion sits atop the hill on Bond Street; it has a commanding view of Middle Georgia. When I was a little boy and in downtown Macon with my family for Christmas shopping, my father would drive us up to the house and park on the street in front; we'd sit and look out at the lights in the city, twinkling with holiday colors. The last time I visited the mansion was at a party hosted by the Georgia Trust for Historic Preservation back in October 2021, one Carey and Christopher attended as well.

BETTY SAMS'S SPINACH AND WATERCRESS SALAD

Ingredients
1 pound fresh baby spinach
1 cup watercress, packed
1 small cucumber, peeled, seeded, and thinly sliced crosswise
3 tablespoons green onions, green and white parts, chopped
1 avocado, peeled and thinly sliced
1 (8.25 ounces) can mandarin oranges, drained
¼ cup fresh orange juice
2 tablespoons sugar
2 tablespoons red wine vinegar
1 tablespoon fresh lemon juice
¼ teaspoon kosher salt
½ cup olive oil
¼ cup pecans, chopped

Directions
1. In a large bowl combine spinach, watercress, cucumber, onions, avocado, and oranges. Set aside.
2. In another bowl, whisk together the orange juice, sugar, vinegar, lemon juice, and salt. Slowly drizzle in the oil to the mixture, whisking the entire time.
3. Pour the dressing over the salad, toss lightly, top with the chopped pecans, and serve immediately.
Serves 8 to 10

A fish course would be served next, and Chris and Carey often turn to Ina Garten for such a recipe. Here I'm using one of my own, which follows closely the Barefoot Contessa's cooking regime of fresh ingredients prepared and cooked simply. I inherited the love of fishing from my mom and dad, two of the most well-known anglers from Middle Georgia in their day. People would comment that "if you see Joyce and John Barrett coming away from the lake without any fish, you *knew* that they weren't biting." This dish is a favorite of mine to serve to a group of people since it can be prepped in advance and cooked quickly at the last moment. You can substitute flounder, red fish, or snapper for the trout if you'd like.

ROASTED RAINBOW TROUT WITH LEMONS & VIDALIA ONIONS

Ingredients
3 tablespoons butter, at room temperature
8 (5- to 6-ounce) boneless trout filets
4 tablespoons fresh-squeezed lemon juice
2 teaspoons kosher salt
2 teaspoons black pepper
2 teaspoons sweet paprika
16 very thin slices lemon
16 green onions, trimmed and sliced in half lengthwise
2 tablespoons olive oil

Directions
1. Preheat oven to 375 degrees.
2. Rub a large baking dish with the butter; place the filets skin side down on the dish in a single layer.
3. Drizzle the lemon juice on the fish.
4. Sprinkle the top of the fish with the salt, pepper, and paprika.
5. Place 2 lemon slices flat, side by side, on each fish; tuck the split green onions between the fish filets.
6. Drizzle the olive oil over the fish, lemons, and onion.
7. Place the dish in the oven and cook 10 to 12 minutes, until just done (the timing will vary on the thickness of the fish).
8. Remove from the oven and set aside. Turn the broiler on high; when fully heated, place the tray in the upper third of the oven for 2 to 3 minutes, watching carefully, until the top begins to turn golden. Serve immediately on warmed plates.

Serves 6 to 8

Carey and Chris chose an outstanding selection for the main course here, one that you don't see grace too many plates at home: it is elegantly and wonderfully pâté-stuffed quail. The recipe comes from the late Dr. Jasper "Jap" Thomas Hogan and his stylish wife, Jean. Carey shares that,

> Jean and Jap Hogan entertained in a grand style that few in Macon
> will ever emulate. With museum-quality silver, linens, and crystal,
> their tables looked like those of European royalty. When Chris and
> I married, Jean gave us a set of their George III salt cellars along
> with twelve Irish linen napkins that were gifted to them by the late

Desmond Guinness. While we treasure them, we use them often and think of the Hogans when we do. Jap was a renowned cook whose creations were in the French tradition of rich sauces—so we actually don't often copy his cooking, but we do try to capture his way of making magic through the use of candlelight.

Carey and Chris enjoy serving this dish with lightly roasted asparagus and a hollandaise sauce (see index for both recipes). In regard to the pâté, there are many found in gourmet markets such as Fresh Market or Whole Foods; Publix and Kroger often carry them as well. You can use either a smooth chicken liver pâté or a rougher grade pâté de maison.

JAP HOGAN'S QUAIL STUFFED WITH PÂTÉ

Ingredients
20 completely dressed quail, wings and legs trimmed
2 tablespoons olive oil
2 teaspoons kosher salt
2 teaspoons black pepper
1 quart cooked wild rice
½ cup sautéed, diced onion
½ cup fresh parsley, minced
½ cup candied ginger, minced
½ cup pâté, either chicken or de maison
2 cups chicken broth

Directions
1. Preheat oven to 350 degrees.
2. Lightly grease 2 large baking pans with the olive oil. Set aside.
3. Sprinkle each quail equally with the salt and pepper. Set aside.
4. In a bowl, mix the rice, onion, parsley, ginger, and pâté until well incorporated.
5. Spoon the stuffing mixture into the cavity of each bird and place the birds breast side up on the prepared baking sheets. Loosely cover the pans with foil and bake for half an hour. Remove the foil and continue baking another half hour. Baste birds with chicken broth every 15 minutes to prevent dryness.
6. Remove from the oven and allow to rest for 10 minutes before serving.

Serves 10

And speaking of exquisite and elegantly presented platters of roasted fowl, let me insert another excellent choice for New Year's Eve. This selection comes from Dr. Jennifer Frum and her husband, Dr. Andrew Herod. Tom and I became friends with these brilliant but oh-so-fun academics when we first moved to Athens. Jennifer serves as the vice president of outreach for the University of Georgia, and Andy is a distinguished research professor of geography, as well head of the UGA Paris study abroad program. Both are die-hard foodies and know their way around a good bottle of wine as well. A Brit, Andy grew up in the historic village of Radlett, in Hertfordshire, about fifteen miles north of London. His father, John, took up cooking after he retired as a senior executive in the liquor exporting business. The following is a recipe John adapted from the famous British chef Delia Smith. It is a pheasant dish infused with both cider and Calvados—apparently the elder Mr. Herod loved using his own products in his cooking. John Herod passed away several years ago, but I have had the wonderful pleasure of meeting Andy's mum, Sylvia, and his world-traveling sister, Jane. It is always a treat for us when the two Herod ladies visit here in the Classic City. And on a side note (you'll see there are many in this book!), Andy and I share the same birth date and birth year, February 6, 1964.

Pheasant with Cream & Apples (Faisan à la Normande)

Ingredients
1 plump young pheasant, fully dressed
1 teaspoon kosher salt
½ teaspoon black pepper
2 tablespoons butter
1 tablespoon vegetable oil
½ cup onion, diced
3 cups apples, peeled, cored, and sliced ¼-inch thick
6 ounces dry cider
5 ounces heavy cream
2 tablespoons Calvados (or brandy)

Directions
1. Season the pheasant on all sides with the salt and pepper. Set aside.
2. Heat the butter and oil in a Dutch oven over medium-high heat. Brown the bird in the hot fat, turning frequently, so that it browns evenly.
3. Add the onion and stir; cook for a few minutes until the onion is soft.
4. Stir in the apples and turn the pheasant over.
5. Pour the cider over the bird, onions, and apples. Cover and reduce heat to low. Cook for half an hour. Remove lid, turn the bird over again. Gently stir the onions and apples, cover, and cook for another 30 minutes.
6. Remove the bird and place it on a warm serving platter. Set aside.
7. Turn the heat up to medium and allow most of the moisture to evaporate; add in the cream and Calvados. Cook 2 to 3 minutes until thickened, stirring. Pour over the pheasant and serve.

Serves 2

Returning to my buddies in Macon, another entertaining practice that I share with Carey and Christopher, especially at large dinner parties where a good deal of food has already been served, is to provide gourmet chocolates and truffles for dessert. We serve ours in antique urn-shaped sterling silver cigarette holders; each person gets their own dish. Such delicacies are also lovely passed from guest to guest in cut-glass bowls or an elegant piece of porcelain. Two or three small truffles, along with a fine glass of champagne, provides just enough "sweet" to end an evening.

At closing of this part of the chapter, I want to thank the Messrs. Pickard and Howard for taking us into their fabulous home and giving us a glimpse of their munificent hospitality. It is no wonder that their parties are of Macon legend.

New Year's Day has probably some of *the* most solid dining traditions in the South, and in almost every home—and most restaurants that are open that day—there will be collards, Hoppin' John, and cornbread on the table or menu. The belief behind these dishes is that eating them on New Year's Day will bring good financial luck for the upcoming year. The verdant leaves of the collards are to provide "green money," the brown peas of Hoppin' John represent coins, and then there is gold from the color of the cornbread. I'm no historian in these areas, but, from what I've read, much of this feast comes from the influence of African Americans, who shaped so many of our foodways in the South. Hoppin' John is an interesting concoction; apparently the recipe was first printed in *The Carolina Housewife* in 1847. One story has it that the dish gets its name from an elderly man named John who sold peas and rice on the streets of Charleston in the 1800s. At our house, I cannot remember a single New Year's Day without these three foods, along with some sort of roasted or fried pork. Pork is also the meat of choice on New Year's Day, and chicken is to be avoided. Why, you ask? Because hogs root forward for their food, making their way into "a good new year," while chickens scratch backwards, which will force you to dwell in the past. My favorite main course to have on a platter for the holiday is Carrie's cubed pork, which was covered with a rich, thick gravy laden with the flavors of onion, garlic, and a hint of hot pepper.

Like Mama, Carrie was one of the greatest influences on my life and figured prominently in my prior two books. She helped raise me like a grandmother—as both of mine had passed away long before I came into the family. Carrie was my teacher and companion, and I spent many a day with her at our cottage on Ball Street. Yes, she was our housekeeper and cook, but she was family as well. I loved her as much as any blood kin that shared our family name. One of her greatest gifts to me was courteousness; she polished my manners up like a bright shiny penny. An especially memorable lesson I learned from her was at the dining table; she claimed that when one finishes eating it is rude and "common" to say, "I'm full." Instead, she instructed, the statement should be, "I've had a gracious plenty." I've passed that phrase along to my great-niece and nephew, and it brings back such wonderful memories to hear them repeat those words. Carrie lives on in our lives through those lessons and the ways to cook she taught me in the kitchen. Here is her mouth-wateringly delicious smothered pork.

Carrie's Soul Food Smothered Cubed Pork

Ingredients
3 pounds cubed pork cutlets, all of approximately equal size (use ⅓ pound per person)
3 teaspoons Lawry's Seasoned Salt
2¼ teaspoons black pepper, divided
1½ cups all-purpose flour

2 teaspoons salt
¾ cup vegetable or peanut oil
½ cup onion, diced
2 tablespoons celery, diced
1 tablespoon bell pepper, diced
2½ cups low-sodium beef or chicken stock
½ teaspoon garlic powder
½ teaspoon onion powder
2 or 3 pinches dried thyme leaves

Directions

1. Lightly moisten the cutlets on both sides with water, then sprinkle each side evenly with the Lawry's and 1 teaspoon of the black pepper.
2. In a bag, or on a large pan, combine the flour, salt, and another teaspoon of the black pepper. Shake, or dredge, each piece of pork to coat. Set these cutlets aside on another pan. Keep all the flour mixture in the bag or on the pan; you will use it in step 5 below.
3. Heat a large cast iron skillet, or other frying pan, over medium-high heat. Add the oil to a depth of ¼-inch. When the oil is heated through (a bit of flour will sizzle), place in 2 or 3 pieces of the pork, being careful not to crowd the pan; the pieces should not touch. Cook over medium to medium-high heat about 5 minutes, browning well on one side. Turn the cutlets over and brown the other side. When each piece is browned, remove the pieces and place on a wire rack.
4. When all cutlets are finished browning, drain off all but 3 tablespoons of the oil from the skillet. If there aren't a full 3 tablespoons, add more. Continuing on the medium to medium-high heat, add the onion, celery, and bell pepper. Sauté, stirring occasionally, 2 to 3 minutes. Make sure to scrape up any of the browned bits of pork or flour left in the pan.
5. Add ¼ cup of the leftover seasoned flour to the pan. Stir to mix well with the oil and vegetables. Cook 2 to 3 minutes, stirring occasionally.
6. Slowly stream in the stock and stir well to mix. Add in the garlic powder, onion powder, thyme, and the remaining ¼ teaspoon of black pepper.
7. Turn the heat up to medium-high and bring the mixture to a boil, stirring constantly.
8. Reduce heat to a slight simmer and cook for 5 to 7 minutes until the gravy thickens and coats the back of a spoon.
9. While the gravy is thickening, preheat your oven to 350 degrees.
10. In a large, lightly greased baking dish—9x13 or big enough so that most of the cutlets are in one layer, with just a bit of overlapping—pour in 1 cup of the gravy and spread with a spatula. Place the cutlets on the gravy, and then pour the remaining gravy on top. Cover tightly with aluminum foil.

11. Bake for 30 to 35 minutes until the gravy is hot and bubbling. Remove the pan from the oven, and turn the cutlets over, making sure that each piece is covered in gravy. Place the pan, uncovered, back into the oven and allow the tops to brown, cooking for another 20 minutes.
12. Serve immediately with rice or mashed potatoes. (This dish may be made a day ahead and reheated in the oven, covered. It also freezes well.)

Serves 8

Many people make their Hoppin' John with dried black-eyed peas, which is totally fine and makes a good dish. However, I prefer using the small field pea or pigeon pea, which can be found in the store under the Dixie Lily brand. Or, when I can get them, Sea Island red peas from the Marsh Hen Mill on Edisto Island are another favorite. These little fellows have a distinctive taste, and the "pot liquor" that results from their cooking provides a much richer flavor for your rice than grains simply cooked in water.

Hoppin' John

Ingredients
2 cups dried brown peas, or Sea Island red peas
2 slices bacon
2 cups onion, chopped
1 cup celery, chopped
¼ cup bell pepper, chopped
4 cups chicken stock
4 cups ham stock*
1 large bay leaf
¼ teaspoon black pepper
1½ cups regular grain white rice (not instant)

Directions
1. Rinse the peas and drain well; pick through and discard loose casings or stems. Place the peas in a large pot, and cover with water by 2 inches. Bring the pot to a boil, stir, and cover tightly.
2. Remove from heat and allow to sit for 1 hour, covered. Drain the peas, discarding the water, and rinse again. Set aside.
3. Place the bacon in a large pot or Dutch oven and cook over medium heat until crisp. Set the bacon aside. In the rendered fat, sauté the onions and celery for 3 to 4 minutes, stirring, until the vegetables are softened. Add the bell pepper, stir, and cook another 2 to 3 minutes.

4. Crumble the reserved bacon and place it, the drained peas, stock, bay leaf, and black pepper into the pot/Dutch oven. Bring to a boil, stir, and reduce heat to a steady simmer. Cook, uncovered, stirring occasionally, until the peas are soft, about 2 hours.
5. When the peas are done, drain the pan, keeping the liquid, and reserving the peas and vegetables.
6. Pour 3 cups of the reserved liquid, which should be a rich brown color, into a smaller pot. Bring it to a boil; add the rice, stir. Cover, and reduce heat to low. Cook 20 to 22 minutes. Do not remove the cover while cooking. Remove from heat and allow to sit for 5 minutes.
7. Place the peas and vegetables back into the large pot/Dutch oven. Add the cooked rice and stir. If you'd like a moister consistency, add a half-cup or so of the reserved liquid. Heat over medium-high until hot; serve immediately.

Serves 8 to 10
Better than Bouillon makes an excellent ham stock concentrate; if you can't find ham stock, or make your own, substitute 4 cups of additional chicken stock, and add 1 cup of diced, smoked ham to the pot just before cooking.

The following is exactly the way Mama and Carrie would cook their collards although Carrie was a bit heavier handed with the red pepper flakes than Mama.

Collard Greens

Ingredients
2 tablespoons vegetable oil
1 cup onion, chopped
4 cups low-sodium chicken stock
1 ham bone, or 2 cups smoked ham, cubed
¼ teaspoon red pepper flakes
2 pounds fresh collard green tops, large stems/veins removed, and torn into 3- or 4-inch pieces, rinsed

Directions
1. In a very large stockpot, heat the oil over medium-high and sauté the onion for about 3 to 4 minutes until soft, stirring.
2. Add the stock, ham, and red pepper. Bring to a boil, cover, and reduce heat to a steady simmer for about 5 minutes.

3. Add the collards and bring back to a boil. Stir well, reduce heat to a steady simmer, and cover slightly. Cook 25 to 30 minutes until the collards are tender and a dark, forest-green color. Stir occasionally.
4. Remove from heat and serve. If there is a good bit of liquid in the pot still, ladle out the servings with a slotted spoon.

Serves 8

This recipe was one of my mom's favorites; this dish was a house specialty at the historic "New" Perry Hotel in my hometown. A superlative confection, it is a real showstopper; prepare it for your family and see why it was—and still is—a Middle Georgia favorite. It goes naturally with the roast pork and other New Year's Day menu items.

New Perry Hotel Shredded Sweet Potatoes

Ingredients
3 pounds sweet potatoes (about 9 medium potatoes)
8 tablespoons butter, divided
1½ cups sugar
¾ cup white corn syrup
¾ cup water
1½ cups pineapple juice
½ teaspoon cinnamon (optional)

Directions
1. Preheat oven to 350 degrees.
2. Peel the potatoes; shred the peeled potatoes by hand into a gallon of water. Drain and rinse well, drain again; shake the colander to remove any excess water.
3. Grease the sides and bottom of a 9x13 baking dish with 2 tablespoons of the butter.
4. Evenly spread the prepared potatoes into the dish.
5. In a saucepan, mix the sugar, corn syrup, and water; cook over medium-high heat until the sugar is completely dissolved and a simple syrup is made.
6. Add the remaining 6 tablespoons of butter to the simple syrup. Stir until melted.
7. Pour the pineapple juice over the potatoes.
8. Pour the simple syrup over the potatoes.
9. Sprinkle the cinnamon over the tops of the potatoes.

10. Bake for 35 to 40 minutes until the potatoes are beginning to become translucent and the edges have browned slightly.

Serves 8 to 12

The cornbread recipe is simple, but make sure you use whole milk buttermilk, not the reduced- or no-fat varieties—otherwise the taste and texture will suffer. Too, and I don't care what *anybody tells you*, you do NOT put sugar in cornbread. Not now, not ever. Period.

Cornbread

Ingredients
¼ cup + 2 tablespoons vegetable oil
2 cups White Lily or Martha White cornmeal mix
1¾ cups whole-milk buttermilk
1 egg, slightly beaten

Directions
1. Preheat oven to 425 degrees. Oil a cast iron skillet, or 8x8 baking pan, with 2 tablespoons of the oil. Place the oiled skillet in the hot oven.
2. In a large bowl, mix together the cornmeal mix, buttermilk, egg, and remaining vegetable oil. Stir until just incorporated but without any lumps.
3. Remove the hot skillet from the oven and pour in the batter. Place the skillet back in the oven, reduce the heat to 375 degrees and cook for 15 minutes, or until the top turns a golden brown.
4. To serve, remove from the oven and allow to sit 5 minutes before slicing. Serve with pats of butter.

Serves 6 to 8

Chess pies are popular in the South; they are easy to make, and everyone seems to enjoy these rich custards. My choice here is a chocolate variety that is really, really good with a dollop of whipped cream. I'd ask Mama and Carrie for this pie each new year.

Chocolate Chess Pie

Ingredients
1 cup sugar
2 eggs, slightly beaten
8 tablespoons butter or margarine
1 square of unsweetened chocolate

Pinch of salt
1 teaspoon vanilla extract
1 (9-inch) pie crust, unbaked
Whipped cream for garnish

Directions
1. Preheat oven to 325 degrees.
2. In a bowl, combine the sugar and eggs; beat well.
3. Melt the butter and chocolate in a saucepan. Remove from heat and allow to cool for about 5 minutes.
4. Pour the melted chocolate and butter into the sugar and egg mixture; add the salt and vanilla and mix well. Pour the filling into the pie crust and bake for 30 to 35 minutes, until the middle sets.
5. To serve, remove from heat and allow to cool 20 minutes or so before slicing. Serve with whipped cream.

Serves 6 to 8

Chapter 2

St. Patrick's Day

Many cities in the South celebrate the feast of St. Patrick on March 17, the day this patron saint of Ireland supposedly died—with the most popular celebration being in Savannah, Georgia. Known as the Hostess City of the South, Savannah certainly earns this moniker as she welcomes upwards of 750,000 guests for the annual "wearing of the green." In the USA, the parade in Savannah is second in size only to that of New York City, which in terms of population alone is pretty impressive.

Savannah, one of the busiest ports in our country, has been a mosaic of immigrants since the city was founded in 1733. Surnames from spots across the globe are represented here today, the descendants of the thousands of folks who climbed the high bluffs from the river below and up into the New World. The Irish were a large part of those settlers, with some even arriving with Georgia founder General James Edward Oglethorpe; the second royal governor of the colony, Henry Ellis, was an Irishman.

The celebration of St. Patrick's Day in Georgia's first capital dates back to 1812, when a handful of prominent Irish residents formed the Hibernian Society in Savannah to aid poor immigrants from their home country. (*Hibernia* is the classical Latin name for Ireland, from the word *hibernus*, meaning "wintry.") In 1824, the society president called on local residents to join him and his fellow Hibernians to attend Mass and then walk through the streets of the city in honor of St. Patrick's Day—and with that invitation, Savannah's annual parade was born.

Today the procession has grown to include more than 250 floats, bands, and other groups, and it lasts between three and four hours as it winds its way through Savannah's historic district. Tom and I attended for many years, walking a good bit of the route, stopping at various parties and gatherings along the way for a Bloody Mary (or two) and plenty of hearty brunch fare. As the crowds have grown over the years, though, our participation waned. Like with the Macy's Thanksgiving Day parade in New York City, we now watch the festivities from our kitchen television.

While the St. Patrick's Day parade gets international attention for its length and the uber party-like atmosphere, the holiday in Savannah still, at its heart, is a family and religious affair with many decades-old traditions.

One such activity is the gathering on Madison Square the day before the parade to honor members of the military, past and present. In the midst of the square, atop a granite pedestal, is a 15.5-foot-high bronze statue of Revolutionary War hero William Jasper, whose parents were from Ireland. Part of the wording on the base reads, "To the memory of Sergeant William Jasper, who, though mortally wounded, rescued the colors of his regiment, in the assault on the British lines about the city, October 9, 1779. A century has not dimmed the glory of this Irish-American soldier whose last tribute to civil liberty was his life."

Another celebration of the Irish heritage is the Celtic Cross Ceremony. Following mass at the Cathedral of St. John the Baptist, parishioners and guests process to Emmet Park. This city common, a beautiful greenspace filled with live oak trees draped in Spanish moss, is located on Bay Street overlooking the Savannah River. The park was once called "the Irish Green" as it was a gathering spot for Irish families in the Old Fort neighborhood; it was later renamed for Irish orator and patriot Robert Emmet in commemoration of his death. The procession culminates in a ceremony where a wreath honoring Irish families and Irish history is placed at the foot of the large and impressive Celtic cross monument, which is hand-carved of Irish limestone.

Mass is celebrated as well each St. Patrick's Day in Catholic churches throughout the city, and then there is always the "greening of the fountains" in the downtown city squares. The largest and most famous of these fountains is the impressive Forsyth Park structure located in the north end of the thirty-acre square. Inspired by one created for London's Crystal Palace Exhibition, the 150-year-old ornate cast-iron sculpture was manufactured by Janes, Beebe & Company in Bronx County, New York, which also created iron work for the dome of the US Capitol and railings for the

Mary Ann Smith and DeAnne Mitchell
in front of the historic Harper Fowlkes House

Brooklyn Bridge. Seeing the brightly painted white tritons of the fountain spray out enormous streams of clover-green water is quite the sight.

Family culinary rituals are found throughout the city as well, and I'd like to share with you those of my dear friend DeAnne Mitchell and her lovely mom, Mary Ann Smith. These two stylish and business-savvy ladies own Convention Consultants, a high-end boutique tour and conference planning company. Mary Ann has been Tom's best friend for more than fifty years (and speaking of traditions and rituals, he has given her each year a sterling silver Gorham Christmas ornament since they met; she now has fifty-two with which to adorn her tree). I came to know DeAnne and Mary through Tom, and they have both been wonderful blessings throughout my adult life.

Mary Ann's Irish grandmother and grandfather were from County Mayo and County Roscommon, respectively. Their son, Mary Ann's father, John Michael Brennan, was a well-known attorney in Savannah. Besides being a partner in the prestigious firm of Bouhan, Williams, & Levy, Mr. Brennan served for over forty years as the attorney for the Catholic diocese. A few of the long list of esteemed and distinguished honors this extraordinary gentleman received from the Irish and Catholic communities includes being named a Knight of St. Gregory by Pope John XXIII, serving as president of the Savannah Hibernian Society, and leading the city's St. Patrick's Day parade in 1971 as grand marshal.

In 1997, *Southern Living* featured a multipage story about Mr. Brennan, his family, and the annual St. Patrick's Day family dinner served at Mary Ann's home. What a place to have a dinner or party! The four-story historic structure, built in 1818 and remodeled in 1875, is of Italianate design and boasts twelve-foot ceilings, candlelit crystal chandeliers, and an array of fine artwork and furnishings. (On a side, note Mary Ann hosted a black-tie cocktail party for forty folks in her renowned home for my fortieth birthday, and what a treat that was!)

The meal around the dining table is laden with traditional classics you hear about when the topic of an Irish dinner comes up in conversation: corned beef and cabbage, beef stewed in Guinness beer, and Irish soda bread. All the recipes presented here are from DeAnne and her mom, along with this note from DeAnne:

My Granddaddy would always sign any card or letter to us with this blessing:
May the road rise up to meet you.
May the wind be always at your back.
May the sun shine warm upon your face;
The rains fall soft upon your fields and until we meet again,
May God hold you in the palm of His hand.

For a festive aperitif, and to cheer Mr. Brennan's memory, here is a tasty cocktail with a green theme, a grasshopper.

Grasshopper

Ingredients
1 ounce *green* crème de menthe
1 ounce *white* crème de cacao
2 tablespoons heavy cream

Directions
1. Mix the ingredients well with crushed ice in a cocktail shaker (or other container with a lid).
2. Strain into a chilled glass to serve.

Serves 1

There's nothing like an Irish coffee to start a big St. Patrick's Day celebration. This famous cocktail was created by chef Joe Sheridan of Limerick, Ireland, in 1943. It has become a huge hit here in the US since those days of World War II. Erin Go Bragh!

Note: While there are only four ingredients, use the best coffee you can find and follow the instructions carefully. Just pouring everything into a mug at once won't work.

Irish Coffee

Ingredients
6 ounces very hot water
2 teaspoons dark brown sugar, packed
6 ounces strong coffee
1½ ounces Irish whiskey

1 ounce heavy cream, whipped until just firm

Directions
1. Pour the hot water into an Irish coffee glass, or other mug, and allow to sit for 1 minute to warm.
2. Pour the water out.
3. Add the brown sugar to the glass and then pour in the coffee. Stir until completely dissolved.
4. Pour in the whiskey, stir a time or two, and then gently place the whipped cream on top of the liquid. Serve immediately.

Serves 1

The following corned beef and cabbage dish is probably the most well known of all the Irish recipes, at least here in the states. DeAnne cooks hers in a crock pot, making it a "one-dish wonder."

Crock Pot Corned Beef and Cabbage

Ingredients
5- to 6-pound corned beef
3 onions, sliced
4 small Yukon gold or other waxy yellow potato*
Spice package[†] that comes with the beef (usually allspice, peppercorns, mustard seeds, and coriander)
2 bay leaves
4 cloves fresh garlic, minced
2 to 3 cups water
1 medium head of cabbage, cut into small wedges
Spicy brown mustard as accompaniment
Parsley for garnish

Directions
1. Rinse the meat several times under cool water to remove excess salt.
2. Place the onions in the bottom of the crock pot, followed by potatoes, the corned beef, spice package, bay leaves, and garlic.
3. Pour in the water, enough to cover all ingredients. Cook on low for 3 hours.
4. Add the cabbage on top, pushing it down into the water. Continue cooking on low for another 5 to 7 hours until the beef is tender.
5. Remove the meat from the pot and set on a tray; cover with foil and allow to rest for 15 minutes. *Slice by cutting across grain* and place on a platter.

Remove and discard the bay leaves; arrange the potatoes and cabbage around the sliced meat to serve.

* If you are worried that the potatoes will be cooking too long, you can leave them out of the recipe; just cook and serve separately.

† If the spice packet is not included, you can substitute by using pickling spices.

Serves 6 to 8

An alternative to the corned beef, or a pairing if you're doing a buffet dinner for a crowd, would be this rich and delicious beef stew braised in Guinness beer and vegetables. And don't save it just for St. Patrick's Day; make a pot for a cold, wintry night and serve it with the cheesy potatoes and a loaf of the hot, crusty Irish soda bread (recipes follow).

Beef and Guinness Stew

Ingredients
2 pounds stew beef (in 2-inch cubes)
1 teaspoon salt, divided
1 teaspoon black pepper, divided
3 tablespoons vegetable oil, divided
2 tablespoons flour
Scant ⅛ teaspoon cayenne
2 cups carrots, peeled and cut into 2-inch rounds
2 large onions, chopped
1 garlic clove, crushed
2 tablespoons tomato paste, dissolved in ¼ cup water
1¼ cups Guinness
1 teaspoon fresh thyme, finely minced (or ½ teaspoon dried)

Directions
1. Preheat oven to 300 degrees.
2. Toss the beef with ½ teaspoon of the salt, ½ teaspoon of the pepper, and 1 tablespoon of the oil.
3. In a bowl add flour with the remaining salt, pepper, and the cayenne—toss beef a few pieces at a time into flour mixture. Set the floured pieces aside.
4. Heat the rest of the oil in a large skillet over medium-high heat. In batches, brown meat on all sides, making sure the pieces do not touch or crowd the pan. Too many pieces in the pan will not produce a good crust/browning.

Set the meat in a lightly greased Dutch oven or baking dish and scatter the carrots on top.

5. Reduce heat to medium and add the onions and garlic to the skillet in which you browned the beef. Stir well for a minute or two, then add in the tomato paste mixture, stir, cover, and cook 3 to 4 minutes.
6. Uncover the pan and add the Guinness and thyme to the skillet; increase heat and bring to a boil.
7. Pour the mixture over the beef and carrots. Cover, place in the oven, and cook 2 to 3 hours until meat is tender.

Serves 6 to 8

The carrot recipe here is a perfect side dish both for the corned beef and cabbage entrée and the beef stew with Guinness.

Bourbon Carrots

Ingredients
5 to 6 cups water
1 teaspoon salt
3 pounds carrots, peeled and cut into 2-inch-long diagonal slant pieces
4 tablespoons butter, melted
6 tablespoons brown sugar, packed
¼ cup bourbon

Directions
1. Bring water and salt to a boil in a large pot. Add the carrots.
2. Return to a boil and cook 6 to 7 minutes. Carrots should be tender but not mushy.
3. Drain all of the water from the pan; add butter and brown sugar and cook for 3 to 4 additional minutes, stirring occasionally.
4. Add the bourbon and cook 3 more minutes, again stirring occasionally. Serve immediately.

Serves 6 to 8

This next dish teams well with the Guinness stew. It's also good with just about any other meat dish, from sliced ham to grilled chicken. DeAnne gets rave reviews on this specialty.

Cheesy Mashed Potatoes

Ingredients
3 pounds small white potatoes, peeled
1 tablespoon kosher salt
8 tablespoons butter, at room temperature, divided
1½ cups half-and-half, at room temperature, divided
½ cup sour cream
½ cup white cheddar cheese, hand-grated
½ teaspoon black pepper

Directions
1. Put potatoes and salt into a large pot and cover with water. Bring to a boil and cook 20 to 30 minutes until potatoes are tender. Drain and set aside in the same bowl you cooked them in.
2. In a separate pan over low heat melt 4 tablespoons of the butter and ¾ cup half-and-half.
3. Mash the potatoes to break them up into small pieces; slowly add the melted butter and half-and-half, mixing them together on the lowest speed of mixer.
4. Then, by hand, fold in the remaining butter and half-and-half, followed by the sour cream, cheddar cheese, and pepper. Fold together until just mixed. Serve immediately.

Serves 6 to 8

Any good Irish family knows "waste not, want not," so, if there is corned beef left over from the main course, this hot Reuben dip is out of this world as an appetizer for family and friends the next day. Or, the dip can be an hors d'oeuvre if you choose to serve the beef and Guinness stew as your main course. Regardless, it is an excellent choice to serve in celebration of St. Patrick's Day.

Hot Reuben Dip

Ingredients
16 ounces cream cheese, at room temperature
1 pound cooked corned beef, chopped finely
2 cups Swiss cheese, hand-grated
1 cup sauerkraut, drained well
½ cup sour cream

½ cup Thousand Island dressing
1 loaf Irish soda bread (recipe follows)
Note: For those of you who don't have time, or the inclination, to make your own bread, traipse on over to Publix or Fresh Market and find a loaf of pumpernickel or whole grain; either will work just fine.

Directions
1. Preheat oven to 400 degrees.
2. In a large bowl, combine cream cheese, corned beef, Swiss cheese, sauerkraut, sour cream, and dressing; mix well. Set aside.
3. With a sharp, serrated knife, cut a hole in the top of the loaf, leaving a 1-inch border around the circumference. Remove the interior bread, cutting it into bite-sized pieces. Leave 2 inches thickness for the bottom of the loaf. Use the pieces for the dip.
4. Spoon the dip mixture into the hollowed loaf of bread.
5. Wrap the loaf and dip in aluminum foil, place on baking sheet, and bake until hot and bubbly, about 20-25 minutes. Remove from the oven and allow to sit for 5 minutes before serving.
Note: If you have leftover dip, you can put in a casserole dish, keep it warm, and add dip to brown bread bowl as needed.
Serves 12 to 16 as an appetizer

This warm, rustic, and crackly bread holds a lot of tradition with Irish families, and it is a superb choice to sit alongside your corned beef and cabbage or beef and Guinness stew. While there are several variations on the bread from region to region on the Emerald Isle, DeAnne's version is the one most folks would be familiar with—a round, browned dome that has a cross cut into the middle. Some hold that the cross in the bread was to force the devil to be driven out while baking or to let the wee fairies escape; it was also thought to bring blessings upon the house. For culinary reasons, the incision allows the dough to rise without splitting. Make sure to have plenty of Irish butter, such as Kerrygold, to slather on your chunks of bread.

Irish Soda Bread

Ingredients
4 cups Irish-style flour, such as Odlum's or King Arthur Irish-Style
1 teaspoon salt

2½ tablespoons sugar
1 teaspoon baking soda
2 teaspoons baking powder
1½ cups whole milk buttermilk
2 tablespoons melted butter

Directions
1. Preheat oven to 400 degrees; lightly grease a baking sheet and line it with lightly greased parchment paper.
2. Mix the dry ingredients together in a bowl, making a well in the middle. Pour the buttermilk and melted butter into the well and stir with a fork until just blended; don't overmix.
3. With a spatula, fold the dough onto a floured surface.
4. With floured hands (to keep the dough from sticking to your fingers) knead the dough 8 to 10 times, or until the mixture holds together well.
5. Roll the dough into a large ball and place on baking sheet. With a sharp, serrated knife cut a cross about an inch deep into the middle of the loaf, making the incision 4 inches long and about 2½ inches wide.
6. Place the loaf in the oven and cook 40 minutes or until a toothpick inserted in the middle comes out clean. Cool on a baking rack before slicing (or pulling apart).

Makes 1 loaf, enough for 8 people

A sweet Irish ending here for St. Patty's Day is a simple but oh-so-delicious treat, crème de menthe brownies. And yep, they come from a box. I know there are bakers out there who can create the most luscious and velvety smooth brownies from scratch, but JSB ain't one of them. And I promise—if you serve any Ghirardelli brownie, your friends will think you either bought the little babies at a gourmet store or cooked them yourself. This Irish-inspired creation uses crème de menthe for a sublime taste combination with the rich chocolate.

Crème de Menthe Brownies

Ingredients
1 box Ghirardelli dark chocolate or double chocolate variety brownie mix
8 tablespoons butter, at room temperature
2 cups powdered sugar
¼ cup green crème de menthe

Directions
1. Preheat oven to 325 degrees.
2. Prepare brownie mix and pan according to package directions. Cook, and then cool brownies on a rack. When completely cooled, cover and refrigerate until cold.
3. Mix the butter and powdered sugar in a food processor or large mixer until blended well.
4. While blending, add crème de menthe 1 tablespoon at a time. The resulting mixture should have a smooth consistency.
5. Spread the icing over the cold brownies and return to the refrigerator to chill the icing. Remove brownies from refrigerator for 20 minutes before cutting. Store in an airtight container.

Serves 6 to 8

This next recipe is not tied directly to St. Patrick's Day, but is a famous Savannah libation—the city's most famous—that was introduced to me by Mary Ann and DeAnne. Chatham Artillery punch is a delicious and sublime drink that belies the impact it can have on one's constitution. It has been called the "strongest punch in history" and has "vanquished many a hearty man." While no one is absolutely certain of the origin of the concoction, it has been said that it was created for George Washington when he came to the city on a presidential tour; at the time he presented two cannons to the fortification of Chatham Artillery—thus the punch's name.

The drink is not too sweet, you don't taste the alcohol, and it goes down quickly and delightfully. And it will literally kick your ass if you aren't cautious! I've bottled it and given it away as Christmas presents (minus the champagne, which has to be added at the end). Too, in a devilish mood, I served it at a Diocesan (Episcopal) dinner many years ago—and that night turned out to be one of the most enjoyable on record for the clergy, lay people, and conventioneers. I was asked to plan the night's entertainment and food for the annual convention. A jazz and rock band of local Episcopalians was secured, we rented a historic event space large enough to hold our group, and a local caterer and florist finished up the package. I was told that beer and wine could be served, but not a full bar; the appearance of all those bottles of hard spirits would not seem appropriate. However, an alcoholic punch would be fine. *Hee-hee.* I did put a sign by the punch bowl with a disclaimer that Chatham Artillery punch contained "the hard stuff." People loved it, and it wasn't too long before the whole crowd, including the bishop, was on the dance floor doing the Electric Slide. People still talk about that convention to this day!

In making the recipe, you have to allow the mixture to sit, in a covered container, for at least a week, if not three or four, though it doesn't have to be refrigerated.

Chatham Artillery Punch

Ingredients
2 quarts green tea
2¾ cups fresh squeezed lemon juice (about 9 large lemons)
2½ cups dark brown sugar
2 quarts Catawba wine (or a sweet rosé or white zinfandel)
2 quarts Santa Cruz rum (or other light rum)
1 quart Hennessey (or other cognac)
1 quart gin
1 quart rye whiskey
1 pint cherries
1 pint cubed pineapple
2 bottles of champagne

Directions
1. In a large 3-gallon container, mix the tea, lemon juice, and brown sugar. Stir well to dissolve.
2. Add the liquors, stir well, and cover the container tightly. If needed, place the punch in smaller containers. Store in a cool, dark place for at least 1 week. I suggest 3 to 4 weeks.
3. When ready to serve, pour the mixture into a punch bowl over a cake of ice. Add the cherries and pineapple and champagne (in proportion to the size of the punch bowl; for example, if it holds a gallon, then place in half the cherries and pineapple, and one bottle of the champagne). If not using a punch bowl, you can also serve by pouring the mixture into individual glasses filled with ice cubes (don't use crushed ice) and garnish with a cherry, a piece of pineapple, and a splash of champagne.

Serves 25 to 50 people depending on their constitution and stamina!

Chapter 3

Easter

Easter—the most religious of Christian holidays—holds numerous culinary customs across the South. For Catholics and Episcopalians, who often observe a strict Lenten season of little or no meat, it is time to again visit the local butcher. For children, the promise of chocolate bunnies, jelly beans, and candied eggs is cause for excitement. Many cooks look forward to the new crop of tender vegetables that were planted early and escaped the ubiquitous seasonal cold snap. And for generations, the sight of a freshly grated coconut cake sitting atop an antique cake plate, a festival all to itself, has been the epitome of Easter foods.

The entire day for a family in the South can mean one feast after another. The morning begins perhaps with richly frosted cinnamon buns or fat homemade sausage biscuits before dashing off to observe sunrise services. The dinner following church may mean a dozen or more deviled eggs—made with creamy mayonnaise, a liberal dose of tangy yellow mustard, and sprinkled with chopped sweet pickles—a baked ham, macaroni and cheese, fresh green beans, and just-off-the-vine yellow-neck squash cooked with a sweet Vidalia onion. For those families who celebrate their big Easter meal at supper, many sideboards offer a mouth-watering roasted leg of lamb, studded with fresh garlic and rosemary and served with mint jelly. Setting alongside may be little red new-potatoes swimming in sweet butter and a sampling of tiny English peas.

Memories and stories of Easter gatherings abound, too. My mind always goes back to the fishing outings we'd have in the afternoon after church, sometimes on the creek banks of Big Indian, out at Rigdon's ponds, or visiting Aunt Martha and Uncle Telford on Lake Blackshear. Mama would put together a picnic hamper with a feast of sweet, smoky ham, pimento cheese sandwiches, potato salad, and all of the fixings. The coconut cake would be cut into individual pieces and wrapped in aluminum foil (we didn't know what cling-wrap was until I was almost a teen). I can still remember licking the frosting and grated coconut off those pieces of crinkled foil after I had devoured my piece. Nothing like the appetite of a growing boy.

One story I always recall at Easter is from spring 1968, just past my fourth birthday. I had been waiting in anticipation all week for my basket of candy and colored eggs. That Saturday night after supper I ran back and forth from window to window to see if I could catch a glimpse of Peter Cottontail hopping down the sidewalks of Ball Street. While my energy and enthusiasm were tolerated by my parents, my fifteen-year-old sister was way past finding my excitement cute. She told me that the Easter Bunny *hated* little blonde boys with pointy cowlicks and would be bringing me rotten buzzard eggs in my basket. Just as she finished those distressing words, I spotted something bright and flickering out one of the dining room windows. I pressed my nose to the glass and immediately hollered back to Mama and Daddy, "FIRE!"

My parents rushed down the hall to see flames shooting from the bedroom windows of the Murphys' house next door. Mama ran to the phone—we only had one then, and it was a rotary dial—and called the fire department, which was right across the street.

Fortunately, the Murphy family was not home, and because of my precocious inquisitiveness about the Easter Bunny, the firemen were alerted in time to salvage most of the house. The next day I was awarded not one but two large slices of that heavenly coconut cake, and there was a crisp five-dollar bill in my basket. I waved that Abe Lincoln under my sister's nose and sang a little, "nah-nah-nah-nah" to her when out of range of my folks. "Rotten buzzard eggs," indeed.

In this chapter I have a few recipes that are meaningful to me and bring back fond recollections of this special spring holiday. In addition, you'll find other stories and recipes from friends across our region, such as the twist on the Easter celebration from my buddies Barbara and Carter Hubbard. Tom and I met the Hubbards over thirty years ago when we moved across the street from the couple and into our first home in Savannah's historic Ardsley Park. Having a Saturday morning cup of coffee on our side porch a week after settling in, we observed the Hubbards packing their Malibu station wagon with boxes, suitcases, duffel bags, and a cooler. A bike was strapped to the back, and we could see Barbara and Carter, along with their only child, Carter Jr., hugging in the driveway. We could tell there were some tears. Come to find out the youngest Hubbard was headed to Athens for his first year at the University of Georgia. As "Little Carter," as we came to call him, pulled out of the driveway, Barbara and Carter followed and stood arm in arm in the street, waving goodbye until the car turned the corner and was out of sight. At that point Tom turned to me and said dryly, "Johnathon, it looks like we've moved in next door to Ozzie and Harriet."

Since then, we have been on countless trips with Barbara and Carter. And, if I had a dollar for every time we had supper together, I could go buy myself a nice new set of Le Creuset pots and pans.

Barbara and Carter love to entertain and are warm and wonderful hosts. One spring, mutual of friends of ours, Charlotte and Andy, were to be married, and the Hubbards threw them a wedding party with a holiday theme. Guests arrived to find the standard Savannah open bar, a dining table full of Barbara's exquisite hors d'oeuvres, and a stack of children's brightly colored straw Easter baskets.

After the guests were well underway with their libations and tomato sandwiches, the Hubbards gathered the group and handed a basket and flashlight to each couple. There weren't any children present at this soiree, so many of the guests were thinking to themselves, "Oh, please, no, don't make me go outside in front of all Ardsley Park and hunt Easter eggs…."

Barbara and Carter were inwardly tickled to see the strange looks on their guests' faces and watched as they smiled nervously at one another.

"Well, gang, we know how you all *love* Easter!" Carter said, clapping his hands once, loudly. "And what better way to have fun and celebrate not only the holiday but the pending nuptials of our dear friends (applause sprinkled across the crowd for Andy and Charlotte) than with one of the holiday's most favorite of traditions!"

Again, you could tell that most guests were *not* looking forward to scavenging for candied eggs. They'd much rather stay inside and drink Carter's single malt and have another pickled shrimp.

Hunting Easter Eggs, Perry, Georgia, 1969.
No buzzard eggs here, Sis.

Barbara and Carter Hubbard,
having dinner at the Chatham Club, Savannah, 2019

"Won't this be *fun*, everyone? I am so excited you all are here and that we can have such a great time together!" Barbara sang out, smiling broadly to the group. She was enjoying watching the effort people made to look well-mannered.

"But before we get started," Carter continued, "we need to let you in on a twist to our adventure outside." He paused for a moment and looked back over the room. "You see, you won't be hunting for chocolate bunnies or colored eggs."

People looked sideways at one another, their curiosity piqued. Carter and Barbara were both Sunday school teachers at St. John's; hopefully this wouldn't be a scripture lesson. Shortly their fears were allayed.

"No Easter eggs, folks. Sorry, I know you're disappointed," Barbara laughed. "Rather, you are on a hunt for two hundred mini-bottles of liquor and liqueurs that are hidden across the front yard!"

Cheers went up from the group; this game wouldn't be so bad after all.

Carter escorted the crowd to the front door with a last bit of information. "Don't leave any spot unturned; those bottles are in the camellias, the azaleas, under the boxwoods, and all places in between!"

Soon the cadre of well-dressed ladies and gentlemen—it could have been an ad for Brooks Brothers and Talbots—was piling out onto the manicured St. Augustine grass, spiritedly (tongue in cheek) and competitively looking for their prizes of Jack Daniels, Beefeater, and Bailey's Irish Creams. When someone found a favorite, you'd hear a shout of "Yes ma'am!" or maybe a loud "Woo-hoo, *Go Dawgs!*" Each of those partygoers, many who had been friends since childhood, were transported back thirty-plus years for a game of seek-and-find. Picture that scene in your mind—just wonderful fun.

Barbara is an excellent cook, and she finds Easter one of her favorite times to be in the kitchen. She has several recipes I dearly love, but for sake of space I've narrowed it down to two of my favorites: grilled leg of lamb and a curried fruit compote. The lamb is butterflied, marinated, and grilled. It is absolutely splendid—and I will stand next to Carter while he carves it, and he kindly allows me a bite or two as he places the slices on the platter. Prime spot in the house at that point in time!

Grilled Butterflied Leg of Lamb

Ingredients
1 boneless leg of lamb, 5 to 6 pounds, butterflied
2 teaspoons kosher or sea salt
1 or more teaspoons black pepper, to taste
4 cloves garlic, peeled
2 tablespoons fresh rosemary leaves
2 tablespoons mint leaves
Zest of 1 lemon
½ cup red wine
½ cup extra virgin olive oil
Fresh parsley for garnish

Directions
1. Sprinkle the entire piece of lamb with the salt and pepper.
2. Prepare the marinade by placing the remaining ingredients, except the parsley garnish, in a food processor and pulse until well blended.
3. Coat the meat with the marinade and place the lamb in a large freezer bag. Pour any unused marinade in the bag and seal.
4. Refrigerate for 3 to 4 hours (or overnight).
5. Remove from the refrigerator half an hour before grilling. Take the leg of lamb from the bag and discard the excess marinade.
6. Turn all grill burners on high; brown the meat 4 minutes on each side. Reduce heat to low and cover the grill; cook 35 to 45 minutes (130 degrees for medium rare). On a charcoal grill or other cooker, such as a Big Green Egg, you will have to adjust cook times and procedures.
7. When done, remove from grill and cover with aluminum foil; allow the meat to rest for 15 to 20 minutes before carving.

Serves 6 to 8

Barbara's curried fruit compote is a staple on my Easter dinner buffet. Use fresh fruit if available, but a selection of frozen varieties will work as well. My favorite items to include are peaches and tart cherries, along with pineapple and pears. Any variety of fruit will do; if using jarred or canned varieties make certain to drain well. As for the curry, I recommend buying a small container of a reputable brand; though it will cost a bit more, you'll use less than one that comes in bulk, and there are few of us who will use up a jar of curry in a season.

Curried Fruit Compote

Ingredients
4 tablespoons butter
⅔ cup dark brown sugar, packed
1 teaspoon curry powder
¼ cup dry or sweet sherry
6 cups assorted fruit, such as sliced peaches, pears, plums, pineapple, tart
  cherries

Directions
1. Preheat oven to 350 degrees.
2. Melt the butter in a saucepan over medium heat; add the sugar and whisk
   until melted.
3. Whisk in the curry powder and the sherry.
4. Place the fruit in a baking dish; pour sugar mixture over the fruit and stir to
   mix.
5. Cook for 45 minutes until the fruit softens; stir twice during baking.
6. Serve with a slotted spoon. Can be stored in an airtight container and refrigerated.
Serves 6 to 8

In terms of personal and family favorites, the following are some delecta-
bles found in my kitchen during Easter. The first, a casserole of asparagus
and peas, is an excellent side dish for a baked ham or roasted leg of lamb;
I dearly love it. My mom made this dish each Easter and on other special
occasions; hers included cream of mushroom soup and canned asparagus.
When I was a kid, the tall cans of asparagus from LeSueur were considered
an exotic—we didn't grow it (too hot in Middle Georgia) and asparagus
was pretty pricy on the shelves of the Piggly Wiggly. And for those of you
who weren't around in that decade, particularly in a small Southern town
such as Perry, let me assure you that there wasn't a fresh spear to be seen
at any of our local grocery stores. I don't think I even ate a fresh piece of
asparagus until in my late teens and on a 4-H trip to Washington, DC. In
an updated version of the casserole, I make my own cheese sauce instead
of using mushroom soup, and the vegetables are not from a can. But I'd
still sit down and happily gobble down my mama's version, which was
always delicious, if she were only here to make it for me.

JSB's "Updated" Asparagus & Pea Casserole

Ingredients
6 tablespoons butter, at room temperature, divided
4 tablespoons olive oil, divided
8 ounces fresh mushrooms, sliced
¼ cup green onions, white and light green parts only, chopped
¼ cup flour
2 cups whole milk, warmed
½ teaspoon salt
⅛ teaspoon black pepper
1½ cups sharp cheddar cheese, hand grated
1 pound fresh asparagus, bottom woody portions (2 inches or so) removed and discarded
2 cups frozen baby English peas, thawed and wiped dry with paper towels
1½ cups Panko breadcrumbs

Directions
1. Preheat oven 350 degrees.
2. Grease a 11x7 baking dish with 2 tablespoons of butter; set aside.
3. In a saucepan, heat 1 tablespoon of the olive oil over medium-high heat. Add mushrooms; sauté, stirring occasionally. Cook until moisture has evaporated and mushrooms are starting to brown, about 7 minutes. Set aside.
4. Melt the remaining butter in a separate pot over medium heat; add the green onions and sauté for 2 to 3 minutes. Add the flour and whisk, cooking for 2 minutes or so.
5. Into the onion mixture, stream the milk, whisking. Continue to whisk until the mixture is thickened, about 5 minutes.
6. Add the salt, pepper, and cheese; whisk until cheese is melted.
7. Spread half of the asparagus spears and half of the peas into the buttered baking dish; on top layer all of the sautéed mushrooms. Spread half of the cheese sauce over the mushrooms, followed by the remaining asparagus and peas; cover with the rest of the cheese sauce.
8. In a bowl, thoroughly mix the breadcrumbs and remaining 3 tablespoons of olive oil. Spread the oiled crumbs over the dish, pressing down slightly into the sauce.
9. Bake 35 to 40 minutes until hot and starting to bubble. (If the crumbs start to brown too quickly, cover with foil).

Serves 6 to 8

This next specialty is one of my mom's, and while I gussied up her asparagus casserole dish, I've left this one completely as-is, going back to her days in Ninnie's kitchen in the 1940s. The recipe is straightforward, with few ingredients, but it's the best you'll ever taste. Over the years, as Southern cooking has become more popular, many cooks have done some serious experimenting with this dish. I've sampled a number of attempts by folks who fuse the yolks with a variety of spices and ingredients that took the old deviled egg to places it has never been before. And to be honest, I never cared for any of those trips abroad. I like mine the way Mama made them, with real mayonnaise, yellow mustard, sweet pickles, and a good dash of black pepper—along with her secret add-in, juice from the sweet pickle jar. Here is her recipe.

Deviled Eggs

Ingredients
12 large eggs
¼ cup mayonnaise
2 teaspoons yellow mustard
1 teaspoon sweet pickle juice
2 tablespoons sweet pickles, minced
¼ teaspoon black pepper
Salt to taste
Paprika, parsley, or pimento for garnish

Directions
1. Place the eggs in a single layer into a large pot and cover with water by 1 inch. Bring to a full boil, then reduce the heat and cook 8 minutes over a low boil. Move the eggs gently a time or two while cooking to center the yolks. Remove eggs from pot with a slotted spoon and place them in a pan of ice water; allow to chill for 5 minutes.
2. Peel the eggs and cut each in half lengthwise. Place the yolks in a mixing bowl and set the whites aside. Mash the yolks with the tines of a fork, or with the back of a spatula until creamy and smooth.
3. Add the mayonnaise, mustard, pickle juice, pickles, and black pepper to the mashed yolks. Stir and mix well. If you'd like the mixture a bit softer, add in a tiny bit more pickle juice, mayonnaise, or mustard. If needed, add a pinch of salt as well.
4. Mound the yolk mixture into the whites with a piping bag or spoon; place the eggs in a container, in one layer, with a tight-fitting lid. Chill for 2 to 4

hours. May be garnished with sprinkles of paprika or parsley, or a slice of pimento.

Serves 12 as an appetizer

Many people enjoy the thin haricot verts that are so popular on menus, and I am a fan of them as well. But for Easter I like to wander back to my Middle Georgia roots and fix a pot of fresh green snap beans cooked with a bit of ham or bacon and rich chicken stock. And please, please…do *not* use frozen green beans. Trust me on this. They just, aren't, well…*good*.

Fresh Green Snap Beans

Ingredients
2 quarts fresh green snap beans, washed, drained, stringed, and snapped into 2-inch pieces
1 quart chicken stock
3 slices of bacon, or 1 cup smoked ham, cubed
Black pepper to taste

Directions
1. Place all ingredients in a large stock pot. Cover and bring to a boil.
2. Stir, reduce heat to a low, steady simmer, and partially cover with lid.
3. Cook for 30 minutes or until tender, stirring occasionally.

Serves 8

Many folks love little red new potatoes at Easter. These were always on our buffet. So good and so easy!

Tiny Red New Potatoes

Ingredients
16 golf-ball sized new potatoes, washed and scrubbed (but not peeled)
2 tablespoons salt
3 tablespoons butter, melted
¼ teaspoon black pepper
¼ teaspoon kosher salt
3 tablespoons fresh parsley, finely minced

Directions

1. Place the potatoes and salt in a large pot with enough water to cover by 2 inches. Cover and bring to a full boil. Reduce heat to a gentle boil, uncover, stir, and cook until fork tender, about 12 minutes.
2. Drain and place the hot potatoes in a serving bowl or tray. Drizzle with the melted butter, then sprinkle with the black pepper and salt. Top with the parsley and serve immediately.

Serves 8

When inquiring on social media and with friends about Easter food traditions, two items came up frequently: pimento cheese and macaroni and cheese. What about combining the two? I set about trying my hand at putting these classics together and found it to be really, really good.

Just as Uncle Jed coaxed Granny to use a phone for the first time on *The Beverly Hillbillies* ("Come on Granny, give it a whirl!"), I urge you to try this unique casserole.

Baked Macaroni and Pimento Cheese

Ingredients

1 pound small elbow macaroni, cooked to package directions and drained
8 tablespoons butter, divided
3 tablespoons onion, minced
3 tablespoons flour
1 cup whole milk, heated until just hot
1 cup heavy cream, at room temperature
1 pound sharp cheddar cheese, hand grated
¼ teaspoon kosher salt
¼ teaspoon red pepper flakes
1½ teaspoons Dijon mustard
¾ cup roasted red bell peppers, diced (such as Mt. Olive or Mancini jarred brands)
2 cups finely ground Cheez-It, Pepperidge Farm Goldfish, or other cheese-flavored crackers

Directions

1. Preheat oven to 350 degrees.
2. With 2 tablespoons of the butter, grease a 9x13 baking dish. Set aside.

3. Over medium heat, melt 3 tablespoons of the butter in a large, heavy-bottomed saucepan; add in the onions and cook for 1 minute, stirring continuously.
4. Add the flour to the onions and whisk together thoroughly, cook for 2 minutes. Pour in the heated milk and stir constantly until thickened, about 3 minutes.
5. Stir in the cream and mix together well until the mixture comes to a low simmer.
6. Add the cheese and stir until the cheese is completely melted.
7. Add the salt, red pepper flakes, and Dijon mustard; stir to incorporate.
8. Stir in the diced roasted peppers and the cooked pasta; stir until mixed.
9. Spoon the mixture into the buttered baking dish.
10. Melt the remaining 3 tablespoons of butter and mix in a small bowl or food processor with the cracker crumbs. Spread the buttered crumbs evenly on top of the casserole.
11. Bake until the top starts to brown slightly and the filling is hot and bubbling, about 35 to 40 minutes. Allow to cool for 5 minutes before serving.

Serves 6 to 8

On my quest for favorite Easter recipes, Copper Pennies were mentioned again and again. My friend Ann Freeman, a Claxton, Georgia, native who now lives on the beautiful Gulf Coast in Nokomis, Florida, shared this with me:

There are more modern "copper penny" recipes featuring complicated "from scratch" sauces. This one is the traditional recipe…a tribute to women from previous generations who were thrifty and creative and could take a can of tomato soup and vegetables from their gardens and literally make memories! My Grandmother Edwards was the traditional family holiday cook, but it was my Aunt Helen who stole the show at Easter. She was most certainly not the traditional "Southern woman." You were more likely to find her behind the push lawn mower than in the kitchen. This easily assembled dish was her signature contribution…just the name was enchanting and enticed the children to try the vegetables, even after we discovered that there weren't actual pennies in the mix!

Copper Pennies

Ingredients
1 pound carrots, peeled and cut into very thin rounds
1 medium green pepper, finely chopped
1 medium onion, finely chopped
1 can Campbell's tomato soup
1 cup sugar
¾ cup white vinegar
¼ cup salad oil
1 teaspoon Worcestershire
1 teaspoon dry mustard
Salt and pepper to taste

Directions
1. In a medium saucepan, sauté the carrots, peppers, and onions with a little water until just tender, about 3 to 4 minutes; drain and cool.
2. In a large bowl, combine all other ingredients and whisk until sugar dissolves. Add carrots, peppers and onions. Cover and chill overnight before serving.

Serves 4

This oh-so-very-Southern dish of half-pear salad is one of my favorites, no matter how much fun some of my "out of the region" friends make of it. It is hard to find in restaurants now—it's gone the way of such wonderful old establishments as the Magnolia Room at Rich's in downtown Atlanta, though the Colonnade there up the road on Cheshire Bridge still offers it. I was heartened to learn that a friend's seven-year-old daughter, Kinney, says that it is one of her favorites; perhaps the tradition will continue on. Let's hope so.

Half-Pear Salad

Ingredients
6 lettuce leaves
6 canned pear halves (if you can find any homemade, those are the best)
3 tablespoons mayonnaise
3 tablespoons shredded cheddar cheese
6 Maraschino cherries

Directions
1. Place a lettuce leaf on each of 6 plates; place a pear halve, cut side up, on top.
2. Spoon a bit of the mayonnaise on each pear, sprinkle with the shredded cheese, and top with a cherry. Serve chilled.

Serves 6

People claim that the South is the casserole capital of the world, and to a point that may be true; we can put most anything in a Corningware dish with some cheese and make it taste good. This confection is a delight of many at Easter; it has a bright fresh taste that just "sings spring" to your taste buds, and it is great spooned alongside a piece of ham or fried chicken.

My good buddy Katrina Bowers, whom I met at Rock Eagle 4-H Center more than forty years ago, contributed the recipe. This Elberton, Georgia, native—who now lives in Athens—is a tremendous hostess and cook, and anything she does, she does with her whole heart!

Pineapple Casserole

Ingredients
2 tablespoons butter, at room temperature
2 (20-ounce) cans pineapple chunks
6 tablespoons flour
1 cup sugar
2 cups sharp cheddar cheese, hand grated
8 tablespoons butter, melted
1 sleeve (about 1 cup) crushed Ritz or other butter-flavored crackers

Directions
1. Preheat oven to 350 degrees.
2. Grease a 2-quart baking dish with the room temperature butter. Set aside.
3. Drain the pineapple, and reserve 6 tablespoons of the juice. Set aside.
4. Mix the flour and sugar in a bowl; slowly stir in the juice.
5. Add in the pineapple chunks and cheese; stir to mix well.
6. Spread the pineapple and cheese mixture into the buttered baking dish.
7. In a plastic bag, or bowl, combine the melted butter and crushed crackers; mix so that all crumbs are coated.

8. Spread the buttered cracker crumbs evenly over the top of the casserole and bake for 30 minutes until hot and bubbly. Allow to sit for 5 minutes before serving.

Serves 6 to 8

Another favorite for the spring holiday is a strawberry pretzel salad. This special concoction of tart berries and Jell-O, along with salty pretzels and sweet cream cheese, is a flavor sensation. Easy to make, it will be a hit for your next gathering. The following recipe comes from my great buddy Janis Owens in her cookbook, *The Cracker Kitchen*. She's a native of the Florida Panhandle (a region that can still be considered "Southern"), and her culinary compilation is a go-to for me. It's one you would enjoy for the sheer entertainment of her storytelling—as well as her fabulous cooking instructions. In the introduction for the recipe, Janis writes, "I can't think of a meal that wouldn't be improved upon by the addition of this modest little fruit and cheesecake dish." So true!

Strawberry Pretzel Salad

Ingredients
2 cups thin pretzels, crushed
12 tablespoons butter, melted
3 tablespoons light brown sugar, packed
8 ounces cream cheese, at room temperature
1 cup powdered sugar
8 ounces whipped heavy cream (or 8 ounces Cool Whip)
1 (6-ounce) box strawberry Jell-O
2 cups boiling water
1 (10-ounce) container frozen strawberries (or 2 cups cooked fresh strawberries, frozen)

Directions
1. Preheat oven to 350 degrees.
2. In a bowl, combine the pretzels, butter, and brown sugar. Press the pretzel mixture into the bottom of a 9x13 pan. Bake for 10 minutes and set aside to cool completely.
3. In a mixing bowl, beat together the cream cheese and powdered sugar until smooth.

4. To the beaten cream cheese mixture, fold in the whipped cream (or Cool Whip) and mix well; evenly spread over the pretzels and place the pan in the refrigerator to chill.
5. In another bowl, place the Jell-O; pour in the boiling water and stir for a moment to dissolve.
6. Add to the Jell-O the frozen berries; stir until separated.
7. Pour the gelatin/fruit mixture over the chilled cream cheese/whipped cream. Refrigerate several hours or overnight.

Serves 8 to 10

When sending out the note on social media for favorite Easter dishes, several people responded about their love of yeast rolls, hot cross buns, and other egg breads. I'm not much of a baker myself, though I can whip together a pan of biscuits before you can say "bourbon & soda"—and my cornbread is very good. Generally, if I want a yeast roll, I turn to Sister Shubert. However, I do have one recipe here from my friend Ali Martin Merk you should try. Ali is an elementary school art teacher who lives up the road from me in Commerce, Georgia. She grew up in Miami, and Italian egg bread was an annual custom with her family at Easter. Here is her story about her grandmother's specialty and the recipe:

> My Gram is a feisty little Italian lady. Both her parents immigrated through Ellis Island. She always has been an entrepreneur, and much of my work ethic comes from her. For most of my childhood she owned a bakery in a craftsman's village south of Miami. We made the most amazing memories creating delectable goodies with her and my Papa Alan. In fact, I won a blue ribbon at the Dade County Youth Fair in the breads division with this recipe. Not as impressive as my best in show mulberry pie, but this bread recipe is a showstopper. It can be made in big, impressive wreaths, straight braid loafs, or individual knots. Easily doubled and a go-to for gift giving.

Note: There's an option to include whole eggs—and that means uncooked, whole eggs in the shell. While they are mostly for décor (look online for photos), Ali says the eggs are edible after baking.

Gram's Italian Egg Bread

Ingredients
2½ cups all-purpose flour
¼ cup sugar
1 teaspoon salt
1 packet yeast, or ½ teaspoon bulk yeast
⅔ cup whole milk
2 tablespoons butter
2 eggs
1–2 teaspoons vegetable oil

Additional ingredients
Egg wash or melted butter for baking risen loaf
3 to 5 clean raw dyed eggs for decoration (optional)
Powdered sugar glaze for serving

Directions
1. In stand mixer with dough hook, combine 1¼ cup of the flour, sugar, salt and yeast; mix.
2. Combine milk and butter in a small saucepan; heat until milk is warm and butter is softened but not melted.
3. With mixer on low, add the milk and butter to the flour mixture.
4. Add the eggs and another ½ cup flour; beat well.
5. Add the remaining flour slowly. When the dough has pulled together, knead on hook for 2 minutes, then turn it out onto a lightly floured surface and knead until smooth and elastic—a poke should bounce back.
6. The amount of flour can be adjusted based on humidity. Having a bit more on hand to add to the hook while kneading is good idea. The bread should mostly be clean on the bowl sides but still a little sticky in the bottom of the bowl.
7. Lightly oil a large bowl, place the dough in the bowl and turn to coat with oil. Cover with a damp cloth and let rise in a warm place until doubled in volume, about 1 hour.
8. Punch the dough and turn it out onto a lightly floured surface. Divide the dough into 3 portions. Roll into ropes and shape into a braid, being sure to pinch and seal the ends to hold the braid.
9. Move the braid to a greased sheet pan. If using whole eggs in the decoration, snuggle them in the braid at this step. Cover with damp towel and let rise in a warm spot about 45 minutes.

10. Carefully brush risen loaf with melted butter or egg wash (one beaten egg with a teaspoon of water). An egg wash will make a shiny, mahogany finish, while butter will yield a matte finish.
11. Bake in a pre-heated 350 degree oven 20 to 30 minutes. It should be golden brown and make a hollow sound if you thump it.
12. Drizzle with a powdered sugar glaze when cooled.

Powdered sugar glaze: Mix 2 cups sifted confectioner's sugar with 4 tablespoons liquid. For a vanilla glaze, use whole milk for the liquid and ½ teaspoon vanilla extract. For an almond flavor, use the whole milk but add almond extract instead. For lemon, substitute 4 tablespoons fresh squeezed lemon juice in lieu of milk.
Serves 6 to 8

I've written about Aunt Polly (Ida Pauline) in both my previous books; she was one of my father's two elder sisters who helped raise him after their mother died in 1920. A wonderful lady who excelled at all things culinary, she worked magic in her cheerful and sunny pastel-yellow kitchen. Aunt Polly was also an excellent gardener, and you'd find the most beautiful zinnias, phlox, asters, roses, marigolds, and a host of other flowers abloom in the summertime. Another hobby was fishing: that little lady straight knew how to bait a hook (with gloved hands, of course) and reel in some of the fattest bream and perch that could be found in Middle Georgia.

Her coconut cake recipe is a basic 1-2-3-4 cake with a 7-minute frosting. She baked one for my father every year on his birthday; just as sure as the sun rose in the east, Aunt Polly would have one of these wonderful confections waiting and ready for him on August 18. It was also a gift to our family each year at Easter. I hope you enjoy this sweet memory from my family.

Coconut Cake

Ingredients
8 tablespoons unsalted butter, at room temperature
2 cups sugar
4 large eggs, separated
3 cups all-purpose flour
2 teaspoons baking powder

1 cup whole milk
½ teaspoon vanilla extract
¼ teaspoon lemon extract
7-minute frosting (recipe follows)
3 cups sweetened, flaked coconut

Directions
1. Preheat oven to 350 degrees.
2. Grease and flour three round 8- or 9-inch cake pans, then line the bottoms of the pans with lightly greased and floured parchment paper. Set aside.
3. In a large bowl, cream together the butter, sugar, and egg yolks with an electric mixer.
4. In a separate bowl, sift together the flour and baking powder.
5. Mix the extracts with the milk in a small bowl.
6. To the creamed butter, sugar, and eggs, add the flour mixture and the milk mixture alternately. Start and end with the flour, mixing continuously. Set aside.
7. In another bowl, beat the egg whites until gentle peaks form.
8. Gently fold the beaten egg whites into the cake batter.
9. Pour the batter into the prepared cake pans.
10. Bake for 25 to 30 minutes, until done. Remove the layers from the oven and cool on a wire rack. Cool completely before frosting.

Serves 12 to 16

7-Minute Frosting for a 3-Layer Cake

Ingredients
2¼ cups sugar
3 large egg whites
⅜ cup cold water
1½ tablespoons white corn syrup
⅜ teaspoon cream of tartar
1 teaspoon vanilla extract

Directions
1. In the bottom of a double boiler, bring about 3 inches of water to a steady simmer over medium-high heat.
2. In the top of the double boiler, beat together the sugar, egg whites, water, corn syrup, and cream of tartar for 1 minute, until well incorporated.

3. Place the top of the double boiler with frosting base from step 2 over the simmering water and beat at high speed for 7 minutes. Remove from heat and add vanilla. Continue to beat until the icing is thick and forms firm peaks. This may take several more minutes.
4. Spread between layers and on the top of the cake; sprinkle the coconut evenly on the tops and sides of the frosted cake.

Another fine Southern lady who knows how to make a proper dish for Easter or any other special occasion is the elegant Lynda Cowart Talmadge of Twin City, Georgia. From her beautifully appointed Queen Anne–style family home, which itself looks like a finely decorated cake with multiple gables, a white baluster-lined porch, and a rounded gazebo crown, Lynda creates culinary delights that are sought-after from the four corners of our state and beyond. I have the privilege of knowing Lynda, the widow of former US Senator Herman Talmadge, through my work with 4-H. Mrs. Talmadge is one of our most ardent supporters and has assisted our youth for decades through her generosity. Here she generously provides the recipe for her renowned lemon cheese cake. This confection, with its moist and delicate layers and magnificent lemon curd icing, is a stand-out dish.

If you've never made this cake before and read through the recipe, you may say to yourself, "Goodness gracious, JSB has evidently left out a main ingredient." Well, no, I haven't—this classic, old-school recipe has not the smallest morsel of cheese in it. Apparently, the name of the cake comes from the icing itself, which is a lemon curd. In days past, folks used the word "curd" as they would "cheese," and my guess is our forebears thought "lemon cheese cake" a more pleasant descriptive than "lemon curd cake." On a side note, several people wrote to me that they iced this cake with a 7-minute frosting—such as with Aunt Polly's cake in this chapter—and then filled the layers with the lemon curd. Regardless of which way you put it together, iced white or completely finished with the curd, be prepared to get a chorus of "oohs" and "ahhs" from your family and friends.

Lynda Talmadge's Lemon Cheese Cake

Ingredients
½ cup Crisco shortening
16 tablespoons butter, at room temperature
3 cups sugar
5 large eggs, at room temperature
3 cups cake flour, such as Swans Down
½ teaspoon baking powder
1 cup whole milk
2 teaspoons pure vanilla extract
Lemon curd icing (recipe follows)

Directions
1. Preheat oven to 350 degrees.
2. Grease and flour 3 (9-inch) baking pans; set aside.
3. In a bowl, cream together the Crisco and butter; add the sugar gradually and continue to beat until the mixture is light and fluffy.
4. Add the eggs one at a time to the bowl, beating after each addition.
5. After all eggs are incorporated, add the flour alternately with the milk, beginning and ending with the flour.
6. Stir in the vanilla. *Do not overbeat! Mix until just well-blended!*
7. Spread the batter evenly into the prepared cake pans and bake 25 to 30 minutes.
8. Remove the cake layers from the oven and allow them to cool in the pans for 5 minutes or more before turning them out onto a rack to cool completely.
9. Frost with the lemon curd icing, or 7-minute icing with lemon curd between the layers.

Serves 12 to 16

The elegant cake baker, Lynda C. Talmadge, of Twin City, Georgia

Lynda shares that the lemon curd icing recipe is her mother's.

Lemon Curd Icing

Ingredients
5½ tablespoons all-purpose flour
9 tablespoons freshly squeezed lemon juice
Zest from 1 large lemon (about 1 tablespoon)
1 cup boiling water
2 cups sugar
½ teaspoon salt
3 large eggs, beaten
4 tablespoons butter, room temperature

Directions
1. In the bottom of a double boiler, bring water to a moderate boil.
2. Sift the flour into the top of the double boiler and set it over the boiling water (in step 1).
3. Whisk into the flour the lemon juice, zest, boiling water, sugar, and salt, mixing together making sure there are no lumps from the flour.
4. As the mixture heats, slowly drizzle in the beaten eggs, whisking as you go (it's good to have a second pair of hands with this step!).
5. Continue cooking until the curd coats the back of a metal spoon, and when you draw your finger down the back of the spoon to make a line, the gap stays. This curd needs to be very thick.
6. Whisk in the butter, 1 tablespoon at a time, until well blended. Keep the curd over the hot water for another 2 minutes, whisking.
7. Take the curd from the stove, set aside, and allow to cool completely before spreading on and between the baked layers.

Makes icing for 3 (9-inch) layers

Chapter 4

Summer Holidays: Memorial, Independence, and Labor Days

As family and friends, and the nation, come together to celebrate those who died in the service of our country, the birthday of the USA, and for the works of laborers who helped shape these fifty states, food is at the center of the festivities. In the South, as always, we pull out all the stops when it comes to showcasing our culinary traditions during these hot-weather holidays. Now some of you might point out that Memorial Day doesn't occur in the summer, but it *is* on the cusp of the season, and many of the dishes we enjoy for all three of these national commemorations are often repeated from one holiday to the next. For the sake of this book, I've combined these summer celebrations into one chapter; grilled hot dogs, hamburgers, barbeque, potato salad, and apple pie are just a short part of the list of the items we Southerners enjoy whether it's Memorial Day, the Fourth of July, or Labor Day.

A big part of my affection for these dates and long weekends is that most of the celebrating is done outside with picnics. I love being outdoors, and these casual al fresco meals allow me to munch on a chicken leg and pimento cheese sandwich while enjoying Mother Nature at the same time. My parents never had to encourage me to go outside and play—if anything, they would have to drag me in when it started to get dark. Barefoot and shirtless most of the time, I'd spend the day playing baseball, riding my bike, fishing down the hill on Fanny Gresham creek, or working with friends to construct some sort of fort in the woods. Because I often came home streaked in sweat and with dirt rings around my neck, Carrie would make me wash off with a water hose before setting foot in the house. How I loved those carefree days of summer.

Let's move along—as you know I can get on a tangent and lead us down any number of talking paths—to some of the South's most popular and traditional summer holiday recipes and dishes. Starting with appetizers and hors d'oeuvres, some of the favorites include the stalwart classic, pimento cheese, as well as pickled okra and Texas caviar. We covered deviled eggs in the previous chapter on Easter; tomato sandwiches, pineapple sandwiches, and some spicy but sweet bread and butter pickles are provided in another chapter—so don't worry, we're good there!

Pimento cheese is a straightforward recipe, but some folks on the modern food scene like to experiment with this dish, much to the consternation of myself and other purists. What supposedly started as a Northern dish (yet was perfected by Southerners—are you surprised?) contains just a handful of basic ingredients: sharp cheddar cheese, pimentos, mayonnaise, black pepper, and maybe, if the cheese is incredibly sharp, a pinch of sugar. How many of you recall having lunch at the old Len Berg's in Macon and relishing a plate featuring pimento cheese on gummy white bread, and a fat, crispy fried chicken breast? Lord, how I miss that restaurant! Besides a summer sandwich, my mom would also stuff celery stalks with pimento cheese as a picnic appetizer, and at other times serve it as a dip with potato chips. For those of you on a low-carb diet, pimento cheese pairs excellently with fried pork skins. Yep, you read right, pork skins! The smoky flavor and crunch of the *chicharrones* are perfect with pimento cheese's tart, smooth creaminess; trust me, people love these together.

My recipe is below and the only thing I have changed out from my mom's old classic is that I use a jar of fire-roasted red bell peppers instead of the pre-diced pimentos. Same pepper, just a different cut—and the fire-roasting gives the pepper a better depth of flavor.

And for this recipe, and most any other calling for cheese, I don't recommend using the packaged, pre-shredded brands—which are coated with cellulose to keep the cheese from sticking together. This coating takes the moisture out of the cheese *and* prevents it from absorbing the taste and flavor of other ingredients in a recipe. If you use a pre-shredded variety here, you will be disappointed in the result.

Pimento Cheese

Ingredients
1 pound sharp cheddar cheese, hand grated
1 cup mayonnaise (no "lite" mayo allowed, at all, no ma'am, no sir!)
1 (12-ounce) jar fire-roasted red peppers, drained and chopped
½ teaspoon black pepper

Directions
1. Place all ingredients in a large mixing bowl and stir until well blended.
2. Cover tightly and refrigerate 4 to 6 hours, or overnight. Serve as a sandwich, with crackers and/or potato chips, with a bowl of fried pork skins: plain or barbequed!

Makes 6 to 8 sandwiches or enough hors d'oeuvres for 12 to 16

A perfect companion on the nibble table this time of year with the pimento cheese is a platter of chilled pickled okra. Choose small, baby pods that are tender and just enough for a bite or two. These crunchy and mouth-puckering snacks are also wonderful to serve as a flavorful garnish for a Bloody Mary. My recipe here calls for fresh dill, garlic, and a number of easily accessible spices, along with a spear of cayenne pepper to give the okra some kick. Just make sure when plucking the okra from the jar you don't accidentally plop that green pepper in your mouth instead. You'll be in for a hot surprise if you do!

Spiced Pickled Okra

Ingredients
2 quarts white vinegar
1 quart water
½ cup salt
12 whole, fresh green cayenne or jalapeño peppers
12 large sprigs of fresh dill
12 garlic cloves, crushed but each clove intact
2 tablespoons black peppercorns
2 tablespoons mustard seeds
120 pods of okra (about 6 pounds) of uniform size, rinsed and drained

Directions
1. Bring the vinegar, water, and salt to a steady simmer in a boiler.
2. Place the peppers, dill, and garlic in 12 sterilized pint jars.
3. Measure out and add to each jar ½ teaspoon peppercorns and ½ teaspoon mustard seeds.
4. Place the okra in the jars, pointed end down, about 10 per jar, or until packed.
5. Pour the hot vinegar solution over the okra and seal.

Makes 12 pints

I met my friend Celeste Bollinger Stroud from Cochran, Georgia, while we were at Georgia Southern University. She and I had some wonderful times together in Statesboro—or "the 'Boro" as we referred to it—much of which included beer out of a keg, wine out of a jug, and a good bit of 80s rock and roll playing from a cassette player. Any of you remember Mother's Finest? One of the best Southern rock bands, ever. Anyway, while I was still living in a dorm, Celeste had her own apartment, and, taking after her wonderful mama, Miss Bonnie, my buddy was a great cook. She would often bring back from Cochran fresh produce and groceries from her mama's pantry and fix up all sorts of dishes for her hungry friends. One favorite munchy we enjoyed was her Texas caviar, also known as cowboy caviar. This dish was originally created by Helen Corbitt, head chef for Neiman Marcus in Dallas for almost twenty years. Mrs. Corbitt was asked to serve a menu using only Texas-grown ingredients for New Year's Eve in 1940. She came up with this dip as a result, and since it was being served in the fancy setting of the Houston Country Club, she dubbed it, tongue-in-cheek, "Texas Caviar."

Note that a key ingredient in Celeste's recipe, red pepper relish, is made in the 'Boro by the fine people at Braswell's. Mr. Albert Braswell started this company making small batches of pear preserves in 1946, and Braswell's has grown to now be the top seller of pepper jelly, fig preserves, and pear preserves in the US, *plus* it holds the spot of being the seventh-largest jam, jelly, and preserve manufacturer in the country. Go Georgia agriculture and food industries!

Texas Caviar

Ingredients
1 cup Vidalia onion, diced
1 cup green or red bell pepper, diced
1 cup red ripe tomato, seeded and diced
1 (15.5-ounce) can black eyed peas, rinsed and drained
1 (15.5-ounce) can shoepeg corn, drained
1 (8-ounce) Jar Braswell's Pepper Relish, or other comparable sweet pepper relish
1 (8-ounce) bottle zesty Italian dressing
Tortilla chips or Fritos to serve alongside

Directions
1. In a bowl, combine all ingredients except for the chips, and stir well.
2. Cover tightly and refrigerate 4 to 6 hours before serving.
Serves 12 to 16 as an appetizer

Hot weather calls for chilled salads, and many people today turn up their high-falutin' culinary noses at iceberg lettuce. And while the distinct taste of baby arugula, the sweet bite of watercress, and most any of the mesclun greens are totally appetizing, they fall short of the cold crunch of crispy iceberg during the days of summer. The classic wedge salad can be found on many menus, especially at high-end steakhouses, and it is quite good. You don't need a recipe for it, though. Just cut a head of iceberg into wedges, drizzle on a dollop of good bleu cheese dressing, and scatter atop chopped tomato, green onions, crumbled bacon, and voilà!

My choice here to share with you is the old-school layered salad, one that has graced many a table, especially at a Baptist church-on-the-grounds picnic. It combines a number of complementary flavors and textures and is excellent alongside a piece of fried chicken, some barbeque, or sliced ham. Of special note: this salad *has* to sit, covered and refrigerated, for at least eight hours or overnight to turn out properly.

Layered Salad

Ingredients
1 head iceberg lettuce, torn into bite-sized pieces
1 cup celery, diced

1 cup green onion, both the white and green parts, diced
1 cup green or red bell pepper, diced
1 cup frozen (don't use canned!) English peas, defrosted, drained, and wiped dry with paper towels
¾ cup mayonnaise
½ cup good quality ranch dressing
½ teaspoon Worcestershire sauce
½ teaspoon sugar
1 cup sharp cheddar cheese, hand grated
1 (12-ounce) package bacon, cooked very crisp and crumbled (you can substitute a 4.3-ounce packet of pre-cooked bacon crumbles—crisp them in the microwave for about 30 seconds before serving)

Directions
1. Place the lettuce on the bottom of a baking dish that is at least 3 inches deep.
2. On top of the lettuce, layer in order the celery, green onions, bell pepper, and lastly the peas.
3. In a bowl, whisk together the mayonnaise, ranch dressing, Worcestershire sauce, and sugar. With a spatula, carefully and evenly spread the mixture over the peas.
4. Cover tightly and refrigerate overnight. Sprinkle the cheese and then the bacon on top just before serving.

Serves 6 to 8

Another summer side-dish of choice is potato salad. In *Rise and Shine!* I shared my mom's decades-old recipe, which was made with russet potatoes, onions, sweet pickles, boiled eggs, mayonnaise, yellow mustard, and a good dash of black pepper. The following recipe is another that I dearly love, and so does Tom. It is similar to the one served at the historic Exchange Tavern in Savannah and features the tang of sour cream, the crunch of fresh celery, and the piquant spice of garlic and green onion.

Sour Cream Potato Salad

Ingredients
3 pounds firm potatoes, such as Yukon gold, scrubbed and washed, unpeeled, and cut into 1½-inch cubes
1 tablespoon salt
¾ cup celery, diced

¼ cup green onion, both white and green portions, diced
1 cup sour cream
½ cup mayonnaise
1 tablespoon Dijon mustard
1 teaspoon garlic powder
¼ teaspoon black pepper

Directions
1. Place the potatoes in a large boiler along with the salt and cover with cold water by 2 inches. Bring the potatoes to a boil, reduce heat to a steady simmer, and cook until done, about 8 to 10 minutes. Stir occasionally while simmering.
2. Drain the potatoes; do not rinse.
3. Transfer the drained potatoes into a large mixing bowl. Add the remaining ingredients and fold together gently so as not to break the potatoes. Cover the bowl tightly and refrigerate at least 4 hours or overnight before serving.

Serves 6 to 8

It's easy to select entrées for the summer holiday party because everyone loves a grilled hamburger or hot dog. Those are pretty easily done, so I don't include them here. If you don't know how to make a hamburger, or don't have time, Fresh Market as well as Publix—and other grocery stores—provide pre-made ones that are good. My favorite is the commercial bacon cheddar burger. Yum, yum, yum!

On polling friends and folks on social media, fried chicken and barbeque, especially ribs, come in as favorites as well. In terms of the yard-bird, so many other more accomplished cookbook writers have already covered the dish. Scott Peacock and Edna Lewis come to mind; their recipe and instructions provide an extraordinary platter. But like any good dish of fried chicken, it takes extensive effort, a keen eye and nose, and the willingness to clean up a messy kitchen afterwards. My recipe here is a simple one: order out! Ingles does an excellent job with fried chicken, as does Publix, not to mention Popeye's or KFC. You can also look to your local restaurants, such as in my hometown of Perry with Skipper John's, or down in Milledgeville at the Shrimp Boat. You can order a big pan for a party from my friends at either Carey Hilliard's or Barnes in Savannah, and you simply cannot beat the drumsticks and breasts that come out of

B&J's in the little coastal town of Darien, Georgia. I say let the experts do the frying so that you view the fireworks with the rest of the gang—and not fret about what to do with that pan of leftover hot grease.

As for ribs, I fix them often but admit to not being a purist—instead of cooking them over the coals the whole time, mine are baked in the oven and then finished on the grill; they turn out very tender, and with plenty of crusty charring and a smoky taste.

If in a hurry, you can always buy ribs from one of your favorite BBQ joints. In terms of cost, you can't fix baby backs any less expensively than letting Fincher's in Macon do the job. But standing outside over the grill and sipping a cold beverage can be a lot of fun.

JSB's Barbequed Ribs

Ingredients
6 pounds baby back pork ribs, cut into 3- to 4-rib portions
1 teaspoon unseasoned meat tenderizer
1 teaspoon black pepper
1 teaspoon garlic powder
1 teaspoon onion powder
1 teaspoon dried thyme
Hickory, mesquite, or other wood chips
1 cup or more of your favorite BBQ sauce

Directions
1. Preheat oven to 350 degrees.
2. Sprinkle both sides of the meat with the meat tenderizer; pierce the ribs with a fork at one-inch intervals on both sides as well.
3. Season the meat evenly with the black pepper, garlic powder, onion powder, and thyme.
4. Completely wrap each portion in aluminum foil and seal. Place the packets on a large baking tray, seam side up; cook for 2½ to 3 hours or until the ribs are fork-tender. During the last 30 minutes of cooking, prepare your grill and wood chips.
5. When done, carefully remove the rib sections from the packets. Spread each piece with barbeque sauce. Place the ribs on the prepared grill; close the lid to smoke. After 10 minutes, turn them over; spread on any additional sauce if you'd like. Close the lid again and allow to cook for another 10 minutes or so. Serve immediately.

Serves 6 to 8

A third entrée is often used as an appetizer, but this dish is such a hit, and with such a great story behind it, that I like to put out an enormous bowl and let folks feast. Made a day in advance, these pickled shrimp are excellent with a slice of tomato pie and a scoop of layered salad sitting on the plate.

The recipe comes from the late, great Pat Conroy, one of the masters of Southern literature. Pat was also a renowned cook and penned the well-received *The Pat Conroy Cookbook: Recipes and Stories of My Life*. I had the incredible fortune of meeting Pat and his equally talented and lovely wife, Cassandra King (who wrote the foreword to this book) through our buddy Janis Owens. The first time I spent any length of time with Pat and Cassandra was the summer of 2015 when Janis, Cassandra, and I were featured as a part of the Laurel Garden Kitchen Tour in Highlands, North Carolina. Tom and I were invited to Pat and Cassandra's cottage for a casual pot-luck supper, and I can't even recall what I brought I was so nervous about meeting them. The worries were all for naught; they were the most gracious and laid-back of hosts and we felt right at home. Pat talked to each of us with genuine interest, warmth, and great humor; it was a night I'll always remember.

One of Pat's favorite dishes was pickled shrimp, and he perfected a recipe that is, hands-down, the best I've ever had. Cassandra shared that she adds a pinch of sugar along with Pat's ingredients and says, with her dry wit, "I like mine better, as I told him." Pat loved the dish so much that he wrote in his cookbook, "When a good friend dies, I take two pounds of shrimp for the mourners. When a great friend dies, I go to five pounds. When I die, I fully expect all the shrimp in Beaufort to be pickled that day."

I was honored with being invited to Pat's wake at the Beaufort Yacht Club. And based on the countless bowls of pickled shrimp offered at the reception, I doubt that there wasn't a single, solitary shrimp to be seen in the waters off South Carolina's Low Country coast on that bright and sunny, but sad, March day.

Pat Conroy and Cassandra King at their home, Beaufort, South Carolina

Jane Pearson Hulbert with her daughter, Beth Beckham Henderson, the night Beth was crowned Miss Westfield, The Westfield School, Perry, Georgia, spring 1981

Pat Conroy's Pickled Shrimp

Ingredients
6 quarts water
4 tablespoons + 2 teaspoons kosher or sea salt
4 pounds large, wild-caught US shrimp, peeled and deveined
2 cups onions, thinly sliced
8 bay leaves
2 (2-ounce) bottles capers, drained and chopped
½ cup fresh lemon juice
2 cups cider vinegar
1 cup olive oil
2 teaspoons garlic, minced
2 teaspoons celery seeds
2 teaspoons red pepper flakes
2 pinches sugar, per Cassandra
Fresh sprigs of parsley and sliced lemons for garnish

Directions
1. In a stockpot over high heat, bring the water and 4 tablespoons kosher salt to a rolling boil. Add the shrimp and cook until just pink, about 3 minutes. (The shrimp will continue to "cook" in the marinade.) Drain and set aside.
2. Mix the remaining ingredients except for the garnish in a large bowl. Toss in the shrimp and stir to fully coat. Cover tightly and marinate overnight in the refrigerator.
3. When ready to serve, drain the excess marinade from the container, and place the shrimp in a large, decorative bowl. Garnish with the parsley and lemon slices.
Serves 8 for a main course, 20 for hors d'oeuvres

The best squash casserole ever sampled in my life, and there have been many, is from my wonderful buddy Carol Cordray, a native of the granite capital of the world, Elberton, Georgia. She now lives in a fine pile of a historic home in Atlanta's historic Virginia Highlands. The two of us worked together for over a decade at Junior Achievement—she was the comptroller and I a major gifts officer. Both accountants by trade who loved to cook and indulge in adult beverages, we bonded during that time and have remained friends long since we left our old jobs. Carol has an excellent sense of humor, so I'm sharing here a story she relayed. It was in

Cook & Tell but bears repeating just to give you a glimpse of her observant wit, particularly about small-town life in the South.

It was 1977; I was just out of graduate school when I landed a job as an assistant controller in a paper mill in Brewton, Alabama. Brewton was a pretty little place where, as in most small Southern towns, everyone knew everyone, perhaps too well. They followed the whereabouts of each by where their cars were parked, since everyone knew the make and model of every car in town. There was one fellow, though, John Paul David, who had four cars, so it was impossible to determine his whereabouts. What single person has four cars? I was not the only one who was curious about that and suspected something nefarious.

How I love my Carol!

Carol Cordray's Squash Casserole

Ingredients
3½ pounds yellow squash, sliced into ¼-inch-thick rounds
2 cups onion, chopped
1 quart chicken broth
1 teaspoon kosher salt
¼ teaspoon white pepper
2 tablespoons butter, at room temperature
4 large eggs
2 cups half-and-half
8 ounces sharp cheddar cheese, hand grated and divided
1 sleeve Ritz crackers, crushed and divided
4 tablespoons butter, melted

Directions
1. Place the squash, diced onions, chicken broth, salt, and pepper in a large pot. Bring to a boil, stir, and cook with a steady simmer over medium heat for 30 minutes. Stir occasionally during cooking.
2. Preheat oven to 350 degrees. Grease a 9x13 ovenproof casserole dish with the room-temperature butter.
3. In a bowl, beat the eggs, then whisk in the half-and-half. Set aside.
4. When the squash and onions are cooked, pour the vegetables into a colander and drain well.

5. Place the drained vegetables back into the pot you cooked them in and mash together. Mix in ¼ cup of the cracker crumbs and ¼ cup of the cheese. Spread the combined ingredients into the buttered baking dish.
6. Pour the whisked eggs and half-and-half over the squash mixture.
7. Sprinkle the remaining grated cheese over the top of the casserole.
8. In a small bowl, combine the remaining cracker crumbs and the melted butter. Stir to coat the crumbs. Sprinkle the buttered crumbs on the top of the casserole.
9. Bake at 350 degrees for 45 minutes until bubbly and the breadcrumbs turn a deep gold color. Remove from the oven and allow to rest for 10 minutes before serving.

Serves 8

Garden fresh, just-off-the-vine tomatoes are hailed as a nectar of the gods in the South. During their growing season in the summer, there would always be a platter of sliced tomatoes, along with cucumbers, radishes, and green onions on our dining table for supper. The favorite way to eat them was in a sandwich, sprinkled with a touch of salt and black pepper, or a shake or two of Lawry's, on white bread with mayonnaise. Mama would also can the tomatoes as the season progressed; there would row upon row of quart jars in our pantry to be used in soups and stews during the winter.

For a summer holiday picnic or party, besides the ever-loved sandwich, I offer two other ways to use the tomatoes as an excellent side dish. One is to slice them crosswise, place the slices on a platter, sprinkle with a bit of balsamic vinegar and olive oil, season with kosher salt and black pepper to taste, and finish with sprigs of fresh basil. On the side, have a bowl of Duke's mayonnaise for folks to spoon on a dollop or two with their serving.

Another is a tomato pie that is served either warm or at room temperature. You cannot ask for a better accompaniment to fried chicken, or Pat Conroy's pickled shrimp, than this dish. Friends rave over it, and I've shared the recipe dozens of times. A key ingredient in this recipe is the Dijon mustard—a trick learned decades ago from a Savannah matriarch, and she was spot-on with the addition. Enjoy!

Summer Tomato Pie

Ingredients
1 unbaked deep dish pie shell
1½ pounds red, ripe tomatoes
1 teaspoon Dijon mustard
¼ teaspoon black pepper
1 cup plus 3 tablespoons freshly shredded Parmesan cheese, separated
1 teaspoon fresh thyme, minced
¼ teaspoon kosher salt
3 tablespoons mayonnaise
1 tablespoon olive oil

Directions
1. Preheat oven to 350 degrees.
2. Line the bottom of the pie shell with aluminum foil and fill with 1 cup dried beans or pie weights; bake for 10 minutes. Remove the foil and beans/weights and set the shell aside.
3. Cut the top quarter off each tomato and carefully remove the pulp and seeds (I use my fingers). Discard the pulp and seeds. Slice the seeded tomatoes crosswise ¼-inch thick, and lay the slices on paper towels; pat dry.
4. Brush the bottom and sides of the pie shell with the Dijon mustard.
5. Place one slightly overlapping layer of tomatoes in the bottom of the shell; sprinkle with a bit of the black pepper, cheese, thyme, and salt. Continuing layering until the shell is full.
6. In a small bowl, whisk together the mayonnaise and olive oil. Place dollops of the mixture evenly on the tops of the last layer of tomatoes, and carefully spread out to evenly coat the slices.
7. Place the pie on a cookie sheet and bake for 20 minutes. Remove from the oven and sprinkle the remaining cheese on top of the pie. Place back in the oven and cook for another 15 to 20 minutes until the cheese is melted into the mayonnaise and the top has browned slightly.
8. Remove from the oven and allow the pie to cool completely, 20 to 30 minutes, before slicing.

Serves 6 to 8

There is nothing as American as apple pie, so the saying goes, and I dearly love a piece with a scoop of ice cream, or, as my mom enjoyed, with a slice of melted cheddar cheese. I prefer fruit pies and cobblers more than cakes or cookies, and I serve them often to guests for a dinner party. Mine usually are done in a rustic manner, cooked in Ninnie's cast-iron skillet in which she fried chicken; it is 10.5 inches in diameter and 3 inches deep. The following creation for the summer holidays is a cross between a pie and a cobbler in that, though the dessert is round, the crusts don't meet. True, it isn't as pretty as a lattice-work pie, but it is a lot less work and, too, you're going to cover the top with either ice cream or whipped cream, so the bowl needn't look like it stepped off a magazine cover. If you don't have a deep-dish cast-iron pan, a round casserole dish with the same proportions will work just fine. Too, use any other fruit that you might like—peaches, blackberries, and blueberries are wonderful choices—just leave off the step of simmering the fruit in water, and adjust the spices to your taste.

Deep Dish Apple Cobbler

Ingredients
6 cups baking apples, peeled, cored, and cut into 2-inch cubes (or other fruit of choice)
3 cups water
¾ cup sugar
2 teaspoons flour
½ teaspoon cinnamon
¼ teaspoon nutmeg
2 tablespoons butter, melted
3 tablespoons butter, at room temperature
1 package rolled piecrusts (2 crusts)
1 egg, whisked together with 1 tablespoon water
Whipped cream or vanilla ice cream

Directions
1. Preheat oven to 350 degrees.
2. Place the apples in a pot with the water; bring to a gentle boil. Decrease heat to a steady simmer, stirring occasionally. Cook 3 to 4 minutes, until apples are just soft to the touch.
3. Drain the apples well and add back to the pot you cooked them in. To the apples, fold in the sugar, flour, cinnamon, nutmeg, and the 2 tablespoons melted butter. Set aside.

4. Rub the 3 tablespoons of room temperature butter on the bottoms and up the sides of your baking dish. Unroll one of the piecrusts and place it on the bottom of the pan. A portion of the crust will go partially up the sides.
5. Pour the apple mixture into the baking dish on top of the bottom pie crust; unroll the other crust and place it on top. You will need to crimp or fold the edges some as there will be some overlap on the sides.
6. Brush the whisked egg and water on the top crust. Cook for 45 to 50 minutes until the juices bubble up on the sides of the pan and the crust is a golden brown.
7. Remove the cobbler from the oven and allow it to rest for 10 to 15 minutes. Scoop into bowls and serve with whipped cream or vanilla ice cream.

Serves 6 to 8

The summer isn't summer without a good, creamy banana pudding, and these desserts are prominent on Memorial Day, Independence Day, and Labor Day. Mom's meringue-topped version was featured in *Rise and Shine!* while *Cook & Tell* shared Big Mama Junnie's banana pudding recipe, thanks to her grandson, my good buddy Wes Goodroe. Here I have a delectable variation that is light, not overly sweet, and uses shortbread cookies instead of vanilla wafers; the result is excellent.

This recipe is from my colleague and friend Kathy Bangle, a senior development officer at the University of Georgia. Kathy is one of those wonderful folks with a perpetually sunny disposition; her smile can light up the entire UGA campus. Kathy received the recipe via her friend Carol White Daniel, whom she met at Presbyterian College in Clinton, South Carolina. Their close group of girlfriends from those college days have been gathering together the first weekend in November for thirty years. It was at one of those annual gatherings that Carol introduced her variation of this classic to her former classmates.

Shortbread Banana Pudding

Ingredients
3 cups whole milk
1 (5.1-ounce) box vanilla instant pudding
1 cup sour cream
1 (12-ounce) container Cool Whip, softened
2 boxes Lorna Doone shortbread cookies, divided with 6 cookies left aside

6 large bananas, peeled and sliced in ¼-inch rounds

Directions
1. In a large bowl, whisk together the milk and pudding mix.
2. Fold in the sour cream and softened Cool Whip. Set the mixture aside.
3. Line bottom of a 11x7 pan with a layer of cookies, then bananas, followed by some of the pudding mixture. Repeat, ending with the pudding as the final layer.
4. Cover tightly and refrigerate 4 to 6 hours, or overnight. When ready to serve, crumble the remaining 6 cookies and sprinkle on top of the pudding.
Serves 6

The finale for this chapter is the quintessential Southern summer dessert, homemade peach ice cream! This version, worthy of a Golden Churn award, comes from the mother of Macon's Beth Beckham Henderson; Beth was one of my best friends at the Westfield Schools. Her mother, Jane, grew up on her family's farm in Peach County, where, yes, they raised peaches. And the family continues the tradition today at Pearson Farms. As a child, I was in awe of Miss Jane, who to me was the prettiest lady in all of Perry and who had such an incredible, elegant style about her. Like Jackie-O, but from Middle Georgia.

Jane's recipe is one of the simplest, yet the best, that can be found. It has only four ingredients, and all you do is add them together and churn. No fussing with cooking a custard or worrying about raw eggs. This version is now my go-to recipe each summer. And if you don't want peaches (why wouldn't you, though?) substitute drained crushed pineapple, mashed bananas, or blueberries. Sublime dessert, bar none.

Jane's original recipe was a "blender full of crushed peaches, and two cans each of condensed milk and sweetened evaporated milk, vanilla extract." I've had to modify here because blender sizes have changed over the years, as have churns. When I was a boy, our churn held two full gallons, and we turned the contraption by hand. People now use commercial-size blenders that hold a great deal more than the old models, and ice cream makers come in counter-top sizes, much smaller than when I was an eight-year-old. Speaking of being eight years old, and peach ice cream, Daddy had made a big churn late one afternoon, and we were sitting outside at dusk enjoying the dessert. Our house sat right across the street from a big swath of woodlands, with Fanny Gresham creek at its center; we saw all sorts of wildlife even though we lived in town. Well, that night as I was propped on the back doorstep, savoring my ice cream, a big old black snake slithered right past me and made his way into the crawl space underneath our house. My cousin sitting next to me screamed, threw his bowl of ice cream, and ran off. I was like, "Dummy. That snake certainly didn't want any of your ice cream." And I kept right on eating without missing a spoonful.

Note: Ingredient quantities in the recipe below are based on the size of your ice cream churn.

Jane's Homemade Peach Ice Cream

Ingredients

	4-quart	3-quart	2-quart
Crushed, ripe peaches	6 cups	4 cups	2 cups
Evaporated milk, 12-ounce can	3	2	1
Sweetened condensed milk, 14-ounce can	3	2	1
Vanilla extract	1½ teaspoon	1 teaspoon	½ teaspoon

Directions
1. Combine ingredients in a bowl, stirring to mix.
2. Add to your churn and follow the churn instructions.
Serves 4 to 10

Chapter 5

Halloween

It amazes me how Halloween has grown into such an enormous celebration, it seems, over the past decade. When I was a young'un, our costumes were bought at the local 5&10; the masks were hard plastic and capes were sewn from some mystery faux-fabric akin to a lightweight tarp. How I loved those vampires, Casper the Friendly Ghosts, horned devils, and fairy princesses. Today the children look like they're ready to sashay down a Paris runway in the latest Dior-inspired ghoul fashion. Too, as a kid, Mama and Daddy would help me carve a single pumpkin so that we'd have a gap-toothed jack-o'-lantern sitting on the front porch. Flash-forward to today, and folks decorate their yards like they are replicating a Stephen King or George Lucas movie set. I first noticed this recent extravagance when I was visiting at the home of my high school buddy, Tom "Boone" Thomson, whose house is on historic Main Street of beautiful Franklin, Tennessee. (If you love charming small towns, you should have Franklin on the top of your bucket list.) It seemed each stately home in that town had been tastefully and professionally decorated for Halloween from a Neiman Marcus catalog. My mind kept tallying what I figured the costs to be—hey, I'm a CPA and a fundraiser, so I think in terms of money and dollars—and I know that a cool couple of thousand here or there wasn't off the mark.

Years ago, at least in Perry, population around 2,600 when I was in kindergarten, folks still made Halloween treats. My sweet Aunt Lil would spend hours in the kitchen making bright red candied apples and Rice Krispy treats for the youngsters who came up her front porch. That practice has gone out of style for a variety of reasons, unfortunately. Now I'm not complaining, please don't think me a curmudgeon; these new outfits and decorations are impressive, and I'm amazed at what can be seen now from year to year. It's just a big change from my years of trick-or-treating.

Some of my favorite memories of spending time with my dad are around this holiday. He made it an annual tradition to have a father-and-son day where he would take me to the Halloween carnivals held at local schools. How I loved those cool fall days, getting in the truck to drive out to Kings Chapel Elementary and then to Tucker Elementary for a full day of festivities. Away from Mama's watchful eye, we would eat big fat barbeque sandwiches made by the lunchroom ladies, munch on bags of roasted peanuts, and relish a couple sweet clouds of cotton candy. We bought tickets for games such as the balloon pop, ring toss, pick a duck, and for my absolute, all-time, most favorite Halloween carnival activity: the cake walk. The chance to win one of those beautifully iced confections sent me into a rush similar to a gambler's high at a Vegas roulette table. Out of the six or seven years of playing, I only got the prize once, and what a joy that was! I can recall the electric charge of the air as the needle touched down on the 45 rpm and still hear clearly the strains of "Baby Elephant Walk"—as the competitors circled, warily watching one another and listening carefully to repeated sounds of the tuba coming from the record. The good Lord answered my simple but repeated prayers that afternoon: when the song abruptly stopped, I was smack dab in front of the lone wooden chair and plopped myself down with a thud. Success! And to make the win even sweeter, the cake was a richly decadent—and appropriate to the holiday—devil's food cake, thickly frosted with a vanilla buttercream icing. To this day I can't bite into a piece of devil's food cake and not think about Halloween, my dad, and my one triumphant cake walk.

While I cherish my childhood memories of Halloween, there is a great deal of fun to be had today, and my friends in Savannah—as Savannahians are apt to do—make the most of the holiday. And Tom and I began a most enjoyable tradition of October 31 revelry when we moved to the 100 block of East 45th Street back in 1995.

We had sold our 1800-square-foot downtown row house to live in the first of Savannah's streetcar suburbs, Ardsley Park. Originally built by Mr. C.S. Rowland, our new house was of Italianate style and featured exterior walls scored to look like stones, a four-columned front door, twelve curved urns, and eight deep planters—all substantially constructed of poured concrete. A third story with dormer windows and a slate roof capped off the historic structure. Leading up to the house were twin twelve-foot-wide walkways, and on both the east and west sides of the house were matching eight-columned porches running the length of the house. The house had incredible street presence, and we had admired it for years. When we saw that it was for sale, we put in a contract and purchased it immediately.

The house had been owned for years by the Whitehead family, and while the interior remained elegant, it needed a complete renovation. We expanded the kitchen to include what was the butler's pantry, put in all new bathrooms, upgraded the wiring and plumbing, painted, hung wallpaper, and stripped and stained all 4,500+ square feet of wooden floors. While all of this work was going on, we camped in the house: the refrigerator, microwave, and coffee pot were outside on the west porch, and our beloved housekeeper, Sally, washed our dishes in one of the old bathtubs. It was an adventure.

We worked on renovations all summer, and by the time Halloween rolled around we were ready to have people by and do a bit of entertaining with a casual trick-or-treat cocktail party for our neighbors. Tom and I provided the open bar and the main course: a big pot of chili and all the accoutrements. We asked the guests to bring an hors d'oeuvre for the adults and candy to give to the kids as they came calling that night. While we had the bar and the food set up inside, the real fun was outdoors. Tom and I lined up sixteen dining chairs along both sides of the two front entrances as well as on the top of the porch. Folks fixed their libations and took a seat, candy in laps. When the children arrived, they promenaded up one walkway, across the front porch, and then down the second walkway, getting treats all along the way. Fun was had by all! Folks loved seeing these cutie-pies in their Halloween attire, and the kids felt like they had hit the jackpot, getting sweets from more than a dozen folks in just one stop. As the years went by, word spread of our mega-candy emporium, and at one count we had more than three hundred children through in a two-hour period. A lot of parents in the area would plan to have us as the last stop, so they could go inside and fix themselves an adult beverage and snack on some of our plated fare.

The recipes I'm including below are some favorites from those parties on 45th Street, as well as one from my mom, and another for you to replicate so that you can sample my cake-walk victory back in 1972. Hope you find them all frighteningly delicious!

Our house on Savannah's East 45th Street,
where we started our Halloween party tradition

Thomas Eugene and me at a Savannah Halloween party.
Yes, that is a lamp shade Tom is sporting.
And yes, it did light up; you just pulled the tassel.

The first here is my chili, and admittedly it is pretty darn good. It isn't as tomato-y and acidic as some I've sampled, as I have two secret ingredients: beef stock along with unsweetened cocoa powder. These additions give a richer depth of taste to the dish than you usually find at Wendy's—though that little red-headed girl does a good job when you're in a rush and don't have time to make your own. And I'll pat myself on the back and say that I just won the Winterville Chili Cook-Off contest this past week, a feat I'm mighty proud of. How many entries were there? Well, only three. But those ladies made some mean pots of the stew, and the competition was nonetheless stiff. Or so I keep telling myself.

I serve this dish with a choice of sides, including sour cream, shredded cheese, jalapeños, green onions, and cilantro. A platter of hot buttered corn bread muffins and a cold beer complete the meal.

Halloween Chili

Ingredients
2 pounds ground chuck beef
1½ teaspoons kosher salt
1½ teaspoons black pepper
2 tablespoons olive oil
2 cups onion, diced
½ cup green bell pepper, diced
5 cups low-sodium beef stock (more if you want a soupier chili)
6 tablespoons chili powder*
1 (6-ounce) can tomato paste
1½ tablespoons unsweetened cocoa powder
1 tablespoon cumin powder
2 teaspoons garlic powder
2 teaspoons onion powder
1½ teaspoons dried oregano
2 bay leaves
1 (28-ounce) can reduced-sodium or no-salt diced tomatoes
1 (12-ounce) jar fire-roasted red bell peppers, drained and chopped
3 (15.5-ounce) cans of beans (I use one of each dark red kidney, light red kidney, and black beans; you can use any of those three that you wish.)

Directions
1. On a tray or platter, break apart the ground chuck loosely. Sprinkle it with the salt and black pepper, then toss together lightly; set aside.
2. Place a large Dutch oven or heavy-bottomed pot over medium-high heat. When hot, add the olive oil. When the oil becomes fragrant and just smoking, add the meat. Brown the chuck for about 2 minutes. Stir, and continue cooking until done, 6 to 8 minutes.
3. Remove the meat with a slotted spoon and place in a bowl; set aside. Keeping the heat on medium-high, add the onion and bell pepper to the pot and sauté for 5 to 6 minutes, until tender and wilted. Don't allow them to brown.
4. Add the meat back to the pot along with the stock, stir well, and bring to a good simmer.
5. Add the chili powder, tomato paste, cocoa powder, cumin, garlic and onion powders, oregano, and bay leaves. Add the diced tomatoes, roasted red bell peppers, and beans. Stir well. Bring the chili back to a steady simmer, reduce heat to low, and cook for 30 minutes, stirring occasionally.
6. Serve immediately or refrigerate and reheat the next day. Serve with assortment of toppings.
* *Read the label carefully on your chili powder. Some contain more salt than chili.*

Serves 8

One of my dearest friends is Lisa Lacy White, who grew up in the nearby town of Fort Valley, Georgia, just one county over from me. Lisa was the first woman to serve as president of the Georgia Historical Society, and I worked with her for several years as a trustee on that board. Through that role we traveled together with a lot of jollification to a number of Georgia towns. Whether eating fried catfish at Coleman's Lake or sipping bourbon in the Hay House, we always were quick with a joke and a laugh.

For parties, one of Lisa's signature hors d'oeuvres is a platter of sesame-toasted crab rolls. People "ooh and ahh" over these delicacies, and there never is one left on the serving tray.

One of the main ingredients in this recipe—Velveeta—will probably come as real surprise to you. Yes, Velveeta. "And you just said something with Velveeta is a delicacy? It cannot be," you are saying to yourselves. But yes, these are absolutely delicious: the combination of butter, sweet lump crab, and that famous cheese "product" makes for a soft, heavenly hors d'oeuvre. Trust me that I would *not* spend thirty-five dollars a pound for crab to waste it in a so-so dish. Prepare these for your next party and expect to receive beaucoup compliments. If anyone asks about the recipe, just coyly say that the filling is "lump crab and my rendition of an American Mornay." Wink, wink.

Sesame Toasted Crab Rollups

Ingredients
20 slices soft white loaf bread, crusts removed
½ pound Velveeta or American-style cheese, cubed
1 pound butter (4 sticks), divided
1 pound lump crab meat, drained and carefully picked for shells
2 cups sesame seeds

Directions
1. With a rolling pin, roll out each slice of bread until thin; set aside.
2. In the top of a double boiler, melt the Velveeta and 2 sticks of the butter. Stir well—the cheese and butter will separate—and set the pot aside to cool for 5 minutes.
3. To the cooled cheese/butter, fold in the crab and stir gently until well mixed, being careful to not break the lumps of crab.
4. Spread a few tablespoons of the crab mixture on one side of each piece of bread and roll up like a pinwheel.
5. Melt the remaining 2 sticks of butter. Brush each rollup with butter, and then roll each piece in sesame seeds.
6. Place the seeded rollups, seam side down, on a baking tray in one layer; cover loosely, and chill 2 to 4 hours.
7. Slice each chilled roll into four pieces and place the slices on a lightly sprayed cookie sheet. Toast under the broiler, 3 to 5 minutes, until the tops start to turn golden brown. Serve immediately.

Makes 80 pieces
Note: Halve the recipe if you don't need this many rollups or freeze the un-used, untoasted rollups in an airtight container. Thaw slightly and cook.

To this day one of my favorite snack foods is Chex Party Mix. Mama would make a double batch at Halloween and give pint-sized bags to the adults who'd bring their kids by to trick-or-treat. The slow cooking of the crunchy cereal, peanuts, pretzels, and pita chips—with that bath of butter, Worcestershire, seasoning salt, and garlic—gives the homemade version a much better taste than any commercial brand. And it is great with a cold beer or martini!

Old-School Chex Party Mix

Ingredients
8 tablespoons butter
3 tablespoons Worcestershire sauce
1 teaspoon Lawry's Seasoned Salt
1 teaspoon garlic powder
1 teaspoon onion powder
¼ teaspoon black pepper
9 cups Chex cereal—any combination or variety: rice, corn, and/or wheat
2 cups cocktail-style roasted peanuts
1½ cups bite-size pretzels
1½ cups garlic-flavored bagel chips

Directions
1. Preheat oven to 250 degrees.
2. In a small pan, melt the butter. Stir in the Worcestershire sauce, Lawry's salt, garlic powder, onion powder, and black pepper. Mix well.
3. Place the cereal, nuts, pretzels, and bagel chips in a large bowl. Drizzle the melted butter mixture on top; toss gently and thoroughly coat all ingredients.
4. Pour the Chex into a large baking pan with sides. Bake for 1 hour, stirring every 15 minutes.
5. Remove from heat and allow to cool. Store in an airtight container.
Makes a scant gallon

This next recipe, a staple at Ardsley Park cocktail parties, is always served at our Halloween get-togethers. A legacy hors d'oeuvre, it is from the well-beloved and most elegant of Savannah hostesses, the late Leonora "Noni" Huguenin Victor. Tom and I lived around the block from Miss Noni and her husband, Jules, a Savannah physician. Noni grew up on her father's ancestral home of Roseland Plantation just across the Savannah River in Coosawatchie, South Carolina; she met Dr. Victor while a nursing student. Miss Noni was the epitome of graciousness and possessed impeccable taste. On a side note, the Victors' middle child, Jules Victor III, known as Bubba, followed his father's footsteps into the medical profession; he was my doctor when I resided in Savannah. Upon first meeting him, I thought to myself, "this fellow doesn't look like any 'Bubba' I've ever met before." Tall, blonde, and blue-eyed, Jules III is as strikingly handsome as his mother was statuesque and lovely. Nicknamed by his older sister, who could not pronounce "Jules" as a youngster, Bubba is a helluva doctor and a helluva guy.

Now if anyone by chance raises an eyebrow because this recipe is a gelatin mold, let me tell you: If Noni Victor liked and served it, then HRH Queen Elizabeth II herself would welcome this creamy and flavor-filled dish at Balmoral.

Noni's Cocktail Egg Mold

Ingredients
1 envelope unflavored gelatin
½ cup cold water
½ teaspoon salt
Juice of 1 lemon
Dash (or 2) Tabasco
1 cup mayonnaise
¾ cup celery, minced
¼ cup onion, minced
¼ cup stuffed olives, minced
6 hard-boiled eggs, minced
Crackers

Directions
1. Soften gelatin in cold water; dissolve the mixture in a double boiler (or microwave) with the salt, lemon juice and Tabasco. Allow to cool; add the rest of the ingredients and whisk to mix thoroughly.
2. Pour mixture into a 4-cup, lightly greased mold. Refrigerate. Can be made 2 days ahead.
3. Unmold and serve with crackers.
Serves 12 to 16 as an appetizer

Another hors d'oeuvre favorite, aptly coming with the word "devil" in it for Halloween, has been a go-to recipe for my dear friend Carolyn Stillwell, who loves, loves, loves Halloween. Her beautiful 1920s brick home would be decorated from top to bottom with witches, goblins, black cats, and various other assortments of ghoulish creatures. These treats combine the exotic sweetness of dates, the smokiness of bacon, and the rich creaminess of Stilton cheese. Easily made in advance, these are a crowd favorite and come off the platter like bats in flight.

Devils on Horseback

Ingredients
24 toothpicks
24 large dates, pitted
⅓ cup bleu, Stilton, cheddar, or cream cheese at room temperature
12 slices bacon, regular, not thick sliced, cut in half crosswise

Directions
1. Soak toothpicks in a pan of water and set aside.
2. Preheat oven to 400 degrees.
3. Stuff each date with ½ to ¾ teaspoon of cheese.
4. Wrap each stuffed date with a piece of bacon; secure with a toothpick.
5. Place the dates on a lightly greased cookie sheet; bake for 25 minutes or until the bacon is cooked through and is crisping on the edges.
6. Remove to a wire rack to cool. Can be made ahead and refrigerated in an airtight container until ready to serve.
Makes 24 pieces (enough for 12 to 16 people)

Just down the block from us lived the well-hailed and beloved Herb Traub, who slept in the same bed in the same home he was born in on August 31, 1917, until he passed away in 2008. Herb was one of Savannah's most well-known native sons. An international ambassador for the city, Herb brought to life and owned the award-winning, world-famous Pirates' House restaurant. With the original buildings dating to the 1700s, his culinary showplace is still in operation today, sitting a block above the Savannah River. It is said that pirates gathered in these old wooden structures, consuming copious amounts of rum, and kidnapping unsuspecting men to serve as sailors. Robert Louis Stevens mentions the Pirates' House in *Treasure Island*, along with introducing readers to the infamous Captain John Flint.

Aside from being his neighbor, I also had the honor of being a fellow Rotarian with Herb in the Rotary Club of Savannah. He was an inspiration to me and to countless others. Active in dozens of civic affairs until the week he died at age ninety, his motto was "I'd rather wear out than rust out." Herb was quite a man.

This next dish is one that he brought to our Halloween gatherings, and the base recipe can be found in *The Pirates' House Cook Book*. My copy from 1998 reads that 60,000 copies had already been sold; in the book, which Herb gifted to me, he inscribed the following:

> Dear J—Here's hoping that you will enjoy every calorie-free morsel…and always remember that "La bonne cuisine est la base du veritable bouheur!"*
>
> Your friend in the one hundred block—H.S.T 06/20/98
>
> *Old French proverb…"Good cooking is the basis of true happiness!"

Cheers to you, Herb; your spirit still lives on, mightily felt, in your hometown on the coast.

Crab and Shrimp Au Gratin

This dish is excellent with a side of Savannah Red Rice (see index) and a side salad.

Ingredients
2 quarts water
½ cup Old Bay seasoning
1 pound medium, fresh-caught American shrimp, peeled and deveined
3 tablespoons butter
3 tablespoons flour
1½ cups whole milk, at room temperature
½ cup cream, at room temperature
2 cups medium sharp cheddar cheese, hand-shredded and divided
½ teaspoon salt
⅛ teaspoon black pepper
1 pound claw crab meat, picked over to remove shells

Directions
1. In a medium sized pot, bring the water and Old Bay to a boil. Add the shrimp, stir, and cook 2 to 3 minutes, until just done. Drain and set aside.
2. Preheat oven to 350 degrees.
3. In a heavy-bottomed pot, melt the butter over medium-high heat; don't allow it to brown. Sift in the flour, and whisking constantly, cook for 2 minutes.
4. Drizzle in the milk, whisking, and then the cream. Cook 4 to 5 minutes until thickened.
5. Sprinkle in 1 cup of the shredded cheese; stir until the cheese is melted. Add the salt and pepper, stir, and remove from heat.
6. Gently fold in the shrimp and crab into the cheese sauce. Pour into a lightly greased or buttered 2-quart baking dish. Top with the remaining 1 cup of shredded cheese.
7. Bake for 30 to 40 minutes, depending on the depth of the baking dish, until the cheese is melted and the casserole is heated through. Remove from oven and allow to rest for 10 minutes before serving.

Serves 4 to 6

The combination of the chocolate in this cake and the vanilla-laced creaminess of the frosting is a perfect combination. My recipe is uncomplicated and can be easily made into two (9-inch) round layers, 24 cupcakes, a 9x13 pan for squares, as well as a regular sized (12-cup) Bundt or tube pan. And don't you know the strains from "Elephant Walk" are going round and round in my head right at this moment!

Devil's Food Cake

Ingredients
1 cup boiling water
¾ cup unsweetened cocoa powder (not Dutch process)
½ cup whole milk
1½ teaspoon vanilla extract
2 cups all-purpose flour
1½ scant teaspoons baking soda
½ teaspoon salt
½ pound (2 sticks) unsalted butter, at room temperature
1¼ cups dark brown sugar, packed
¾ cup white sugar
4 large eggs, room temperature
Vanilla buttercream frosting (recipe follows)

Directions
1. Grease and flour the bottoms and sides of pans of choice. If using cake pans or Bundt/tube pans, you should also grease and flour wax or parchment paper and line the bottoms of those pans. Set aside.
2. Preheat oven to 350 degrees with rack set in the middle of the oven.
3. Pour the boiling water into a mixing bowl with the cocoa; whisk well until smooth. Add in the milk and vanilla and whisk until fully incorporated.
4. In another bowl, sift together the flour, baking soda, and salt. Set aside.
5. In large mixing bowl, beat together over medium speed the butter and sugars until light and fluffy. Add in the eggs, one at a time, beating well after each addition.
6. To the butter, sugar, and egg mixture beat in the dry ingredients and the cocoa mixture. Do this in three batches, starting and ending with the flour.
7. Divide the batter evenly into the pan(s) and spread smooth with a spatula or spoon. Bake 25 to 30 minutes for the 9-inch pans, 35 to 40 minutes for a 9x13 pan, or 40 to 45 minutes for a Bundt pan. For cupcakes, bake 18 to 20 minutes. The cake is done when it starts to pull away from the edges of the pan and a toothpick inserted comes out clean.
8. Place the cake(s) on a wire rack for 10 to 15 minutes. Invert the cakes onto the rack and remove the paper. Allow to cool completely, at least 30 minutes to an hour. I prefer to place them in the fridge for a while to firm even more.
9. Frost and serve.

Serves 12 to 14

Vanilla Buttercream Frosting

Ingredients
6 tablespoons butter, at room temperature
⅓ cup Crisco
⅛ teaspoon salt
4½ cups confectioners' sugar
2 teaspoons vanilla extract
⅓ cup heavy cream

Directions
1. Beat the butter, Crisco, and salt until light and fluffy.
2. Add half of the sugar to the butter mixture and beat slowly until fully blended.
3. Add the vanilla and half of the cream and beat until fully blended and fluffy.
4. Add the remaining sugar and cream in 2 more batches, beating until fully incorporated and fluffy.

Makes approximately 4 cups, enough for a 2- or 3-layered cake, or 24 cupcakes

Chapter 6

Thanksgiving and Christmas

Now some of you may roll your eyes at the fact that Thanksgiving and Christmas are included in one chapter, considering me a philistine in that I can't seem to separate the significance of the two holidays. Well, that is fine—I'm pretty thick-skinned and can shrug the criticism off easily (well, not really, but my sensitivity isn't the subject of this book. Maybe I'll explore my idiosyncrasies later in an autobiographical tell-all, haha.)

But seriously, the food of autumn and winter blended a great deal in my home growing up; the same tastes, smells, and dishes lasted from the first frost through early spring, especially on Turkey Day and with Jesus' birthday. In addition to a robust hen or capon (Daddy didn't care for turkey) and a fat pork roast, cornbread dressing and beautifully glazed candied yams were ever-present at 1209 Ball Street at Thanksgiving and Christmas. During both holidays there would be a buffet of vegetables that had been harvested during the summer and either canned or placed in one of Mama's deep freezers: tiny baby butter beans, creamed corn, a squash casserole filled with cheese and Vidalia onions, and a big pot of snap beans cooked with the tiniest red potatoes that Mama or Carrie could find. We'd also have a congealed side dish called Moon Salad that was a favorite from Miss Mildred Evan Warren's 1967 publication *The Art of Southern Cooking*, which consisted of lime Jell-O, cream cheese, pineapple, and chopped pecans. In terms of sweets, both holidays meant pecan and sweet potato pies, a red velvet cake, a fruitcake along with fruitcake cookies (a specialty of my mother's), Aunt Hazel's divinity, Aunt Lil's lemon crisp cookies, and Aunt Polly's butterscotch haystacks.

I'll also share here—and admit—that I begin celebrating both Advent and Christmas at Thanksgiving. When I'm pulling the turkey out of the oven on the fourth Thursday of every November, you can hear me singing "Come, Thou Long Expected Jesus," and then "Joy to the Word" while spreading whipped cream on the sweet potato pie. My tree is up, and the house decorated over the Thanksgiving weekend, and it stays put until the twelfth day of Christmas. In the Barrett-White household, we follow Lady Mary Crawley's observance, and I paraphrase: "Here at Downton we do things properly. The tree does not come down until Epiphany."

Rushing the season, you say? Ecclesiastically speaking I am, much to the chagrin of my parish priest. Yes, yes, Advent is Advent and Christmas is Christmas, so on and so forth, but by now he should know that he is preaching to deaf ears. My gratitude in November is for many blessings, including the coming Christmastide. To me the benedictions of the American holiday flow naturally right into Advent and Christmas, and I get caught up in the enthusiasm. As with Psalm 95:2, "Let us come before him with thanksgiving, and extol him with music and song." I just love Christmas!

My favorite remembrance from my childhood was the decorated cedar tree that was always centered between the two front windows of our living room. Until I was a teen, our tree was cut in the woods on a cousin's property and delivered home in the back of Daddy's pickup truck. Those cedars were crisply fragrant, and the limbs stiff and upright, until, as my friend Nancy Fullbright in Savannah says, that "they'd fall out all pretty with the weight of the decorations." Strings of opaque lights the colors of the rainbow glowed brightly; glass beads were draped in swags along with hard-foil tinsel, Shiny Brite ornaments hung in careful place, icicles glittered from every limb, and a lighted gold metal star crowned the top. Each year now, more than three dozen of those vintage decorations from youth adorn a special Christmas tree in my kitchen.

Then there are the books and classic movies to be enjoyed during the holidays along with all the food and décor. In terms of reading, I'll pour myself a stiff bourbon and sit down with Truman Capote's *A Christmas Memory* and have a good cry. To cheer back up, I read Fannie Flagg's *A Redbird Christmas* next—what a beautifully told story. A tradition with our friends Barbara and Carter (of the previous chapter on Easter) is to gather for cocktails and dinner to watch *Holiday Inn*, *White Christmas*, *The Bishop's Wife*, *Home Alone*, and *Love, Actually* leading up to December 24. And on my own I'll take in *A Charlie Brown Christmas*. I've mentioned how much I dearly love this holiday, and my favorite part of scripture is

With Daddy in our living room Christmas morning, 1972. I racked up
from Santa with a Krazy Kar, a Hot Wheels set, and a Tonka truck!

My kitchen Christmas tree, all with vintage ornaments from childhood

Dottie and Jim Kluttz on their wedding day

the Christmas story from Luke, which Linus Van Pelt shares with his friends. When my great nephew and great niece were children, I'd recite this passage to them for the blessing on Christmas Eve. And while most all you readers are familiar with those words, bear with me for a moment and take in the beautifully told scripture:

> And it came to pass in those days, that there went out a decree from Caesar Augustus, that all the world should be taxed. ...
>
> And all went to be taxed, every one into his own city.
>
> And Joseph also went up from Galilee, out of the city of Nazareth, into Judaea, unto the city of David, which is called Bethlehem; (because he was of the house and lineage of David:)
>
> To be taxed with Mary his espoused wife, being great with child.
>
> And so it was, that, while they were there, the days were accomplished that she should be delivered.
>
> And she brought forth her firstborn son, and wrapped him in swaddling clothes, and laid him in a manger; because there was no room for them in the inn.
>
> And there were in the same country shepherds abiding in the field, keeping watch over their flock by night.
>
> And, lo, the angel of the Lord came upon them, and the glory of the Lord shone round about them: and they were sore afraid.
>
> And the angel said unto them, Fear not: for, behold, I bring you good tidings of great joy, which shall be to all people.
>
> For unto you is born this day in the city of David a Saviour, which is Christ the Lord.
>
> And this shall be a sign unto you; Ye shall find the babe wrapped in swaddling clothes, lying in a manger.
>
> And suddenly there was with the angel a multitude of the heavenly host praising God, and saying,
>
> Glory to God in the highest, and on earth peace, good will toward men. (Luke 2:1, 3-14, KJV)

Now, getting back to cooking. Holiday food traditions include breakfast or brunch, as well as dinner and supper, so let's start the day with some morning favorites. These first dishes come from four of my friends on Tybee Island: Dottie and Jim Kluttz and Cindy and Craig Meyer. Both couples have long-standing favorites to serve to family and friends and are renowned for their hospitality.

Dottie and Jim moved to Savannah from their native Virginia in 1974; Jim, a graduate of UVA's Darden School of Business, opened and operated a chain of auto-care stores, while Dottie was a nursing instructor at Georgia Southern University. They purchased and restored a large Victorian home overlooking the sand dunes and beach of Tybee's north end. The three-storied structure is part of historic Officer's Row—originally a part of Fort Screven, which was built to fortify and protect Savannah during the Spanish-American War. Dottie said, "It was in need of a total restoration. Palm trees were growing out of the porch. No heat, no AC. It really looked sad, but it was also magical at the same time. We fell in love and polished it up, keeping what made it wonderful. Lucky us!"

Dottie shared that while enjoying life in their new hometown, their traditions from back home in Virginia, especially during the winter holidays, were missed. Realizing that there were many other transplanted couples and single friends in the area who were also without local family, they began inviting over twenty or more folks to celebrate both Thanksgiving and Christmas.

Dottie writes,

Born and bred Virginians living in Savannah, holidays can be lonely, so we decided to host Thanksgiving meals and Christmas breakfasts and call them "our other family" meals. We ask people like us who do not have family living nearby over; everyone was so happy to be together. Each person has a chore to do to make them feel as if they had a real part in the celebration of the day; I put slips of paper with those chores listed on them in a basket, and people draw out their assignment, such as set the table, clear the plates, or say the blessing. I include dishes served in my Virginia home, dishes that had a special meaning to me growing up, such as Nannie's Richmond Spoon Bread and my baked Virginia ham on homemade biscuits. Thanks for letting me share these sweet memories and recipes. I'm excited to see this book—you know how I love stories. The shortest distance between two people is a story.

Dottie is a natural storyteller herself and began the well-regarded Story Keeping program at Hospice Savannah. This initiative helps patients record their life stories so that "they will be remembered not just in one generation, but for generations to come." Dottie speaks fondly of her days with her grandmother, Annie Guthrie, sitting on her front porch, shelling peas, and hearing the stories of days gone by. Her grandmother would tell Dottie of her Christmas recollections as a child, when tree ornaments were handmade, the stockings hung at the mantel were actual socks that had been washed and cleaned that day, and presents for kids included such items as raisins, apples, and oranges.

One of my favorite stories with Dottie is how she and I were competitively bidding against each other, along with another couple, at a charity auction for a stay at Palmetto Bluff. The figures kept going up and up. Finally, we all looked at one another and said something along the lines of, "Hell's bells! There are four bedrooms in this house! Let's just buy it as a group and we'll all go!" And we did, and we had a marvelous time over a long weekend resting, biking, boating, and, yes, eating.

Here is Dottie's special holiday breakfast dishes of ham, biscuits, and spoon bread. Serve these up with a big pan of eggs scrambled with cheese for a morning feast. And I hope when you try them that you'll taste a bit of the Kluttz's wonderful Virginia—and now Tybee Island, Georgia—hospitality.

While Kentucky has its bourbon, Maryland is known for crabs, and Georgia claims fame to peaches, the most well-known culinary delight of the Commonwealth of Virginia is the ham known by the state's name. A Virginia ham is the richer and more flavorful cousin of what we refer to as a country ham. These pork delicacies date back to colonial times and are best known from the town of Smithfield in Isle of Wight County. The hams are from hogs fed on a fattening diet of acorns, nuts, and corn. They are dry-cured with salt and sugar and often pepper-coated and smoked over apple or hickory wood fires. These intensely flavored Virginia hams come to you uncooked. Dottie serves hers with biscuits (recipe follows) with a bit of mayonnaise, and, if the guest likes, a thin spreading of mustard. This ham is also a great dish for supper paired with most any vegetable side dish.

When shopping for these delicacies, know that a Virginia-*style* ham is *not* a true Virginia ham; though the "styled" ones may be lower in price and a bit easier to prepare, the taste is just not the same. That said, and Dottie may hit me with one of her hats the next time I see her for suggesting this, but…if you don't want to bake a whole ham, you can purchase sliced, vacuum-packed ham from online purveyors such as Edwards Virginia Smokehouse. Just follow the cooking directions on the package.

Baked Virginia Ham

Ingredients
1 small Virginia ham (about 15 pounds)
Homemade biscuits (recipe follows)
Mayonnaise and mustard

Directions
1. Completely skin and trim the ham; scrub with a wire brush under running water. Leave a trace amount of fat.
2. Soak overnight in an ice chest, completely immersed in cold water. Change water 2 or 3 times. These steps remove a good bit of the salt used in the curing process.
3. Place the ham in heavy aluminum foil. Pull up sides and add 1½ cups of water. Wrap ham completely in the foil. This retains juices. Place in a large roasting dish.
4. Bake at 350 degrees for 15 to 20 minutes per pound. Center should read 160 degrees.
5. Cool completely prior to slicing. This prevents shredding the ham. Always slice Virginia ham thinly, 2 to 3 millimeters at most.

Serves 12 to 16

Buttermilk Biscuits

Ingredients
¼ cup Crisco
2 cups self-rising flour, sifted
1 cup whole milk buttermilk (not reduced fat or skim!)
Melted butter

Directions
1. Preheat oven to 425 degrees.
2. Cut shortening into flour with pastry blender until the mixture is crumbly.
3. Stir the buttermilk in gently a little at a time until the dough is just moistened. The amount of buttermilk can vary.
4. With a spatula, turn out the dough onto a lightly floured surface. Pat the dough gently into a round that is ½-inch thick. *Do not over handle, or the biscuits will be tough.*
5. Fold the dough over onto itself three times and then press again to ½-inch thickness. Cut out biscuits with a 2-inch round cutter. Do not twist the cutter, but push down in one motion, keeping the sides of the biscuits straight—this allows a higher rise. Flour the cutter after every biscuit or two so not to stick to the dough.
6. Place the biscuits on a lightly greased baking sheet; do not crowd the pan. Cook for 12 to 14 minutes until the tops are just turning golden brown. Brush the tops with melted butter and serve immediately.
Note: The biscuits can be made in advance; cook until just done. Remove from the oven, place on a wire rack until completely cooled, and then place in a gallon zip-lock bag and freeze. To reheat, place the frozen biscuits on a lightly greased cookie sheet, brush the tops with melted butter, and heat until they have golden brown tops in a 350-degree oven.
Serves 8

Spoon bread is a popular dish in Virginia and Kentucky; there is even a festival held each September in Berea, Kentucky, in celebration of this dish. With origins dating back to Native Americans, the recipe is thought to have been first featured in Sarah Rutledge's 1847 cookbook, *The Carolina Housewife*. This rich and velvety variation on cornbread gets its name from its creaminess—in that it is a bread that needs to be served with a spoon and not sliced. The recipe from Dottie is a classic one, and you'll find it an excellent side dish at breakfast with eggs and baked ham, or at suppertime alongside roasted pork or baked chicken.

Richmond Spoon Bread

Ingredients
4 tablespoons butter, melted
¾ cup white cornmeal
1½ cups boiling water
½ cup all-purpose flour
1½ cups whole milk (not 2% or skim)
4 eggs
½ teaspoon baking powder
½ teaspoon sugar
Pinch of salt
Pats of butter

Directions
1. Preheat oven to 350 degrees.
2. Pour the melted butter into an 8x8 pan.
3. Place cornmeal in a mixing bowl. Pour boiling water over cornmeal and mix well. Stir in flour, milk, eggs, baking powder, sugar, and salt. Beat with a wire whisk until smooth.
4. Pour into the buttered pan. Bake until firm and golden, 30 to 35 minutes. To serve, scoop onto plates and top each mound with a pat of butter.

Serves 6 to 8

Just down the road from Dottie and Jim are my friends Cindy and Craig Meyer. Both native Savannahians, they celebrated their fiftieth wedding anniversary in 2021. For the past thirty of those years, the couple has welcomed upwards of twenty folks for Christmas brunch, all who find a wonderful comfort of hospitality and holiday spirit in the Meyers' 1920s home. The two stories of jasmine-covered porches, with ceilings painted "haint blue" to keep out the evil spirits, give visitors perfect venues to sit and enjoy the balmy Christmas weather of the Georgia coast. And always served al fresco with the gentle temperate breezes are Craig's Merry Bloody Mary, and Pops's Eggnog. "Pops" is Cindy's dad, Mr. John Carlton Knight, known to most as either "Coach" or "Jug"—but to family, he is "Pops." Jug's eggnog is the real deal!

On the Meyers' table this feast day guests find a bountiful buffet, including a cheesy egg and sausage casserole, grilled beef tenderloin, roasted asparagus, "brown" grits cooked with beef stock, pickled peaches, tomato aspic, oyster pie, and sour cream and butter drop biscuits. To go along with Dottie's Virginia ham biscuits and Richmond spoon bread, I'm including here for your Thanksgiving or Christmas morning menu the recipes for Pops's Eggnog, the Merry Bloody Mary, and the egg casserole—and my ambrosia. These dishes would be a great way to greet your family and guests on a holiday morning. Cheers from Tybee (and Virginia)!

Pops's Eggnog

This eggnog is rich and thick. Yes, the eggs are raw, so make sure to use fresh, pasteurized ones that have been refrigerated.

Ingredients
1 (750-milliliter) bottle good bourbon
2 cups sugar
12 large eggs, separated
2 quarts heavy cream

Directions
1. In a bowl, whisk together the bourbon and sugar until the sugar is dissolved.
2. In another bowl, beat the egg yolks until thick and a rich, golden color.
3. Whisk in the bourbon/sugar mixture slowly into the beaten yolks.
4. In a third bowl, whip the cream until thick, soft peaks form. Carefully fold in the bourbon and yolk mixture into the whipped cream.
5. In a fourth bowl, beat the egg whites until they are in stiff peaks.
6. Carefully fold the whipped whites into the bourbon/sugar/yolk/cream mixture.
7. Cover and refrigerate 4 to 6 hours. To serve, gently fold the mixture to recombine the ingredients.
Makes 1½ gallons

Craig uses Clamato juice instead of tomato for his Bloodys, which gives a fitting taste of the sea at the beach. It gets a real "zing" from the horseradish—which Craig says is a must, and I agree—and a few other wonderful ingredients that will make you merry on Christmas morn.

Merry Bloody Mary

Ingredients
6 cups Clamato or tomato juice
½ cup prepared horseradish, such as Gold's
¼ cup freshly squeezed lemon or lime juice
¼ cup dill pickle brine
¼ cup Worcestershire sauce
2 teaspoons freshly ground black pepper, plus more for garnish
2 teaspoons celery salt, plus more for garnish
2 teaspoons Tabasco sauce
1 (750-milliliter) bottle of good-quality vodka
Pickled okra, lime wedges, large olives for garnish, made into decorative
   skewers, and celery stalks

Directions
1. In a large pitcher, combine the Clamato or tomato juice, horseradish,
   lemon or lime juice, pickle brine, Worcestershire, black pepper, celery salt,
   and Tabasco. Stir well, cover, and refrigerate at least 6 hours or overnight.
2. Fill glasses with ice. Into each pour 1 to 3 ounces of vodka (depending on
   size of the glass and size of the guest's tolerance).
3. Pour Bloody Mary mixture over the ice and vodka. Stir. Sprinkle black pepper and celery salt on top of the drink and serve with a skewer and celery
   stalk.
Makes 14 to 20 drinks, depending on size

Cindy shared that their breakfast casserole followed the popular recipe
made with eggs, cheese, and sausage, and whatever your other favorite ingredients might be, and then baked. I make this simple but tasty morning
dish often when I have overnight guests. It can be constructed the day
before and cooked the next morning. My version is certainly not high-
brow—because I use, yes, tater tots—but people rave over it. If you'd rather, you can always dice some potatoes, rinse, drain, toss with oil, salt,
and pepper, and bake until golden—to substitute for the tater tots. But
really, why?

Breakfast Tater Tot Casserole

Ingredients
1 tablespoon olive oil
½ cup onion, diced
½ cup red or green bell pepper, diced
2 tablespoons butter, at room temperature
4 cups tater tots, defrosted
1½ pounds bulk Italian sweet sausage, cooked, browned and drained
2 cups cheddar, Monterey Jack, or Swiss cheese, hand grated
8 large eggs
2¼ cups whole milk
2 teaspoons Dijon mustard
2 teaspoons Worcestershire sauce
1 teaspoon black pepper
¼ cup butter, melted

Directions
1. Preheat oven to 350 degrees.
2. Heat the olive oil in a pan over medium-high heat; add the onion and bell pepper and sauté for about 2 minutes, or until just beginning to soften. Set aside.
3. Grease a large baking dish, such as a 9x13, with the room temperature butter. Spread the tater tots evenly in the dish.
4. Spoon the sautéed vegetables around the tater tots.
5. Spoon the cooked sausage on top and between the tater tots and vegetables.
6. Spread the grated cheese over the top of the casserole ingredients.
7. In a mixing bowl, beat together the eggs, milk, mustard, Worcestershire sauce, black pepper, and melted butter until thoroughly mixed.
8. Pour the egg mixture into the casserole dish. Bake 40 to 45 minutes or the center is just set; the top should be beginning to brown. Let dish cool for 5 minutes before serving.

Serves 8 to 10

To round out the menu for breakfast or brunch a little something sweet is needed. Lord knows there are plenty of sugar-filled confections offered up during the holidays, so here is my recipe for a lighter option, ambrosia, another holiday staple on the Southern table. The crisp taste of the citrus, along with the tartness of the cherries, is a nice balance to the more substantial offerings, such as the ham biscuits—since after the morning meal, it is time for a walk on the beach at Tybee.

Ambrosia

Ingredients
24 clementines, peeled and segmented
4 dozen or more fresh, ripe, tart cherries, pitted (if fresh are not available, opt for frozen, tart cherries)
3 cups fresh pineapple, cut into 1-inch cubes
1½ cups flaked coconut
½ cup Cointreau or another orange-flavored liqueur
½ cup sugar

Directions
1. Combine all ingredients; place in airtight container, refrigerate overnight.
2. Stir contents occasionally while chilling to mix flavors. Serve chilled or at room temperature.
Serves: 8 to 10

Now let's move on to dinner, the midday meal in the South. At our house growing up—and continuing now as I jet toward my sixtieth turn around the sun—Thanksgiving and Christmas were similar in terms of what was on the dining table. Until my father passed away in 1998, the centerpiece was a roasted hen or capon, as Daddy never cared for turkey. Today, Tom is the bird chef, and he likes turkey, so…we have turkey. Here I've included instructions for roasting both—exact same routine, just some adjustments to the amount of ingredients and cooking time. And, like John B. Sr., I prefer a capon as well.

People claim many "best" ways to prepare the bird. Wet brine. Dry brine. Butter and herbs under the skin. Savory bread stuffing in the cavity. No, wait, instead, stuff the bird with onions, garlic, lemons, and celery.

Some of the more complicated recipes call for cooking the bird on one side for a while, then flipping it to the other side, then moving it so it is breast-down, all of which read to me like "do the hokey-pokey and turn the turkey around"—sorry, that ain't happening in my kitchen. It is all I can do to get it on the rack upright and into the oven without fail. I'm not going to try and flip a fifteen-pound steaming hot carcass in a pan full of simmering juices—that just spells out big chance for disaster. The first time reading over such a cooking production, I thought to myself, "Lord, I'm tired just reading this diatribe. *Just cook the damn bird!*" My suggestion here is to dress Tom Turkey simply—just make sure you don't overcook and dry it out—and allow yourself time to enjoy the holiday without making the bird dance in the oven. The following recipe will bring out a nicely flavored and tasty fat fowl—without a lot of fuss.

On a side note, I'd encourage those of you with a smaller crowd to try a capon instead of a turkey. Larger than a hen and smaller than an average turkey, a capon is a male chicken that is castrated and fed a rich diet. Without his testes, the bird is less active—allowing him to become fatter, and in the process, making for a more flavorful roast. Shakespeare wrote of their merits in *As You Like It*, in the renowned "all the world's a stage" monologue, speaking of middle age where a man has found his wealth and wisdom:

> All the world's a stage,
> And all the men and women merely players;
> They have their exits and their entrances;
> And one man in his time plays many parts
> His acts being seven ages…
> And then the justice,
> In fair round belly with good capon lin'd,
> With eyes severe and beard of formal cut,
> Full of wise saws and modern instances;
> And so he plays his part.

Roasted Turkey/Capon

Ingredients
1 self-basting turkey, such as Butterball,* 12 to 15 pounds,† or a capon, 8 to 10 pounds†
2 tablespoons kosher salt
1 tablespoon black pepper
Zest of 2 lemons, reserving lemons
1 small onion, quartered

1 stalk celery, chopped
3 bay leaves
4 garlic cloves, whole
Sprig of fresh rosemary
2 to 3 tablespoons olive oil or melted butter
1 cup white wine or dry vermouth
1½ to 2 cups chicken or turkey stock

Directions

1. Preheat oven to 350 degrees.
2. Remove the neck and giblets and rinse the bird with cold water; pat it completely dry with paper towels, including the cavity.
3. Sprinkle the entire bird and cavity with the salt, pepper, and lemon zest. Set aside for 30 minutes at room temperature.
4. Cut the zested lemons in half. Squeeze the juice from them into a small bowl and place the juiced halves in the bird's cavity along with the onion, celery, bay leaves, garlic, and rosemary.
5. Tie the legs with kitchen twine and tuck the wings under the body of the bird.
6. Place the bird on a rack inside a large roasting pan (I like to use a V-shaped rack).
7. Brush the entire bird with olive oil or melted butter.
8. Pour the wine and stock into the bottom of the pan along with the reserved lemon juice.
9. Bake, basting every 45 minutes, until the internal temperature reaches 165 degrees in the thickest part of the thigh.
10. When finished, remove from the oven, tent with foil, and allow to sit at room temperature for 30 minutes before carving.

Serves 8 to 10

* *If you're using a frozen turkey, you'll need 24 hours for every 5 pounds of turkey to defrost in the refrigerator; a 15-pound turkey would need 3 full days.*
† *Allow 1.5 pounds per person; a 15-pound turkey would feed 10 guests.*
‡ *If using a capon, reduce the spices and other ingredients by about a third.*

My mom would make giblet gravy to serve with our bird and cornbread dressing. However, not caring for the texture of the livers and other giblet pieces, I've come up with my own gravy. It has a rich, poultry taste from the drippings of the roasting pan—along with a golden color from tempering two large egg yolks in the recipe. My guests often ask for second helpings. Make the gravy about a half hour before your bird is done and finish with the drippings when you remove the turkey or capon from the oven.

Creamed Gravy

Ingredients
5 tablespoons butter
¼ cup celery, minced
¼ cup shallots, minced (green onion will work as well)
5 tablespoons flour
2 cups low-sodium chicken stock
1 (10.5-ounce) can cream of chicken soup
1 cup heavy cream
½ teaspoon black pepper
¼ teaspoon dried thyme
2 large egg yolks, beaten and at room temperature in a small bowl
½ cup or more drippings from the roasted turkey or capon pan

Directions
1. In a medium-sized pan, melt the butter over medium-high heat. Add the celery and shallots; stir and cook until soft, about 2 minutes.
2. Whisk in the flour and cook, whisking for 1 minute.
3. Stream in the chicken stock, whisking until thoroughly incorporated.
4. Add the cream of chicken soup, whisking for 1 to 2 minutes until the mixture is hot.
5. Whisk in the cream, stirring. Cook for 2 to 3 minutes until thickened and smooth.
6. Add in the black pepper and thyme. Stir to mix.
7. To the beaten yolks slowly stream in 1 cup of the hot gravy, whisking constantly.
8. Pour the tempered egg mixture into the gravy pan and whisk to fully incorporate. Continue cooking over medium heat for 1 minute.
9. Set the gravy aside until the turkey is done.
10. When the turkey is finished, pour in ½ cup or more of the pan drippings to the gravy—depending on the thickness you'd like—and reheat over medium until just under a simmer.
11. Serve over sliced turkey and cornbread dressing.
Makes 4 cups, serves 8 to 10

I don't know that I laid eyes on a real cranberry until my late teens. The Pig (as we affectionately called the Piggly Wiggly grocery store) didn't carry them. Our cranberry sauce at home always came out of the Ocean Spray can before being sliced. Today I make my own, and it is easy-breezy. My recipe uses light brown sugar to give the sauce a bit more depth—and, since I love the taste of cranberries and orange together, a bit of zest is included. This sauce turns out like a jam; with plenty of natural pectin, it gels beautifully. I often place a few batches in jars and give this tangy condiment to friends the week before Thanksgiving.

Cranberry Sauce

Ingredients
2 (12-ounce) bags fresh cranberries (or 4 cups frozen)
1½ cups water
1½ cups light brown sugar
1 tablespoon finely zested orange peel (about 1 large orange)

Directions
1. Add the cranberries, water, and sugar to a heavy-bottomed pot; bring to a boil over medium-high heat.
2. Reduce heat to a steady simmer; cook 8 to 10 minutes, until the berries are very soft.
3. Add the orange zest. Remove from heat.
4. With a potato masher, press the cranberries until the mixture is thick; allow some of the berries to remain partially whole.
5. Cover tightly and chill 4 hours or overnight.
Makes 1 quart and serves 10 to 12

The following recipe was from Ninnie, and I've not changed a single ingredient since it was passed down to me. I inherited many of Grandmother Nipper's cast iron pots and pans, and several of her utensils, some that are more than a hundred years old. Using them when I cook makes the dishes even more special, if only to me.

Ninnie's Cornbread Dressing

Ingredients
3 tablespoons butter, at room temperature
1 (9-inch) pan of cornbread (about 6 cups crumbled) made a day ahead and set on the back of the stove to dry out
3 biscuits (about 2 cups crumbled)

1 quart or so homemade chicken, turkey, or pork stock, at room temperature*
2 cups onion, diced
2 cups celery, diced
3 large hard-boiled eggs, diced
2 eggs, slightly beaten
½ teaspoon black pepper

Directions
1. Preheat oven to 350 degrees.
2. Butter a 9x13 baking pan or large iron skillet with deep sides; it should be
   deep enough to hold 2½ quarts of dressing. Set aside.
3. Crumble the cornbread and biscuits into a large mixing bowl.
4. Pour in half of the stock and mix together with a spatula, mashing until
   there are no lumps. Add additional stock until you get the consistency of a
   slightly soupy batter.
5. Add the remaining ingredients and stir well to mix.
6. Pour batter into the buttered dish; bake until the top turns a golden
   brown, about 50 to 60 minutes. Serve immediately.
Serves 8 to 10

Seafood is extremely popular and bountiful throughout the South, and oysters are often at the top of the favorites list. I love them whether served on the half-shell, fried, roasted, or in a stew. Here I want to highlight another holiday favorite from Virginia to Louisiana, that of oyster dressing. I heard from several folks about this traditional dish, including my hometown friend from Perry, Selecia Young-Jones. Selecia says that the dish was one that her mom, Joyce Jones, and her grandmother, Irva Bridges, made each year at Thanksgiving. Mrs. Jones was the drama teacher at Perry High School and was known for her personal flair and stylish hats; she was a milliner's best friend. Miss Irva had a beauty salon in her home, a big, pretty white clapboard house sitting amidst camellias and pecan trees. I remember it well because Mama would drag me along on some Saturdays to "get her hair fixed," and thankfully there was that big yard to play in and not be stuck inside whiffing Aqua Net and Virginia Slims (this was the late 60s, remember…).

---

* You will need the fat that homemade stock provides; if using a commercial brand add to the mixture 4 tablespoons of melted butter.

Mrs. Jones & Miss Irva's Oyster Dressing

Ingredients
1 recipe for a pan of cornbread
4 slices of loaf bread
1 quart chicken, turkey, or pork stock
1 (10.5-ounce) can cream of chicken soup
4 cups chopped onion
4 cups chopped celery
4 eggs, slightly beaten
1 teaspoon poultry seasoning
½ teaspoon salt
½ teaspoon black pepper
1 quart oysters, drained; reserve the juice

Directions
1. Preheat oven to 350 degrees.
2. Grease a 9x13 baking pan or large iron skillet; it should be deep enough to hold almost a gallon of dressing. Set aside.
3. Crumble cornbread and tear the loaf bread into small pieces in a large mixing bowl.
4. Pour in half of the stock and mix together with a spatula, mashing until there are no lumps. Add additional stock until you get the consistency of a slightly soupy batter.
5. Add in the cream of chicken soup, onion, celery, eggs, and spices. Stir well and mix thoroughly.
6. Test the consistency of the batter; it should be soupy. If more liquid is needed, add in small amounts of the oyster juice until you get the thickness you like.
7. Fold in the oysters, being careful not to tear them.
6. Pour batter into the greased dish; bake until the top turns a golden brown, 50 to 55 minutes (the length of time will vary depending on the depth of the baking dish). Serve immediately.
Serves 8 to 10

While we're on the subject of oysters and winter holidays, there is the ever-so-popular oyster pie, or more sumptuously referred to as escalloped oysters—that graces tables across the Southern coast. This dish is delicious in its simplicity, allowing the natural brine of the oysters to complement the silkiness of cream and the satisfying crunch of buttered crackers. Some people will sprinkle in a splash of sherry, or a bit of cheese; others scatter in minced scallions and celery to add some panache. The following recipe is a basic one; add in the flavors that might make your guests happy.

Escalloped Oysters (Oyster Pie)

Ingredients
4 tablespoons butter, room temperature, divided
½ cup celery, minced
½ cup green onion, white and light green portions, minced
3 cups saltine, Ritz, Townhouse, or other cracker crumbs, coarsely ground
8 ounces butter, melted
1 quart (2 pints/32 ounces) of fresh oysters, drained with liquor reserved
½ teaspoon black pepper
1 teaspoon Old Bay Seasoning, Lawry's Seasoning Salt, or kosher salt
1 teaspoon Worcestershire sauce
½ teaspoon Tabasco
2 tablespoons chopped fresh parsley, either curly or flat leaf
2 cups heavy cream
2 tablespoons dry sherry, optional

Directions
1. Preheat oven to 350 degrees.
2. Using 2 tablespoons of the room temperature butter, grease the bottom and sides of a 9x13 baking dish. Set aside.
3. In a saucepan, melt the remaining 2 tablespoon of room temperature butter over medium-high heat. Add in the celery and onions; sauté for 2 to 3 minutes. Set aside and allow to cool.
4. In a mixing bowl, combine the cracker crumbs and melted butter, tossing well until the crumbs are evenly coated. Take out 1 cup of the buttered crumbs and sprinkle across the bottom of the buttered baking dish.
5. In another bowl, gently toss together the cooled sautéed vegetables, oysters, black pepper, Old Bay, Worcestershire, Tabasco, and parsley. Measure out half of this mixture—about 2¼ cups—and spoon evenly over the cracker crumb layer.
6. Top the oyster layer with 1 cup of the buttered cracker crumbs.
7. Place the remaining oyster and vegetable mixture over the second layer of cracker crumbs.
8. Pour ½ cup of the reserved oyster liquor/juice evenly around the edges of the casserole dish.
9. Top the final oyster layer with the remaining 1 cup of cracker crumbs and press down gently.

10. Slowly and evenly stream the cream (combined with the dry sherry if you choose to include the sherry) over the top of the cracker crumb topping.
11. Place in the middle rack of an oven and bake 35 to 40 minutes until the cream is bubbling and the cracker topping golden. Serve immediately.

Serves 8 to 10

One of Tom's—and it seems lots of folks'—favorite holiday dishes is a green bean casserole; we serve this dish both at Thanksgiving and Christmas. Now on several occasions I've had a "made from scratch" version served by some overly enthusiastic uber hostess who used fresh green beans, made a real cream sauce, and fried her own shoe-string onions. My verdict? Not nearly as good as the old classic with canned mushroom soup and French's French-fried onions—though I do "doctor" mine up with a few extra ingredients.

"Doctored Up" Green Bean Casserole

Ingredients
4 tablespoons butter, at room temperature, divided
8 ounces fresh mushrooms, sliced thinly
4 (14.4-ounce) cans French-style cut green beans, thoroughly drained
1 (10.75-ounce) can cream of mushroom soup
8 ounces sour cream
2 teaspoons soy sauce
½ teaspoon black pepper
1 (6-ounce) container French's French-fried onions, divided
1½ cups sharp cheddar cheese, hand grated
1 cup chopped green onions, white and light green portions

Directions
1. Preheat oven to 350 degrees.
2. Using 2 tablespoons of butter, grease a 9x13 baking dish. Set aside.
3. Melt the remaining butter in a saucepan over medium-high heat. Add the mushrooms; sauté 5 to 7 minutes until tender and just beginning to brown. Set aside.
4. Pour the beans into a large mixing bowl; add in the sautéed mushrooms, the mushroom soup, sour cream, soy sauce, black pepper, ¾ cup of the fried onions, and the cheese. Fold together.
5. Sprinkle the chopped green onions into the bottom of the buttered baking dish. Ladle the bean mixture over the onions and smooth out evenly.

6. Bake, uncovered, for 25 minutes until hot and bubbling on the edges. Remove from oven, stir gently, and top with the remaining fried onions. Return to the oven and bake for 10 additional minutes until the onions begin to brown.
7. Remove from heat and allow to cool for 5 minutes before serving.
Serves 8 to 12

Somewhat of a newcomer to the Thanksgiving and Christmas table—at least in the South—are crisply roasted Brussels sprouts. As a child, the only way these little green bundles were served was boiled in salted water with a bit of side-meat. Until done. Very done. We didn't have them that often because, while a novelty at 1209 Ball St., there weren't, well, good. The dish was *not* my mama's finest hour in the kitchen. These days, Brussels sprouts are on many restaurant menus, not only as an accompaniment, but often offered up as an appetizer for the table to share. The recipe here is one that I've replicated at home based on one of Ina Garten's designs. (Don't you just love her? Style with comfort, taste with ease.) My few changes include the sprinkling of sugar for a bit more caramelizing, a little garlic, a hotter oven, and a tad more roasting time. If you have a convection oven, use it with the roasting option. The big piece of this recipe, and that of many Brussels sprouts, it the addition of balsamic vinegar, usually in the form of a glaze. These glazes can be purchased at your grocer or online, but you can make your own—easy-breezy. This entire dish is simple to make with just a handful of good ingredients and is an excellent presentation on your holiday table.

Crisped Brussels Sprouts with Balsamic Glaze

Ingredients
3 pounds fresh Brussels sprouts
½ cup olive oil
2 teaspoons garlic, minced
½ teaspoon kosher or sea salt
½ teaspoon freshly ground black pepper
¼ teaspoon sugar
8 ounces pancetta, diced into ¼-inch cubes (uncured bacon can be substituted)
2 tablespoons balsamic glaze (recipe follows)

Directions

1. Preheat oven at convection roast to 400 degrees, or on bake 425 degrees.
2. Remove and discard any yellowed, brown, or limp leaves from the sprouts.
3. Cut the bottom section of each sprout so that there is just a bit left next to the green head, then cut each sprout in half lengthwise. Place the halved sprouts, along with any stray leaves or parts, into a large mixing bowl. Make sure to include those loose leaves that fall off; they will crisp and caramelize nicely and are an integral part of the dish.
4. To the mixing bowl add the olive oil, garlic, salt, black pepper, and sugar. Toss to coat the sprouts evenly.
5. Spread the sprouts cut side down on a large nonstick baking dish, making sure not to crowd the pan. Scatter about any loose leaves onto the pan.
6. Sprinkle the pancetta around the cut halves on the pan.
7. Cook for 30 to 35 minutes, stirring once. The sprouts are ready when they begin to brown and crinkle around the edges. Do not worry about the loose leaves in the pan—although well-browned, they will add flavor and crunch to the dish. Remove from the oven, toss with the balsamic glaze, and serve immediately.

Serves 8 to 10

Balsamic Glaze

Ingredients

½ cup good quality balsamic vinegar, such as those offered from Modena or Reggio Emilio
1 tablespoon brown sugar or honey

Directions

1. Stir the vinegar and sugar (or honey) in a saucepan and bring to a steady simmer.
2. Reduce the heat to medium; continue simmering 8 to 10 minutes, stirring occasionally, until glaze is reduced by half and a syrupy consistency. It will thicken as it cools.

Makes ¼ cup or 4 tablespoons

Another favorite during these feast days is a sweet potato casserole. Now while the main part of the dish is the same from recipe to recipe—sweetened and mashed sweet potatoes—the topping is sometimes open for debate. And it seems like everyone has their favorite. Toasted marshmallows? Perhaps a nutty pecan topping? Or maybe a thick, brown sugar praline crust? I'll happily put a healthy serving of any of those selections on my plate. But for my recipe there is an additional and traditional holiday flavor—the distinct taste of gingersnaps.

Also used here are bourbon-infused raisins, cream, brown sugar, eggs, and vanilla. This version is a rich one, and not for those looking for a light and airy soufflé. Trust me, though…fattening though it may be, it is good. Just remember: portion control!

Important note: Do not take a shortcut and boil your sweet potatoes. Doing so loses so much flavor—and it waters down the vegetable as well. Bake them as suggested in the recipe.

Sweet Potato Casserole with a Gingersnap & Pecan Topping

Ingredients
1 cup raisins
1 cup bourbon
2 tablespoons butter, at room temperature
3 pounds sweet potatoes, baked and peeled (about 5 cups)
1 cup light or dark brown sugar
1 teaspoon cinnamon
½ teaspoon nutmeg, freshly grated
¾ cup melted butter, divided
2 teaspoons vanilla
2 eggs, slightly beaten
¾ cup heavy cream
3 cups crushed gingersnaps
1 cup chopped pecans

Directions
1. Preheat oven to 350 degrees.
2. In a small saucepan, bring the raisins and bourbon to a steady simmer. Cook 3 to 4 minutes, stirring occasionally. Remove from stove and set aside to cool.
3. Grease the bottom and sides of a 9x13 baking dish with the room temperature butter; set aside.
4. In a large bowl, add the sweet potatoes, and with a hand mixer (or stand mixer) beat until smooth.
5. Add to the beaten potatoes the sugar, cinnamon, nutmeg, ¼ cup of the melted butter, vanilla, eggs, and cream. Whip together until smooth.
6. Fold in the raisins and any remaining bourbon from the saucepan.
7. Ladle the sweet potato mixture into the buttered baking dish.

8. In another bowl, combine the gingersnaps, pecans, and remaining ½ cup melted butter. Mix well.
9. Evenly spread the cookie and pecan mixture over the top and press gently down just a bit into the sweet potatoes.
10. Bake 35 to 40 minutes until firm. Allow to sit for 5 minutes before serving.
Serves 8 to 10

Congealed salads, while not as popular as they were in the sixties and seventies, still find a home on Southern menus at Thanksgiving and Christmas. Some people feel that these dishes are culinary wonders—to others, they are culinary horrors. I like them—if you don't get carried away with the ingredients. One of my family's favorites that we continue to make during the holidays is Miss Mildred Evan Warren's Moon Salad, and also referred to as Moon Glow salad—perhaps because of its color? The combination of tart lime, sweet pineapple, creamy cheese, and crunchy pecans make a tasty offering. Enjoy it as a first course, side dish, or dessert, and I've been known to have some of the leftovers for breakfast!

Moon Salad

Ingredients
6 ounces cream cheese, at room temperature
1 (3-ounce) package lime-flavored Jello-O
1 cup boiling water
½ cup pineapple juice (use the reserve from the can of pineapple)
1 cup canned pineapple, crushed (do *not* use fresh pineapple as the salad won't congeal)
1 cup pecans, chopped

Directions
1. Beat together the cream cheese and the gelatin until smooth.
2. Add the boiling water and pineapple juice to the gelatin mixture; whip until the gelatin is dissolved and the mixture is fully incorporated. Stir in the pineapple and nuts.
3. Pour into whichever type of container you'd like to use: a baking dish (to slice the salad into squares to serve), individual molds, or a decorative mold.
4. Chill overnight or at least 6 hours before serving.
Serves 8

So far, we've covered the bird, dressings, and several selections of side dishes for the dinner meal. Let's move on to the desserts. There are enough favorites and traditions out there to write a whole book just on Thanksgiving and Christmas sweets; for sake of space here I've had to narrow it down enough to at least get you inspired.

With my family, pies were prevalent at Thanksgiving, and cakes and candies more so at Christmas. I shared earlier my dad's "thumbs down" attitude toward turkey; it was the same in regard to pumpkin pie. He'd turn his nose up at the Yankee gourd and ask instead for one made of the Southern sweet potato. I'm not including a pumpkin pie in *Cook & Celebrate*—no, not to mollify my late father's soul—but because the best recipe you can use is found on the can of Libby's Pure Pumpkin. Why replicate those words here? And like roasting a bird, so many people do their best to complicate the pumpkin pie recipe. Don't bother, really—just do what Libby says and you'll have great results.

As for sweet potatoes, did you know that they are related to the morning glory? Just look at the similar vines and blooms of both plants. Anyway, my favorite way to prepare this Barrett family tradition is based on the recipe from South Carolina's famous food writer and farmer, Dori Sanders. Purchase her book *Dori Sanders' Country Cooking* and enjoy the wonderful stories and delicious recipes. "People tell their life stories through food," Sanders writes. "They talk about how they did it then, and how they do it now. The way they talk tells you who they are."

In my adapted version, I don't roll out my own crust, as Dori does, and I leave out a few things and put in some others. This pie is more of a sweet potato custard, a bit lighter and creamier than most served during the holidays. I've tried many, many sweet potato pies over my life, and this is one that I'm sure you'll enjoy.

Sweet Potato Custard Pie

Ingredients
3 eggs, slightly beaten
1 cup light brown sugar
2 cups baked and mashed sweet potatoes (about 2 to 3 large potatoes)
⅔ cup + 1 tablespoon half-and-half
4 tablespoons butter, melted

1½ teaspoons vanilla extract
½ teaspoon cinnamon
⅛ teaspoon freshly grated nutmeg
1 unbaked deep-dish pie crust
Whipped cream

Directions
1. Preheat oven to 350 degrees.
2. In a large bowl, beat together the eggs and sugar until smooth. Add the sweet potatoes and beat until all three ingredients are well mixed.
3. To the bowl add the half-and-half, butter, vanilla, cinnamon, and nutmeg. Beat well until fully incorporated.
4. Pour the filling into the pie shell. Bake 45 to 50 minutes, until the center is set. Remove from the oven and allow to sit for half an hour before slicing. Serve with whipped cream.

Serves 6

Next is another family favorite, pecan pie. I have two versions here: one in the form of a pie, and the second prepared like a brownie in that you cut into pieces. For the pie itself, I turn to one of my Southern culinary buddies, Jamie DeMent, of Coon Rock Farm near Hillsborough, North Carolina. I had the pleasure of presenting with Jamie a few years back at the Southern Festival of Books in Nashville where we shared with the audience our common love of family and food traditions. Jamie can be seen on several Hallmark channel cooking shows, and her cookbook, *The Farmhouse Chef: Recipes and Stories from My Carolina Farm*, is a go-to for me when needing inspiration. And I certainly found a home-run recipe with her take on pecan pies; in it she uses pure cane syrup instead of corn syrup, and the result is sublime. I inherited my love of cane syrup from my parents and grandparents. We served it on our pancakes, and it was a favorite dessert covering a hot, buttered biscuit after a fish fry or alongside a platter of fried chicken or pork chops. My mother so loved the taste with her fried fish that she would even take cane syrup with her when we would go out to a restaurant for a catfish dinner. Out from the Kate Spade purse would come a small Tupperware container—and without batting an eye she'd pour some over her biscuit. The lady knew what she liked.

In my adapted recipe here, both cane and corn syrup are used. It isn't easy to find real, 100 percent cane syrup in the stores these days—if you can't locate any close by, go online and order from Steen's out of Abbeville, Louisiana. And, too: when purchasing pie crusts, they come in pairs. So just double the recipe here and make two.

Cane Syrup Pecan Pie

Ingredients
2 large eggs
1 cup real cane syrup
½ cup white corn syrup
¼ cup light brown sugar
2 tablespoons plain flour
2 teaspoons vanilla extract
1 cup pecan halves (not pieces)
1 (9-inch) unbaked pie crust
Whipped cream

Directions
1. Preheat the oven to 350 degrees.
2. Beat the eggs together in a large mixing bowl; add the cane syrup, corn syrup, sugar, flour, and vanilla extract. Mix well.
3. Spread the pecan halves evenly in the bottom of the pie crust.
4. Pour the egg and syrup mixture over the pecans.
5. Bake for 50 minutes to an hour, until the center starts to firm well.
6. Allow the pie to cool completely before slicing and serving. Top each slice with whipped cream.

Serves 6

The next recipe, pecan pie bars, comes from my friend Evelyn McDowell Castleberry of Sylvester, Georgia. Evelyn is a great cook, and her posts of supper-time meals on Facebook have me constantly hungry; more than once I've invited myself over for her cooking. Evelyn's mama, Miss Polly, was one of my mother's best friends. Those two ladies had a ball together, and I can still hear them laughing as they sat around the kitchen table exchanging stories.

Evelyn's recipe here is great for a cocktail party or large gathering where you don't want to worry with plates and cutlery—or you just need a bite of the pie, and not a whole slice.

Pecan Pie Bars

Ingredients
1 box yellow cake mix, divided
8 tablespoons (1 stick) butter, at room temperature
4 eggs
½ cup light or dark brown sugar
1½ cup white corn syrup
1 teaspoon vanilla extract
1 cup pecans, chopped

Directions
1. Preheat oven to 350 degrees.
2. Combine 1 cup cake mix, the butter, and 1 slightly beaten egg in a bowl. Mix well to form a dough; press the dough into the bottom of a 9x13 baking dish. Bake for 20 minutes. Remove from the oven and set aside.
3. In a large bowl, whisk together the remaining 3 eggs, the sugar, corn syrup, and vanilla extract. Add ⅔ cup cake mix to the bowl; stir to mix well. Pour onto the baked crust from step 2; sprinkle the chopped pecans on top.
4. Bake for 30 to 35 minutes until set. Cool before cutting and serving.
Serves 12 to 16

One dessert that many look forward to at Christmas is a red velvet cake. This fluffy, slightly chocolate-flavored cake was iced with a 7-minute frosting when I was a child. Over the years it seems that tradition has been replaced by the much-easier-to-make, but equally tasty, cream cheese frosting. The recipe here for the cake layers is the one my mom used, which was published in the 1967 and later editions of *Talk about Good!* by the Junior League of Lafayette, Louisiana. The contributing cook, Mrs. Abeline Stuller, lists the dessert as a Waldorf Astoria red velvet cake. Curious, I searched the internet to see if anything was there about Mrs. Stuller. It appears she was born in 1896, died the year before *Talk About Good!* was published, and is buried in St. Mary Magdalene Cemetery in Abbeville, Louisiana. God rest her cake-baking soul. I wonder if she had this cake at the famous hotel or just used the name because it made the cake sound fancy and rich?

The icing provided at this juncture is Mama's cream cheese frosting. You can also use Aunt Polly's 7-minute frosting found in the Easter chapter (see index). Garnish your cake slices with a bright green sprig of holly, and you'll have a picture-perfect, and quite delicious, hit for you and your guests. This cake just sings "Merry Christmas!"

Waldorf Astoria Red Velvet Cake

Ingredients
½ cup Crisco
1¼ cups sugar
2 large eggs
1 (1-ounce) bottle red food coloring
2½ cups all-purpose flour
2 tablespoons cocoa
1 teaspoon baking soda
1 teaspoon salt
2½ cups whole milk buttermilk
1 teaspoon vanilla extract
1 teaspoon white distilled vinegar
Cream cheese frosting (recipe follows), or 7-minute frosting (see index)

Directions
1. Preheat oven to 350 degrees.
2. Grease and flour three 9-inch cake pans and line the bottoms with greased and floured waxed paper.
3. In a mixing bowl, cream the Crisco and sugar until smooth and creamy.
4. Add the eggs to the mixture, one at a time, beating until smooth.
5. Add the food coloring and mix until well-blended.
6. In a separate bowl, sift together the flour, cocoa, baking soda, and salt. Set aside.
7. In another small bowl, mix together the buttermilk, vanilla, and vinegar.
8. To the Crisco, sugar, and egg mixture, alternate adding the flour mixture and buttermilk mixture, starting and ending with the flour. *Mix until just combined; do not over beat!*
9. Spoon the batter evenly into the prepared cake pans. Bake 20 to 25 minutes until firm; a toothpick inserted into the middle should come out clean.
10. Allow the cakes to cool on a rack for 10 minutes. Turn the cakes out of the pans to cool completely on the racks.
11. Ice with the frosting of your choice.
Serves 12 to 16

Cream Cheese Frosting

Ingredients

8 ounces cream cheese, at room temperature
4 tablespoons butter, at room temperature
1 (16-ounce) box powdered sugar
1 teaspoon vanilla extract
1 tablespoon whole milk, cream, or half-and-half

Directions

1. Beat the cream cheese and butter until thoroughly mixed.
2. Sift in the powdered sugar, a cup at a time, and beat until smooth.
3. Add in the vanilla and milk and continue to beat until fully mixed. Spread on and between cooled cake layers.

Then there is the much loved, and much maligned, fruitcake; I dearly love this candied dessert. Dense, dark, and soaked in a good bourbon or spiced rum, it is the epitome of all things culinary this season of the year. And if you are a Southern foodie, you can't help but think about the warm and bittersweet story of Buddy and his cousin in Truman Capote's "A Christmas Memory": "Oh my! It's fruitcake weather, Buddy!" is a line we all know by heart.

I relish those cold days waking to a sparkling frost and then plunging into the ritual of creating these gems. Tom and I start at Thanksgiving, baking small loaves that will sit tucked in the back of the refrigerator, wrapped in cheesecloth and soaked in spirits, until time to gift them to friends at Christmas. We also make fruitcake cookies, one of my mother's specialties, but I cover that story and recipe in a later chapter.

The recipe I use is based on Ninnie's version, with the inclusion of cane syrup, as well as that of the incomparable Nancie McDermott. Nancie, a native of the Tar Heel State, is renowned as a food writer and cooking teacher. The author of fourteen cookbooks, she creates a fruitcake sensation that's found in her extremely popular *Southern Cakes: Sweet and Irresistible Recipes for Everyday Celebrations*. If you want to know how to bake a stunning-looking and stellar-tasting cake, you need that book in your culinary library.

Note: If you are a teetotaler, you can leave off the bourbon. The cake will still be excellent (but not quite as spirited). Merry, merry!

Spirited Fruitcake

Ingredients

1 cup candied orange slices or peel, chopped
1 cup candied cherries, chopped
1 cup candied pineapple, chopped
¾ cup dried tart cherries, chopped
¾ cup dried apricots, chopped
¾ cup dried plums, chopped
¾ cup dates, chopped
1 cup raisins, golden or dark
1 (750-milliliter) bottle bourbon, divided*
1½ cups all-purpose flour, divided
½ teaspoon salt
½ teaspoon baking powder
1½ teaspoons cinnamon
1 teaspoon nutmeg
½ teaspoon ground allspice
2 cups chopped pecans
2 cups chopped walnuts
½ cup butter, at room temperature
1 cup dark brown sugar, packed
3 large eggs
½ cup blackberry, fig, or grape jam
½ cup pure cane syrup (such as Steen's)
½ cup orange juice

* Drink some, cook with some.

Directions

Make ahead note: In a large bowl or gallon zip-lock bag, combine the dried
  fruits and 2 cups of the bourbon. Allow it to sit, stirring (or shaking) ever 15
  minutes or so, for 2 hours.

1. Prepare pans by greasing and flouring the bottom and sides; as well, grease
   and flour waxed paper for the bottoms of the pans. You can use 1 (10-inch)
   tube pan, 2 (9x5) loaf pans, or 8 miniature (6x3) loaf pans.
2. Preheat oven to 250 degrees.
3. In a mixing bowl, stir in one cup of flour, salt, baking powder, cinnamon,
   nutmeg, and allspice.
4. In a sieve or colander drain the bourbon from the bowl/bag of fruit. Reserve the leftover spirits in a bowl and set aside.

5. Place the drained fruit into a large mixing bowl along with the chopped nuts. Toss to mix. Add ½ cup of the flour to the bowl and toss the fruit and nuts to coat the fruit evenly with the flour.
6. In another bowl, cream the butter and sugar in a mixer over high speed—about 2 or 3 minutes. Add the eggs to the bowl, one at a time, beating after each addition. Scrape the sides and bottoms of the bowl 2 or 3 times to make sure all ingredients are incorporated.
7. To the creamed butter/sugar/eggs, whisk in the jam and cane syrup. Whisk together until mixed well. Add in ½ cup of the flour mixture and ¼ cup of the orange juice. Stir well to mix thoroughly. Repeat with the final ½ cup of the flour mixture and ¼ cup juice.
10. Pour in the fruit and nuts and stir to mix. As you see, there is little flour in ratio to the fruit and nuts, so the mixture will be very thick; it is not pourable.
11. Ladle the batter into your prepared pan(s). Bake 2½ to 3 hours for the 10-inch tube pan or until the center begins to spring back when touched or a toothpick inserted into the middle section of the cake comes out clean. For the 9x5 loaf pans, start checking for doneness at 1 hour 45 minutes. For the 6x3 size, check after 1 hour 30 minutes.
12. When done, place the pan(s) on a wire rack for half an hour or so to cool. Invert onto a flat surface and remove the wax paper.
13. Brush the cake(s) with the reserved liquor saved from the dried fruits. Wrap the cake(s) in cheesecloth and then wrap each in foil. Refrigerate for 2 weeks or more; I "cure" mine for about 6 weeks. Every 4 to 5 days remove the cake(s) from the refrigerator, unwrap the foil *but leave on the cheesecloth* and splash with the leftover bourbon. And when the leftover runs out, use additional spirits.
14. To serve, unwrap from the foil, remove the cheesecloth, and allow to sit for 30 minutes to remove the chill. If you are gifting the cake(s), remove the foil and cheesecloth, wrap in cling wrap, and then wrap again in butcher paper and tie with a decorative ribbon. I use inexpensive holiday tins that I find at Dollar Tree to put these in when gifting.

Serves 16 to 24 for the tube pan, 8 to 12 for each 9x5 pan, and 4 people each for the 6x3 size.

Holiday candies and cookies both hold a multitude of traditions in the South at Thanksgiving and Christmas, sometimes several even within a single family. In our house, two of those featured were my mom's award-winning peanut brittle—hands-down the best you've ever tasted—and my Aunt Polly's chocolate macaroons, rich with the taste of cocoa and peanut

Lillie Mae Owens (my Aunt Lil), left, with her daughter,
Joyce Owens Giles , Elko, Georgia, c. 1952

Giving Aunt Polly a kiss on her eightieth birthday; she lived to be 108!

butter. Both of those stories and recipes are in *Rise and Shine!*, so I won't replicate here. Another two memorable favorites were Aunt Polly's scrumptious butterscotch haystacks and Aunt Lil's lemon crisp cookies. Folks scrambled to get a handful of each—and if you weren't quick, you'd do without. I would deftly scoop us as many as possible into a bag and then hoard them in a secret stash, away from poaching relatives. These recipes bring back such beautiful memories, as these two gracious ladies were like grandmothers to me. Both of my parents' mothers passed away years before I was born, and Aunt Lil and Aunt Polly stepped in to give me a double dose of grandmotherly love. I miss them each and every day.

For the haystack recipe, I have updated the process; Aunt Polly's original recipe instructs the cook to melt the butterscotch and peanut butter in a double boiler while here I use the microwave oven. It makes me appreciate all the changes in the world Aunt Lil and Aunt Polly witnessed. Aunt Lil, born in 1902, was the oldest by a few years. She lived to be ninety; Aunt Polly stayed with us until the astounding age of 108. The two sisters started out riding in a horse and buggy, and at the end of their lives could fly anywhere in the world. Cooking as children meant a wood stove, and they both purchased microwave ovens in the mid-1980s. Pretty amazing when you think about it.

Butterscotch Haystacks

Ingredients
1 cup butterscotch morsels
½ cup creamy peanut butter
½ cup cocktail peanuts
2 cups dry chow mein noodles

Directions
1. Set a piece of wax paper on a flat surface.
2. Place the morsels and peanut butter in a microwavable bowl; heat on medium for 2 minutes. Stir. Heat for another minute, or until completely melted.
3. Add the peanuts and noodles to the bowl; stir well to evenly coat the nuts and noodles.
4. Quickly drop the mixture by the heaping teaspoonful onto the wax paper. Allow them to cool and harden completely. Store in an airtight container.

Makes 2 dozen (which only serves about 2 folks if you have someone like me hovering around the kitchen)

Of all the cookies I've ever tasted, and I mean all of them, these thin bursts of buttery lemon, with their distinctive crunchy brown edges, are my absolute favorites. Give me a dozen and a glass of cold milk and I am one happy, happy fellow.

Lemon Crisp Cookies

Ingredients
2½ cups all-purpose flour, sifted
½ teaspoon salt
½ teaspoon baking soda
8 tablespoons (1 stick) butter, at room temperature
½ cup butter-flavored Crisco
1 cup sugar
1 large egg, lightly beaten
1 teaspoon vanilla extract
2 teaspoons lemon extract
1 tablespoon milk
Additional sugar
Lemon juice

Directions
1. Preheat oven to 400 degrees.
2. In a mixing bowl, sift together the flour, salt, and soda. Set aside.
3. In another bowl, beat together until creamed (about 3 minutes) the butter, Crisco, and sugar.
4. Add the egg, vanilla, lemon, and milk to the creamed mixture and beat for 1 minute.
5. Add the sifted dry ingredients 1 cup at a time to the bowl and beat until well blended. Scrape the bottom and sides of the bowl occasionally to insure all the ingredients are incorporated.
6. Shape the dough into 1-inch balls and place 2 inches apart on a wax paper lined cookie sheet. The cookies will spread when baking, so make sure to allow space.
7. Dip the bottom of a glass in lemon juice and then in sugar. Press down gently onto each of the cookie dough rounds and flatten slightly. Reapply the lemon juice and sugar for every cookie or two.

8. Bake 9 to 11 minutes. The edges will begin to brown while the center remains a golden color. Be watchful as these thin cookies will continue to cook from residual heat when removed from the oven.

9. Allow the cookies to cool 4 to 5 minutes; with a spatula, move them to rest on a wire rack. Make certain that the cookies are at room temperature and completely cooled before putting them in your storage container. If they are still the slightest bit warm, they will lose their crispness.

Makes about 4 dozen cookies

My first memory of divinity candy was from my Aunt Hazel. She was a wonderful cook, and this angelic confection of hers was famed in our family. It was always light, airy, and white as the driven snow. Hazel Grace Nipper McIntyre Lytle was the eldest sister on my mama's side of the family, and while she had a wonderful sense of humor and a glorious laugh, she was no-nonsense as well and was one true steel magnolia. One sideways look from her would even make my outspoken mother sheepish. We lost Aunt Hazel way too early in life to cancer, a disease that has plagued the Nipper family. In *Rise and Shine!*, I shared her famed German chocolate cake recipe—another one of her Christmas specialties. We all miss her greatly to this day.

In my adult years, it has been my friend Nella Maxwell of Savannah who has supplied me with Christmas divinity; she and I have shared some real belly-laughs with one another over the years—and have danced our toes off to some 80s music; we can cut a rug to "You Dropped a Bomb on Me." I call her "Nelda" because my mom always pronounced her name that way. It was sort of like Endora on *Bewitched*, who constantly mispronounced Darrin's name—although Mama loved "Nelda" dearly. More than once I said, "Mama, her name is *Nell-lllla*; there isn't a letter 'd' in it," to which I'd get a bored, sometimes even exasperated look. Shaking her head, wondering why she spent all that money on my education that must not have taken, she'd say, patiently, "That's what I said, honey. 'Nelda.'" Anyway, even after all these years since Mama has left us for that big dining room in the sky, I have my friend's name in my phone spelled as "Nelda." And what does she call me? Joe-Nathan. Long story there— I'd have to tell you that one over a bourbon sometime, but when we see one another, we holler out "NELDA!" and "JOE-NATHAN" and give each other big hugs.

Now Nelda loves Christmas as much as I do and celebrates it in memory of her mom, Ethelyne Williamson Hardee. Miss Ethelyne, raised on a farm about seventy miles due west of Savannah, was a beloved fifth grade teacher at Hancock Day School for twenty-five years. Nelda shares the story of her mama and that most magical of Christmas confections, the sweet little nut-filled clouds called divinity.

My love for Christmas decorations and baking comes from my mother. The aromas and smells at Christmas take me back to my childhood. The Christmas season at my house officially kicked off the day after Thanksgiving. First came the decorating of the house and then the endless days of baking. Mom would bake fudge, bourbon balls, Oreos dipped in white chocolate, almond bark, crescent-shaped wedding cookies, fruit cake cookies, and the all-time favorite, divinity. "The weather," my mom would say, "has to be just right. A cool crisp day with no humidity." Well, living in Savannah—even in December—dry, cloudless days were few and far between. Every morning I would ask my mom if this was The Day. When The Day would finally get here, I would rush home from school. Mom would lay out the wax paper on our dining room table in anticipation of the lovely white cotton that was soon to adorn it. Mom would have all her ingredients lined up and then would stand over the stove, stirring for what seemed like hours for the temperature to be just right to drop teaspoons of the mixture onto the wax paper. We'd both hold our breath, hoping the divinity would hold its shape and not flatten like a pancake. And if the mixture turned into a beautiful white mound, we knew the wait had been worth it!

Christmas Divinity

Ingredients
3 cups sugar
1 cup white corn syrup
½ cup water
¼ teaspoon salt
2 egg whites, at room temperature
1 teaspoon vanilla extract
1 cup finely chopped pecans

Directions
1. Make sure *the day* is here: one that is cool and with little or no humidity. Another critical step is to have *everything* lined up, measured, and ready to use, as the mixture needs to come together at once.
2. Combine first 4 ingredients in a Dutch oven; cook over low heat, stirring constantly, until sugar dissolves.
3. Increase heat to high, and cook, without stirring, until mixture reaches hard ball stage (260 degrees using a candy thermometer).
4. In another bowl, beat egg whites until stiff peaks form.
5. Pour the hot sugar mixture in a thin stream over egg whites while beating constantly at high speed.
6. Add vanilla, and continue beating 5 to 10 minutes, until mixture holds its shape. Stir in pecans. Drop the candy by the teaspoon onto waxed paper.
7. Allow to cool completely. Store at room temperature in airtight containers.
Makes about 3 dozen pieces of candy

Now the eves of both Thanksgiving and Christmas give cause for additional culinary celebrations, and I like to "do it up," especially the night before Christmas. When younger and with more energy, I'd put together a multi-course meal, we'd all feast, and then head off to midnight Mass. As my years have stretched out, though, my stamina has not kept up with the age digits—so now we go to the 5:00 children's Mass, watch the kiddies as they march in dressed as Mary and Joseph, sing a few hymns, and I'm home with cocktail in hand by 6:30 to finish cooking. (Don't worry about my soul; I get up the next morning and go back to church; I'm not short-cutting Jesus on his birthday.)

I have pretty much a standard supper each year; the tradition of what we have and the presentations give me a sense of comfort and, yes, joy, as I roll out the sausage balls just like my mother did and prep that big, fat, juicy prime rib that has been curing in the refrigerator alongside the next day's bird.

The menu here is one that I've seen replicated from dining room to dining room across the South; most all of it can be prepped and ready in advance, so you don't have to rush around in the kitchen, breaking out in a sweat, while the rest of the family sit by the fire and enjoy the lights on the tree.

I start out with two favorites for hors d'oeuvres: the aforementioned sausage balls and a wonderfully rich artichoke, spinach, and Vidalia onion spread. Both dishes can be ready to stick in the oven the moment you get home from singing the last stanza of "Silent Night."

For the sausage balls, attempts have been made by cooks to gussy them up and add in exotics such as shallots, roasted poblanos, imported rich cheeses—all to questionable results. My advice: keep it simple and follow the recipe that has worked for decades: sausage, sharp cheddar, and Bisquick. A few hints here to follow even with this simplicity. First, make sure to grate the cheese yourself; I've already warned about pre-shredded cheese and how cellulose will dry out your dish. Secondly, use a creamier sharp variety, such as Cracker Barrel brand. Thirdly, use a trusted brand of hot sausage—if you know your local butcher does a spicy sausage that isn't blazing, great. If not, choose Jimmy Dean, Johnsonville, Bob Evans—the commercial brands of "hot" that give a bite to the food but won't burn the palate of Great-Aunt Lillibet, who will never, ever, let you live it down.

If you do want to spice them up a bit, serve a side bowl of raspberry and jalapeño jelly, or another other hot, sweet jam to dip the balls in when serving. Leftover hint: if you do happen to have some of these flavorful jewels left over, serve them the next morning at breakfast alongside your fried eggs. Too, they freeze well and can be made in advance; just reheat and serve.

Holiday Sausage Balls

Ingredients
2¾ cups Bisquick
1 pound ground sausage, uncooked
1 pound sharp cheddar cheese, hand grated
1 to 2 tablespoons milk (only if needed)
Raspberry jalapeño jam (optional)

Directions
1. Preheat oven to 375 degrees.
2. In a large mixing bowl, and either with a stand mixer with a paddle, or with your hands (have plenty of Dawn afterward to get the grease off) thoroughly combine the Bisquick, sausage, and cheese. If it's too stiff to make into a ball, add in a bit of milk.

3. Scoop out the dough in heaping teaspoons and roll into balls. Place the balls an inch apart on a lightly greased baking sheet.
4. Bake for 20 minutes until light brown and sizzling. Remove from the oven and place on a wire rack to cool slightly before serving. Serve with a spicy jam (optional). Can be refrigerated in an airtight container and either re-heated or served at room temperature.

Makes 4 dozen

The second hors d'oeuvre offering for your crowd is one of the easiest and quickest you can make, and at the same time be considered fancy party fare. For the best result, use a good mayonnaise—and, for the Lord's sake, not a reduced-fat variety—and real Parmesan cheese that you grated yourself. While this dip can go with any cracker (and some folks serve it with corn chip scoops as well), it is best served on homemade toast points. For Christmas color, garnish with bright green minced parsley and finely minced red bell pepper. Enjoy!

Artichoke, Spinach & Vidalia Onion Dip

Ingredients
2 (14-ounce) cans artichoke hearts
1 tablespoon butter
1 cup Vidalia onion, chopped
1 cup chopped *fresh* spinach, packed
1 cup less 2 tablespoons real mayonnaise
1½ cups freshly grated Parmesan cheese
⅛ teaspoon red pepper flakes
2 tablespoons fresh parsley, minced
2 tablespoons red bell pepper, minced
Garlic toast points (recipe follows)

Directions
1. Preheat oven to 350 degrees.
2. Drain the artichoke hearts. Take each in your fist and squeeze to remove any excess water. Coarsely chop the hearts and place in a mixing bowl.
3. In a saucepan, melt the butter over medium-high heat; add in the onion. Sauté for about 2 minutes, until just starting to become tender.
4. To the artichoke hearts, add the cooked onions, spinach, mayonnaise, cheese, and pepper flakes. Stir to mix well.

5. Spread the mixture into an 8x8 baking dish. (At this point the dip can be refrigerated and cooked later.)
6. Bake for 25 to 30 minutes until the sides of the dip are bubbling and the top beginning to turn golden brown. Allow to sit at room temperature for 10 minutes before serving—it will be hot! Garnish with the parsley and red bell pepper and serve with the toast points.

Serves 10 to 12

Garlic Toast Points

Ingredients
10 to 12 slices thinly sliced sourdough or rye bread
1 tablespoon butter, melted
1 tablespoon olive oil
1 teaspoon garlic powder
½ teaspoon kosher or sea salt

Directions
1. Preheat oven to 400 degrees.
2. With a 2-inch cookie cutter or champagne flute, cut out rounds of the bread and set aside. I don't use the crusts, but you can if you'd like. You should get about 3 rounds per slice.
3. In a small bowl, mix together the butter and olive oil.
4. Set the bread rounds in 1 layer on a nonstick cookie sheet.
5. Brush each round lightly with the butter and oil mixture.
6. Sprinkle ½ teaspoon of the garlic powder and ¼ teaspoon of the salt over the rounds.
7. Turn the rounds over and repeat steps 5 and 6.
8. Bake for 6 minutes and turn the rounds over. Continue baking for another 5 to 6 minutes until the bread is a golden brown and crisp.
9. Remove from the oven and allow to cool on a wire rack. Make certain that the toast is *completely cool* before storing in an airtight container.

Makes 3 to 4 dozen

There are many recipes available for crab bisque and crab stews, and while I adore the taste of crab, it is not easy these days to find local crab, even on the coast of our Southern states. Yes, the local seafood markets may have crab meat, but often it is from Ecuador or someplace far from the shores of the USA. Too, crab meat is expensive, and making the stock a real chore. I have come up with a recipe that uses shrimp instead, and the result is a silky, sherry-laced bisque that is like sipping a creamy taste of the sea. The recipe is in two stages and takes a bit of time; however, it is not difficult and can be made the day before it is to be served. *Important note: Do not overcook your shrimp. If you do, the bisque will be filled with rubbery pieces of prawns that cannot be rectified (unless you are a wizard with magical powers).*

Pair this bisque with a crisp white wine such as a French Sancerre or a pinot blanc from Alsace.

Shrimp Bisque

Ingredients
Stock
2 pounds medium size, fresh USA wild-caught shrimp (heads on if possible)
6 cups low-sodium chicken stock

Bisque
6 tablespoons butter, divided
3 tablespoons carrot, minced
3 tablespoons celery, minced
3 tablespoons shallot, minced
¼ cup all-purpose flour
6 cups shrimp-infused chicken stock
3 tablespoons tomato paste
3 cups heavy cream
½ cup dry sherry
Peeled shrimp from the stock recipe
1 teaspoon kosher salt
½ teaspoon fresh ground black pepper
2 tablespoons olive oil
Chopped parsley or chives to garnish

Directions
Stock
1. Peel, head, and devein shrimp. Place the shrimp in an airtight container and refrigerate.
2. Process the shrimp shells in a food processor, pulsing half a dozen times. Scrape out the shells into a large pot. If you have shrimp heads, add them to the pot as well.
3. Add the chicken stock to the pot. Bring to a boil, stir, and reduce heat. Cook at a low simmer for 15 minutes.

4. Remove from heat and let sit for half an hour. Strain through a sieve into a bowl. Set aside or cover and refrigerate if using later.

Bisque

1. Melt 4 tablespoons butter over medium-high heat in a large Dutch oven. Add in the carrot, celery, and shallot and sauté for 2 to 3 minutes, stirring, until the vegetables are soft. Do not allow the butter and vegetables to brown.
2. Add in the flour, whisk to mix well, and cook for 2 minutes, whisking constantly.
3. Into the flour mixture, stream in the reserved stock, whisking, until it is thoroughly incorporated. Bring to a steady simmer and allow to cook for 5 to 7 minutes to thicken. Stir occasionally during the process so that the flour does not stick to the bottom of the pot.
4. Add in the tomato paste; whisk to fully incorporate.
5. Pour in the cream and whisk together; cook for another 3 minutes, until just under a simmer.*
6. Stir in the sherry; reduce heat to the lowest setting.
7. In a large sauté pan, melt the remaining butter and the olive oil over medium-high heat.
8. Sprinkle and toss the shrimp with the salt and black pepper; add to the sauté pan.
9. Cook, stirring constantly, until just done, 3 to 4 minutes. The shrimp will turn pink and bend together into a C-shape.
10. Pour the cooked shrimp into the bisque, stir well, and ladle immediately into warmed bowls. Garnish with the parsley or chives.

Serves 8 to 10 as an appetizer, 4 to 6 for an entrée

* If the bisque is to be finished at a later time, allow the pot to cool on the counter, cover and refrigerate. Reheat over low until almost to a simmer. Stir occasionally and proceed with step 6.

There is nothing like a perfectly roasted prime rib of beef that can set the stage for a fabulous dinner party. These roasts are not difficult to prepare, so don't be intimidated by the task. Mine is done with Worcestershire Sauce and olive oil, along with a dry rub that creates a crispy and flavorful crust. The secret to this seasoning is coarsely ground black pepper that has been cold smoked in bourbon barrels; you can find it in gourmet grocery stores or online. I have also had success with McCormick's Grill Mates Smoky Montreal Seasoning.

A creamy horseradish sauce is a delicious accompaniment for the meat, and if you'd like, you can save some of the pan juices and have an au jus as well. So many things pair well with this dish, such as the baked rice with caramelized onion and roasted asparagus recipes following—just let your taste buds be the guide. And remember, keep the leftovers! One of the most wonderful breakfast dishes I ever had was in Victoria, British Columbia. The restaurant in the historic inn where we were staying made a hash out of prime rib (I believe the beef was a dinner special the night before) and served it with poached eggs—a stunning way to start the day. You can also cut the meat into strips for a main course salad or make a substantial sandwich. The meaty bones also can be frozen and used later as a base for a big bowl of hearty soup.

Note: Season this roast the day before you cook it, and let it sit, uncovered, on a rack in the refrigerator. Before baking, make sure to let it sit for an hour on the counter to come to room temperature.

Prime Rib of Beef with Horseradish Cream Sauce

Ingredients
1 (7- to 8-pound) 3-rib prime rib of beef
4 tablespoons Worcestershire sauce
2½ tablespoons olive oil
3 tablespoons Bourbon Barrel Smoked Black Pepper (or other good quality smoked-infused pepper blend*)
1 tablespoon kosher salt
1 tablespoon onion powder
1 tablespoon garlic powder
1 tablespoon dried thyme
Horseradish sauce (recipe follows)

* *If using a pepper blend, most of which contain salt, you will need to reduce the amount of salt above to ½ to 1 teaspoon.*

Directions
Day 1
1. Brush the entire roast with the Worcestershire sauce, then with the olive oil.

2. Combine the dry ingredients in a small bowl; sprinkle 1 tablespoon of the mix on the bottom (rib side) of the roast. Rub and pat the rest of the dry mixture into the meat; make sure to cover the entire roast.
3. Set the roast rib side down, fat side up, on a rack in a shallow pan. Refrigerate, uncovered, overnight.

Day 2
1. Remove the roast from the refrigerator and sit at room temperature for 1 hour before cooking.
2. Preheat oven to 350 degrees.
3. Place the roast in the lower third of the oven; cook for 1 hour and 15 minutes. Check your meat at this point; it needs to register 125 degrees in the thickest portion for rare. If you want your meat a little more well done, place back in the oven and cook for another 3 to 5 minutes. Remember: after the meat reaches a temperature of 125 or so, it begins to cook much more quickly, so you will need to monitor often so as to not overcook.
4. Remove from oven and allow to rest for 20 minutes, allowing the juices to center back into the roast. The resting period is important, so do not reduce that timing.
5. To carve, place the roast on a cutting board bone side down—just as you had in the baking dish. Using a large two-pronged fork, hold in place and slice away the bone—it should come off easily. Be sure to handle the prime rib carefully, as you don't want to rub off any of that wonderful crust. With the fork holding the roast in place, slice to the desired thickness, and serve immediately.

Serves 6

Horseradish Cream Sauce

Ingredients
1 scant cup mayonnaise
⅓ cup sour cream
3 tablespoons finely ground horseradish

Directions
1. Mix ingredients; taste and add additional horseradish if you would like a spicier sauce.
2. Cover and allow to chill for 2 hours. Serve with prime rib or beef tenderloin.

Makes 1 ½ cups

On the Southern coast, rice is a staple and has been grown here for centuries. My 4x-great-grandfather, William Withers of Georgetown, South Carolina, was a rice farmer. In the early 1850s he purchased a home in the North Georgia mountains of Habersham County, in the little community of Sautee. There on his property he built a mill on the Soque River and had rice from his plantation sent up from South Carolina to be milled. Family lore has it that his wife did not take well to what she considered "the backwoods" and preferred the social life of Charleston and Georgetown. While Papa Withers would make periodic trips back to the coast, Grandmother moved permanently back to Charleston, never to return to North Georgia. I believe he then took a mistress in his wife's absence—or so it was whispered amongst my elderly aunts when I was a child. When Mr. William Withers died, Grandmother Harriet Taylor Withers let him stay put in Habersham County. He is buried on the old family property in the Nacoochee Valley, underneath a large, lone headstone engraved with the sign of the Masons. The current owner refers to the grave as "our Mr. Withers" and keeps the arbor of mountain laurels and rhododendrons bordering the site trimmed and in a garden setting.

One more family tale about this—and while not about cooking, it is interesting. The day my Grandmother Harriet died, her three granddaughters were sitting on the front porch of one of their homes in downtown Clarkesville, doing needlepoint. According to the story, they each looked up at the same time and spotted a woman walking along the sidewalk behind the boxwood hedge. One exclaimed, "No one told us Grandmother was in town!" They put down their needlework and hurried down the broad steps. When they got to the sidewalk, no one was there. The sisters were puzzled and eventually went back to their work. The next morning, a telegram arrived from Charleston informing the family that Harriet had passed away the afternoon before—right at the time of their sighting. Family ghosts? Perhaps.

Anyway, this next dish pairs wonderfully with the prime rib and can be constructed before you leave for Mass and then cooked alongside the prime rib. While a good, commercial grade rice will work, I'd suggest you'd venture to one of the more flavorful small-batch varieties available, such as a one from the Satilla River area of Georgia or a South Carolina Gold, a crop similar to what Grandfather Withers might have milled.

Too, don't use Vidalias or other sweet onions here. Those wonderful onions have their place in so many dishes, but they often can add too much sweetness rather than the onion flavor necessary here.

Baked Rice with Caramelized Onions

Ingredients
5 tablespoons olive oil, divided
6 cups thinly sliced, non-sweet onions (about 1½ pounds)
⅛ teaspoon kosher salt
¼ teaspoon black pepper
2 tablespoons butter
1½ cups regular white rice (do *not* use an instant brand)
3 cups reduced-sodium beef broth, such as Better than Bouillon
1½ teaspoons Worcestershire sauce
8 ounces fresh mushrooms, sliced

Directions
1. Preheat oven to 350 degrees.
2. Heat 3 tablespoons of the olive oil in a Dutch oven over medium-high heat. Add the onions, salt and pepper. Stir and cover.
3. Reduce heat to medium-low, and allow to cook for 10 minutes, stirring occasionally.
4. Remove lid, and continue to cook for 20 additional minutes, stirring occasionally, until the onions caramelize and turn a dark golden brown.
5. With a spatula, remove onions to a bowl and reserve.
6. Place the Dutch oven back on the stove and turn heat back up to medium-high. Add the remaining 2 tablespoons olive oil and the butter.
7. When hot, add the rice, and stir to coat. Cook 2 minutes, stirring constantly.
8. Add the caramelized onions and remaining ingredients to the pot, stir well, and cover tightly. Place in the oven and bake for 55 minutes.
9. Remove from the oven and allow to sit at room temperature for 10 minutes. Remove lid, stir, and serve.
Serves 6 to 8

Roasted asparagus goes well with so many dishes, and it is one of the simplest sides you can make. If you have your baking dish prepared in advance, these green stalks can cook while the prime rib and rice rest on the countertop. A homemade hollandaise sauce complements this side quite nicely (see index).

Roasted Asparagus

Ingredients
2 pounds fresh asparagus (I recommend using thick stalks here rather than thin ones)
1½ tablespoons olive oil
1 teaspoon kosher salt
½ teaspoon black pepper
Hollandaise sauce (optional; see index)

Directions
1. Preheat oven to 425 degrees.
2. Cut off the lower inch or so of each spear and peel the lower third of each stalk. Place the prepared spears on a baking tray large enough to hold the spears in one layer.
3. Drizzle over the vegetable the olive oil; sprinkle on the salt and pepper. Gently toss—don't tear off the tender tops—to coat each spear.
4. Bake for 10 to 15 minutes, depending on the thickness, giving the pan a good shake halfway through the cooking time. Serve immediately.

Serves 6 to 8

Dessert for Christmas Eve, you ask? A glass of champagne and a passed plate of Mama's fruitcake cookies; the recipe is in chapter 8 (see index).

Part 2

Parties, Get-Togethers,
&
"Gatherins"

Chapter 7

A Twelfth Night Celebration

As I wrote earlier, Christmas is hands-down my favorite time of the year, and celebrating Twelfth Night allows those of us who don't want Christmastide to end at New Year's to extend our "joie de Noël" even further. This ecclesiastical observance dates to the sixth century and continues to be observed in Great Britain and in other parts of Europe. Counting from Christmas Day, the twelfth night of Christmas is January 5. We celebrate Twelfth Night because it is the night before Epiphany, the day the nativity story tells us that the wise men visited the infant Jesus.

There are a number of traditions you might have heard of but perhaps don't realize are tied to Twelfth Night, such as the burning of the yule log that begins on Christmas day and continues until Epiphany, as well as wassail, which is spiced hot cider mulled with apples. Wassail could be a potent drink and led to much merry-making in olden days. Quoting Ogden Nash's "A Drink with Something in It:" "Then here's to the heartening wassail, / Wherever good fellows are found; / Be its master instead of its vassal, / and order the glasses around." The ever-popular king cake that is a New Orleans triumph has its roots in the traditions of Twelfth Night as well, dating back to the Middle Ages. In France it was referred to as *galette des rois* and in Spain heralded as *roscón de Reyes*. Today's king cake is most often made with flaky pastry dough and covered in colored icings. In old Britain, this dessert of the three kings was more akin to what we now consider a dense fruit cake—one that was baked round and wrapped with a paper crown. Instead of a small plastic baby Jesus hidden inside, there would be a bean; whoever found the bean would be "king" for the remainder of the night.

Since I'm a fan of the theater, one story worth telling is that of Robert Baddeley, an eighteenth-century English actor. Mr. Baddeley practiced his art in London at the Theatre Royal Haymarket and Drury Lane. He was quite the dandy; it was said that he "loved as great variety in his amours as in his clothes." Apparently, he loved the traditions of Twelfth Night as well; when he died the sixty-one-year-old Mr. Baddeley left in his will a then-hefty sum of a hundred pounds to the theater. He had instructed that the funds be invested and for the earnings henceforth into perpetuity to "be applied and expended in the purchase of a twelfth Cake or Cakes and Wine and Punch or both of them which...it is my request the Ladies and Gentlemen performers of Drury Lane Theatre...will do me the favour to accept on twelfth night in every year in the Green Room...." The Baddeley cake ceremony continues to this day at Drury Lane.

My friend Mary Martha Greene, the author of the recently released and much-heralded *The Cheese Biscuit Queen Tells All*, hosts an impressive and incredibly festive Twelfth Night party each year. A native South Carolinian who has a deep-rooted love of food and entertaining, Mary spends her time between homes in Columbia and Beaufort. During her more than forty years in government relations, serving for many years on the staff of former governor Richard Riley, this multi-talented lady often used her cooking skills to make friends (and I imagine influence people) in the legislature. I do much the same in my role at the helm of the Georgia 4-H Foundation. Many weekends during the summer find me putting up hundreds of jars of a variety of jams and preserves—from peach to plum to fig to pear—which are then given to donors throughout the year. I took a gift-wrapped jar to one such contributor the other day—someone who can fly to Paris first class, just for lunch, and not blink an eye at the expense—and exclaimed, "Oh, wonderful! I was hoping you'd brought some of your jelly!"

And besides her political acumen and talents in the kitchen, Mary also has a heart the size of her home state: she teaches baking skills each week to at-risk youth and to young adults experiencing homelessness at the Mental Illness Recovery Center in Columbia. She is just wonderful all the way around.

Here are a few paragraphs from our South Carolina friend that tell of her famed Twelfth Night soirée and some of the incredible food she serves to her sizable cadre of friends:

I began the tradition of hosting a Twelfth Night party in 1993 when renovations to my house precluded my annual Christmas Party. Some friends in Columbia who previously held a Twelfth Night celebration had discontinued the tradition, and I asked if it was ok for me to pick up the torch, which they happily agreed. The party quickly became a tradition of mine. I mail the invitations on December 24th, so that they will arrive shortly after Christmas, just when the holiday "let down" is starting to set in. "The Lord of Misrule desires your presence for Twelfth Night Revelry" reads the invitation, usually decked in out purple, green and gold, since Twelfth Night is also the traditional start of the Mardi Gras season. And I always leave my Christmas decorations up for the party, and layer them over with Mardi Gras décor. A huge arrangement of purple, green and gold materials—feathers, Mardi Gras masks and beads, ribbons and pretty much anything else that catches my eye—rises from the main table and up into the dining room chandelier.

I have a tendency, too, to test the limits of the Irish blessing "May your house always be too small to hold all your friends," and the guests usually number between 150 to 200 people. The party extends from the front door and out to the "party house" in the backyard that was built on the foundation of the circa-1930s garage on the property. In keeping with the season, guests are asked to bring a gift for one of my favorite charities, the Women's Shelter, so it's also a "party with a purpose." Guests pile the gifts under the Christmas tree, and a few days after the party, I deliver them to the ladies at the shelter. It extends the joy of the giving even further into the new year.

Food for the party reflects my roots in the South Carolina Low Country, and includes a variety of small-plate dishes, such as shrimp and grits tarts (a recipe I created especially for the party which was published in *Southern Living* magazine), a smoked salmon cheesecake, crawfish spread, South Carolina mustard-based barbeque, steamed asparagus with Parmesan peppercorn dressing, and an array of finger-food sweets. And of course, I have my Aunt Mimi's beloved cheese biscuits available throughout the house. Keeping items bite-sized and self-contained lets guests pick up

Mary Martha Greene in her kitchen, 2021.

My dear friend, the late Sam Zemurray, of New Orleans
and Savannah, at Tom's 65th birthday party

items and place on a plate, rather than having to hover over the food table.

I used to order King cakes from a local bakery, but when it closed, I started making "cheater's king's and queen's cakes." I buy cream cheese Danish coffee rings from the local grocery store, turn them over, and cut a small slit into the underside of the cake, and insert a small plastic baby. Once the cake is flipped back to the right side, I sprinkle the cakes with purple, green and gold decorating sugar, places them on beautiful cakes stands, and no one has to be any wiser! Gold crowns and purple capes await the lucky finders of the babies who are crowned King and Queen for the evening!

And my final rule for the party—even though it's held in January, I get up the morning of the party and turn the air conditioner down as low as it will go. In the South, if there are going to be that many people in the house, it's going to get hot inside, no matter how cold it is outside.

A sampling of Mary's wonderful recipes follows here after my wassail recipe; to get the "whole shootin' match" of her talents, I encourage you to secure a copy of *The Cheese Biscuit Queen Tells All*. There are hundreds of extraordinary dishes in the compilation, and it is a wonderful read as well with stories and tales of the food we Southerners love.

Now every good party should have a signature drink, and, given the history of Twelfth Night, wassail certainly comes to mind. I've "Southerned" the recipe up a bit, and instead of using hard cider and ale, or wine, I make mine with bourbon. It's excellent to serve to a crowd of merrymakers, and to keep on hand to sip upon while sitting by the fire on a cold winter's night. And, hey, if it's too hot to have a warm drink—which isn't unusual in January in the deep South, allow the wassail to cool, pour it over ice, and add a splash of soda!

"Southern" Wassail

Ingredients
6 cups unfiltered apple juice
2 cups bourbon
2 cinnamon sticks
2 whole nutmegs, cracked

10 allspice berries, cracked

Zest of one large orange, cut into strips (make sure there isn't any pith attached)

Zest of one large lemon, cut into strips (no pith)

½ cup honey or brown sugar

Directions
1. Place all the ingredients, except for the honey or brown sugar, in a heavy-bottomed pot. Bring to a boil, reduce heat, and allow to simmer slowly for about 30 minutes. Stir occasionally.
2. Pour through a strainer back into the pot to remove the spices and zest. Whisk in the honey or brown sugar, stir well to melt, and serve.

Makes 8 (1-cup) servings

This Mary Martha Greene original recipe is truly outstanding, and I am so grateful she has shared it with us. It is an impressive hors d'oeuvre and will have your guests "oohing" and "ahhing" as they gobble these morsels down. All the necessary parts of this dish—cooked shrimp, grits tarts, and tasso gravy—require fixing in advance before heating and serving, which I find appealing because, as mentioned before, it allows the host to spend more time with the guests.

Shrimp & Grits Tarts

Ingredients
36 grits tarts
½ recipe tasso gravy
36 prepared and cooked medium shrimp
Fresh chopped parsley for garnish

Directions
1. Preheat oven to 350 degrees.
2. Place the tarts on baking sheet with sides. Neatly ladle 1 teaspoon of gravy in each tart. Top with a shrimp.
3. Bake for 5 to 10 minutes until hot. Garnish with fresh parsley. Serve warm.

Makes 36 tarts

Components for Shrimp Tarts

Grits Tarts

Ingredients
2 cups chicken broth
1 cup milk
2 tablespoons butter
1 teaspoon salt
½ teaspoon white pepper
1 cup regular or coarse ground grits (not instant!)
⅔ cup Parmesan cheese
Butter flavored cooking spray

Directions
1. Preheat oven to 350 degrees.
2. Bring broth, milk, and butter to a medium boil in a large saucepan. Add salt, white pepper, and grits, whisking to make sure grits do not become lumpy. Reduce heat and let mixture cook until thick and grits are done, according to package directions. When soft and fully cooked, add the cheese and whisk until melted. Remove from heat, set aside to cool for 15 minutes.
3. Spray miniature muffin tins liberally with butter flavored cooking spray. You will need 36 (1¾-inch) wells. Spoon 1 tablespoon of grits mixture into each muffin tin, using a tablespoon or #70 cookie scoop. Spray top of grits mixture with cooking spray. Using the small, rounded end of melon baller, or a spoon, press down center of each tart to make a small indentation.
4. Bake for 20 to 25 minutes. Remove from oven and while tarts are still warm, press down centers again with melon baller. Let tarts cool completely. Remove from pans by running dull knife around edge if necessary.
5. Tarts can be prepared to this point, placed on a lightly-greased baking sheet with sides, and covered in plastic wrap. They will keep 2 to 3 days in refrigerator. Tarts can also be filled with tasso gravy ahead of time and refrigerated. Reheat on pan covered with foil in a 350-degree oven for 10 minutes.
Makes 36 tarts

Tasso Gravy

Ingredients
8 tablespoons (1 stick) butter
½ cup tasso ham, diced (country ham can be used if you can't find tasso)

½ cup all-purpose flour
4 cups chicken broth, heated
2 tablespoons parsley, chopped
2 teaspoons Tony Chachere's Original Creole Seasoning

Directions
1. Melt the butter in a heavy skillet over medium heat. Add ham and cook for 2 minutes.
2. Add flour and stir, making a roux, and let cook until roux turns brown and begins to smell nutty, about 3 to 5 minutes.
3. Add half of chicken broth, stirring with a whisk until all flour is dissolved into broth. Add remaining chicken broth and continue to whisk until mixture starts to thicken.
4. Turn down heat and let simmer for 20 minutes. Add parsley and creole seasoning.

Makes 1 quart

Boiled Shrimp

Ingredients
2 quarts water
½ cup Old Bay Seasoning
36 medium-sized shrimp, peeled and deveined (about 1½ pounds)

Directions
1. In a large pot, bring the water to a boil.
2. Add the Old Bay and shrimp, stir, and cook 2 to 3 minutes, or until the shrimp have turned pink and just curled from end to end. *Do not overcook.*
3. Drain the shrimp in a colander and cool for about 10 minutes.
4. Place in a covered container and refrigerate until ready to use.

Mary has another savory tart recipe that includes a fabulous crawfish spread atop tiny red rice muffins. Not to give away too much of her book, I'm not including all the steps for that magical dish, but I am sharing with you the spread itself, which is excellent served on homemade garlic toast points. For those of you who live inland and not near a bayou, crawfish are easily found online by a variety of vendors and can be shipped to you frozen.

Crawfish Spread

Ingredients

1 tablespoon butter
½ cup onion, diced
2 tablespoons green onions, white and green parts, diced
1 teaspoon garlic, minced
3 tablespoons celery, diced
½ teaspoon Tony Chachere's Original Creole Seasoning
1 teaspoon salt
¼ teaspoon black pepper
8 ounces cream cheese, at room temperature
3 tablespoons red pepper jelly
2 tablespoons, fresh parsley chopped
2 teaspoons soy sauce
1 (12-ounce) package cooked crawfish tails, chopped
Garlic toast points (see index)

Directions

1. Melt butter in a medium frying pan. Cook onions and green onions for about 3 minutes. Add garlic and celery and cook for 2 minutes more. Stir while cooking.
2. Remove from stove and add creole seasoning, salt, and pepper.
3. Place cream cheese in bowl of electric mixer. Pour warm onion mixture over cream cheese and allow it to soften. Add pepper jelly, parsley, and soy sauce; mix at low speed until blended.
4. Fold in crawfish by hand. Cover bowl with plastic wrap and place in refrigerator. Chill for 4 to 6 hours or overnight
5. To serve, place the spread in a bowl and serve with the toast points.

Serves 12 to 16

Another item people look forward to each year is Mary's smoked salmon cheesecake, which combines all the flavors we enjoy and associate with smoked salmon all into one bite. The dish also makes a great presentation on a raised glass or silver cake stand.

Smoked Salmon Cheesecake

Ingredients
15 butter-flavored crackers (Ritz or Townhouse), plus more to serve
1½ cups Parmesan cheese, grated and divided
3 tablespoons butter
1¼ cup onion, chopped
4 (8-ounce) packages cream cheese, at room temperature
1 cup sour cream
4 large eggs
8 ounces smoked salmon, chopped, reserving a few strips for top of cake
1 tablespoon dried parsley, or 2 tablespoons minced fresh parsley
¾ teaspoon dried dill or 2 teaspoons minced fresh dill
Peel of 1 lemon, grated
1 tablespoon lemon juice
½ teaspoon salt
¼ teaspoon black pepper
Sprigs of fresh dill, sliced lemons, strips of smoked salmon for garnish

Directions
1. Preheat oven to 350 degrees. Cover bottom of a 9-inch springform pan, or six 4-inch individual pans, with aluminum foil; butter, or spray with cooking spray, the bottom and sides.
2. Crush crackers in food processor and add ½ cup of Parmesan cheese. Transfer to prepared pan(s) and press lightly with back of a spoon to form crust.
3. In a small skillet, melt the butter over medium heat, add the chopped onions. Cook for 5 minutes, or until soft, stirring. Set aside.
4. With a mixer, beat cream cheese and sour cream together until smooth; add eggs and blend until smooth. Add sautéed onions, salmon, parsley, dill, lemon peel, lemon juice, salt and pepper and stir to mix well.
5. Pour mixture into pan or divide evenly among smaller pans. Use reserved strips of salmon to garnish top of cheesecake and add more fresh dill if desired.
6. Wrap cheesecake pan in 2 layers of aluminum foil, 1 turned at a 45-degree angle to create an 8-point star. Roll down sides of foil to create a "collar" around pan.
7. Place pan in larger roasting pan with at least 2-inch-deep sides, fill larger pan with water halfway up sides of cheesecake pan.
8. Bake 1 hour (50 minutes for individual pans). Turn oven off. Allow to sit in oven 1 hour. Remove from oven and cool completely on rack, then refrigerate overnight. Run a knife along edge and remove side from pan. Garnish

with lemon, additional strips of smoked salmon, and fresh dill. Serve at
room temperature with crackers.
Makes 1 (9-inch) cheesecake, serving 20 to 25

As I write about these recipes—with all of their Mardi Gras influence—I
start to think about trips to New Orleans and friends I knew from that
magnificent city. One such splendid fellow was Samuel (Sam) Zemurray
III; he was one of the kindest, most unassuming gentlemen you would
ever meet. Sam was a member of St. Paul's Episcopal as was I, and Tom
had been friends with him for years when we met in the early 1990s. His
grandfather, Samuel Sr., was an example of the quintessential American
success story. A poor Russian Jew who came to the United States in 1891,
he worked at odd jobs in the food industry, selling fruit from a pushcart
in Mobile, Alabama. He saved more than $150,000 by the time he was
twenty-one and founded his own fruit company, Cuyamel Fruits, special-
izing in what was considered at the time an exotic, the banana—earning
him the nickname "Sam the Banana Man." He later became president of
United Fruit Company, now known as Chiquita Banana. Samuel Jr., my
friend's father, was a World War II pilot who was killed in action. Sam
and his mother, along with his brother and sister, moved in with his
grandparents at their Beaux Arts mansion at 2 Audubon Place in New
Orleans; the house was left to Tulane University by Sam Sr. and is now
the residence of the president of Tulane University.

Sam III moved to Savannah to work in the shipping industry in the
1970s and later purchased the more than three-hundred-acre Honeyridge
Plantation in Effingham County, just northwest of Savannah. There he
raised Polled Herefords and was widely known for pioneering in vitro fer-
tilization in calving. Tom decorated the Georgian-style, three story brick
home that sat on the ridge of the property for Sam and wife, Patricia. In
the wood-paneled library of the house was the life-sized portrait of Sam at
age twelve, with his model sailboat on Olmsted Lake in Audubon Park.
As an animal lover, I loved visiting; as soon as you pulled into the long,
winding drive, you'd be met by a pack of various and sundry dogs. Some
were missing an eye, maybe one was three-legged, another just a mixture
of who knows how many breeds. Sam, like my friend Elizabeth Oxnard
(I write about her in the wild game chapter), had a soft, soft heart when it

came to animals. Folks in those parts knew that if they dropped off an unwanted animal, Sam would take them in. His barn was full of cats as well, and you'd see them napping on hay bales or sitting atop the pasture fence posts.

We lost Sam in 2018. His friends miss him greatly. I would love fixing a pot of gumbo when he and Pat would come over for supper; he said it always reminded him of home. So, in keeping with the theme of Twelfth Night, Mardi Gras, and New Orleans, and in honor of Sam, here is my gumbo recipe.

This gumbo does not have a roux, as many of these stews do, but since my version is chocked full of shrimp, smoked sausage, and chicken, it doesn't need any additional thickness. The dish is better made a day in advance and reheated, allowing the flavors to marry. I like to serve the gumbo with hush puppies or buttered biscuits (see index for both recipes) as well as my Mardi Gras salad that follows here.

Chicken, Sausage & Shrimp Gumbo Ya-Ya

Ingredients
1 pound medium wild-caught USA shrimp, peeled and deveined, shells reserved

2 quarts low-sodium chicken stock

2 tablespoons olive oil

½ pound andouille sausage, sliced into ½-inch rounds

5 teaspoons creole seasoning (recipe follows), divided

½ pound boneless, skinless chicken thighs

1 scant cup onion, diced

½ cup celery, diced

¼ cup green bell pepper, diced

¼ cup red bell pepper, diced

¼ teaspoon kosher salt

¼ teaspoon black pepper

1 tablespoon minced garlic

1 (14.5-ounce) can no-salt-added diced tomatoes

1 teaspoon Worcestershire sauce

½ teaspoon Texas Pete or other hot sauce

4 bay leaves

1 tablespoon packed fresh basil, minced

2 teaspoons fresh thyme, minced

2 teaspoons fresh oregano, minced
1½ cups sliced fresh okra, cut into ¼-inch rounds
2 teaspoons filé powder
3 cups cooked white rice
½ cup fresh parsley, chopped

Directions
1. Place reserved shrimp shells and chicken stock in a pot; bring to a boil, reduce heat, stir, and allow to simmer for 15 minutes. Set aside.
2. While the stock simmers, place a Dutch oven over medium-high heat; add the olive oil. When the oil is fragrant and just beginning to smoke, add the sliced sausage rounds and brown, cooking for 3 to 4 minutes. Remove the slices and set aside. Drain off all but 2 tablespoons of the accumulated fat.
3. Sprinkle 2 teaspoons of the creole spice onto the chicken thighs.
4. Continuing on medium-high heat, brown the chicken in the Dutch oven, turning occasionally, until done, about 10 minutes. Set the chicken aside with the sausage.
5. To the Dutch oven add the onion, celery, and peppers, along with the salt and pepper. Continue cooking, stirring constantly, for 2 minutes.
6. Add the garlic, stir, and cook another 4 to 5 minutes until the vegetables are soft and the onions are opaque.
7. Strain the stock into the Dutch oven, pushing down on the shells to get the juices.
8. Add the tomatoes, Worcestershire, hot sauce, bay leaves, fresh basil, thyme, and oregano and 2 teaspoons creole spice. Bring to a boil, and reduce heat to medium-low, stirring.
9. Cut the chicken into bite-sized pieces, and add it, along with the cooked sausage, to the pot. Stir to mix.
10. Add the okra; continue cooking for 15 minutes, stirring occasionally. *Note: At this point, the gumbo can be removed from the heat, and set aside, or refrigerated until ready to serve.*
11. Sprinkle the last teaspoon of creole seasoning on the shrimp; toss to coat. With the gumbo on a steady simmer, add your shrimp, and stir to mix; cook for 3 minutes until the shrimp are just done.
12. Sprinkle filé powder over stew, stirring, and allow to cook 2 to 3 more minutes; the gumbo will thicken slightly.
13. To serve, pour into a bowl, top with ½ cup rice and sprinkle with chopped parsley.
Serves 6

I prefer to make my own creole (or Cajun) seasoning mix so I can control the sodium content. Commercial brands, even from gourmet sources, salt is usually the first ingredient. The items in this creation should be found in most cooks' kitchens.

Creole Seasoning

Ingredients
2 tablespoons sweet paprika
2 tablespoons garlic powder
1 tablespoon kosher salt
1 tablespoon onion powder
1 tablespoon dried oregano
1 tablespoon dried thyme
1½ teaspoons black pepper
1 teaspoon cayenne pepper

Directions
1. Combine all ingredients and keep in an airtight container.
Makes about ½ cup

To go along with the gumbo, how about a festively colored and flavor-filled salad? One of green, gold, and purple? Yes? OK, well, here you go!

Mardi Gras Salad

Ingredients
6 cups green leaf lettuce, sliced into strips (about one small head)
4 cups radicchio, sliced into strips (about 2 heads)
2 cups carrots, peeled and shaved into long strips
¾ cup purple onion, cut into very thin rings
Red wine vinaigrette (recipe follows)

Directions
1. On salad plates, decoratively arrange the lettuce, radicchio, carrots, and onions.
2. Drizzle with the vinaigrette. Serve immediately.
Serves 6 to 8

Red Wine Vinaigrette

Ingredients
3 tablespoons red wine vinegar
1 teaspoon fresh thyme, minced
½ teaspoon garlic, minced
½ teaspoon Dijon mustard
⅛ teaspoon black pepper
⅛ teaspoon sugar
⅛ teaspoon kosher salt
½ cup olive oil

Directions
1. In a small bowl, whisk together all ingredients except the olive oil. When incorporated, slowly whisk in the oil.
2. Refrigerate and store in an airtight container.
Makes ½+ cup

For dessert, most supermarkets, including Publix, offer king cakes during Mardi Gras. My buddy, fellow gourmand Stacy Jennings, swears by Gambino's bakery in New Orleans, which will ship these incredible confections right to your doorstep. Originally from Jesup, Georgia, and late of Savannah, Stacy is a Tulane grad and loves, loves, loves N'awlins.

Or, if you can't find a king cake at the store and are in too much of a rush to wait on a delivery, do what Mary Martha does and create your own from a round supermarket cream cheese breakfast Danish!

Chapter 8

Holiday Tea in Savannah

Before I met Tom, he had a long-standing tradition of having friends by on Christmas Eve for tea, champagne, sherry, and an assortment of wonderful holiday dishes. We have continued the party on through the years, although not always on Christmas Eve. The appearance of children in my family—great nieces and nephews and cousins—sometimes calls us away for the holiday, but the tea still remains a special celebration for us.

Tom taught me an interesting lesson about having a real English tea, and how Americans oftentimes confuse the tradition and name. On many occasions, you see our hotels and resorts promoting "high tea," which is a misnomer. Rarely do you find the proper wording, "afternoon tea," which denotes the tea service people really have in mind, one filled with scones, canapés, petit fours, and other elegant items. High tea was a practice of the working class and was in itself a whole meal.

The origin of afternoon tea is credited to the Duchess of Bedford, a contemporary and friend of Queen Victoria's. The timing for the evening meal as the nineteenth century progressed came later and later in the day, and the duchess felt the need for some refreshment between lunch and dinner. Finding that sandwiches and tea made for an appetizing interlude, she began inviting friends to join her. Soon the practice was an everyday affair among the titled nobility and aristocracy. Guests would receive this repast in sitting and withdrawing rooms, with the delicacies served on low tables, such as today's coffee table. Hence the other name for this meal, "low tea."

High tea, from what I understand, received its designation because it was eaten at the dinner table, which had high sitting chairs, and so the name. This meal also included much heartier fare than that served at afternoon tea, including shepherd's pie, fish, vegetables, and other substantial dishes. Some in England and the British Isles also refer to this repast as "meat tea."

The tea Tom started—and we've continued—is an afternoon tea, and it's one of the most popular gatherings we host. The party was written about in a past issue of *Savuer* magazine.

Here in the States, most people think of tea as a ladies' affair, but our celebration finds a room filled with husbands, sons, and boyfriends as well as the fairer sex. I do bend the rules of tea etiquette somewhat for the fellows, though, making sure that they can easily find our decanters of bourbon and single malt scotch if needing something stronger in their cups.

The mood for this party is always festive; the house is decorated in all its holiday finery, and guests are all in the joyous mood of the season. The men are resplendent in their blazers and monogrammed buttons, and the ladies are an understatement of casual elegance. Occasionally we even have some of our male guests of Scottish heritage come dressed in their kilts.

And if the weather dips below fifty degrees, more than half of our female guests show up in their fur coats. Since there aren't many cold days in Savannah, these prizes don't get to be showcased too often, so our winter tea provides an excellent excuse to don the minks.

I mention the mink coats to give a little background on a funny incident that happened at one of our parties many years ago.

One of our guests called and asked if she could bring her brother-in-law, Ryan Gainey, who was visiting Savannah for the holidays, to the tea. We said yes and thought he would be an interesting addition to the guest list, as he was a nationally known landscape and lifestyle artist with many books to his credit. We knew he'd be a big hit, particularly with the garden club set.

Christmas Eve was so chilly that year it was downright cold, and Tom and I stood at the door greeting guests and repeating over and over "May I take your fur, please?" The finery filled up the closet in the entrance way to our townhouse, and there was enough mink draped over the stair rails to upholster a couch, settee, and several throw-pillows.

Please join us for our traditional

CHRISTMAS TEA

Sunday, December 22nd
three o'clock
3402 Abercorn Street

Thomas Eugene White   Johnathon Scott Barrett

Rsvp 233-0626

An invitation to one of our Christmas tea parties

When we opened the front door to our friend and Mr. Gainey, we both did a double take. We'd never met this gentleman before and just did not expect, after watching our house fill with dozens of conservatively dressed men who were patrons of Ben Silver and H. Stockton, to see a fellow in a large, wide-brimmed felt hat adorned with vibrantly toned stitching, fringe, and silk balls. His was also wearing a waist-length shawl the color of a rich, purple plum.

Tom, who is *never* at a loss for words, paused for a moment taking all this in, and finally said, "So very nice to meet you, please come in. May I take your fur? I mean your coat—no, sorry! I meant to ask, 'May I take your shawl?'" He said "shawl" as if the word itself was a question.

The little incident added a chuckle for the day and one we recall often. Needless to say, he was a popular guest at the party, and people were thrilled to have him, hat, shawl, and all. Sadly, Mr. Ryan died in 2016.

A typical menu for our tea would be some of my Southern scones, an assortment of finger sandwiches, a roasted chicken terrine with cranberry jelly, my mom's fruitcake cookies, Stilton cheese wafers, and a centerpiece of a bûche de noël I would purchase from Gottlieb's Bakery (operated since 1884!). I'd also get my petit fours and curd tarts from the bakery as well.

I read through a number of recipes for scones and came up with the following recipe. It is "Southern" due to the White Lily flour and bourbon-soaked raisins. Serve these with clotted cream and orange marmalade. If you can't find clotted cream, I have a cheater's recipe for it: beat 4 ounces of room temperature cream cheese until very soft, then beat in another 4 ounces of heavy whipping cream. Chill and serve.

Southern Scones

Ingredients
¾ cup white raisins
¼ cup bourbon
2 cups White Lily self-rising flour, sifted
1 tablespoon sugar
2 tablespoons Crisco shortening
2 tablespoons butter, cut into small pieces
1 cup heavy cream

1 egg, separated
Marmalade and clotted cream

Directions
1. Place the raisins and bourbon in a small saucepan; bring to a boil. Stir, remove from heat, and set aside.
2. Preheat oven to 400 degrees.
3. In large bowl, add the flour, sugar, shortening and butter; mix together with a pastry cutter (I use my fingers instead) until the consistency of small grains.
4. Drizzle in the heavy cream and egg yolk, which needs to be lightly beaten. Fold together with a spatula until just incorporated. Drain the raisins (save the liquid to sip in your teacup later) and fold the raisins into the dough.
5. With a spatula, turn the dough onto a floured surface. Knead together a few times, careful not to overwork the bread (lest it turn out tough) and fold over onto itself 3 or 4 times as well.
6. With a floured rolling pin, roll the dough to 1 inch thick. Cut out the dough into small rounds, using a 2-inch cutter or a champagne flute. Place them on a nonstick cooking sheet.
7. Whisk the egg white with 2 teaspoons of water; brush lightly on top of each scone.
8. Place in the oven and reduce heat to 350. Bake for 12 minutes or so until the tops are starting to brown slightly. Remove from heat and place them on a wire rack to cool. May be reheated in a warm oven. Serve with a marmalade of choice and clotted cream.
Makes 12 small scones

I make the canapés and sandwiches into bite-sized rounds so that they are easily handled. I use Pepperidge Farm Very Thin Sliced bread, alternating between wheat and white. I do both cucumber and watercress dressed with softened butter and white pepper. Egg salad is also served, which is made simply with boiled eggs, mayonnaise, a tiny bit of mustard, and black pepper. Bite-sized tomato sandwiches are also popular in Savannah, and I tell of that process elsewhere in the book (see index). You can also find a good deviled ham at Honey Baked Ham, and those little savories are excellent and have a taste of the holidays.

To give a bit more *oomph* to the buffet, I came up with the following recipe. Some folks were leaving from our party right for Mass, and supper for them would not be for several hours. This terrine is a good choice for the fellows in the crowd, too, giving them something a little more sub-stantial to eat without introducing a heavy plate to the buffet. They some-times need more food, particularly if they have found the Scotch decant-ers. You'll find that the roasted chicken and cranberry pair well together; it is one of my most popular holiday party dishes.

Roasted Chicken Terrine

Ingredients
1 whole rotisserie chicken, skin removed, and meat ground finely in a food processor
½ cup celery, minced
½ cup fresh chives, minced (if you can't find fresh chives, use the green parts of green onion)
3 hard-boiled eggs, minced
¾ cup+ mayonnaise
2 tablespoons Dijon mustard
1 tablespoon fresh tarragon, minced (or 1 teaspoon dried)
Several grinds of fresh black pepper
Cranberry sauce (see index)
Wheat or other hearty crackers

Directions
1. Mix all the ingredients well together except for the cranberry sauce and crackers; press tightly into in a lightly greased Bundt pan.
2. Cover and refrigerate overnight.
3. Unmold and place the cranberry sauce in the middle of the terrine. Serve with crackers.

Serves 16 to 20

While many people do not like fruitcake itself, they tend to enjoy candied fruits and nuts served instead as a cookie. The following recipe is one that my mother used. For decades she made these at Christmas and gave away as gifts in decorative tins; they are a real taste of the holidays.

Mama's Fruitcake Cookies

Ingredients
1⅓ cup butter, at room temperature
1⅓ cup dark brown sugar
4 eggs

1½ teaspoons baking soda
1½ teaspoons cinnamon
1 teaspoon nutmeg
½ teaspoon allspice
Pinch of salt
¾ cup whole milk
1½ teaspoon vanilla extract
4 cups plain flour
1 cup candied cherries, chopped
1 cup candied pineapple, chopped
1 cup dates, chopped
1 cup candied orange slices or peel, chopped
1 cup dark raisins
1 cup white raisins
6 cups chopped pecans or walnuts

Directions
1. Preheat oven to 325 degrees.
2. In a mixer, cream butter and sugar until very smooth.
3. Add eggs one at a time, mixing constantly over medium speed.
4. Add soda, cinnamon, nutmeg, allspice, salt, milk, vanilla, and flour. With a sturdy spoon or spatula, mix until fully incorporated—the batter is thick and sticky.
5. Add fruit and nuts; stir until fully mixed together. With this step, you may need to use your hands.
6. On a lightly greased cookie, sheet, place dough by the tablespoonful, leaving an inch between cookies.
7. Bake for about 12 minutes, or until just beginning to brown.
8. Place the cookies on a wire rack and allow to cool completely. Store in an airtight container. The cookies also freeze well to serve later.
Makes about 4 dozen cookies

I wanted another savory item to serve at tea and balance the sweets; I came up with this recipe, which I call Stilton wafers. This robust and flavorful shortbread is my English variation on the Southern cheese straw.

Stilton Wafers

Ingredients
2 cups English Blue Stilton Cheese, rind removed, at room temperature

8 ounces English or Irish Butter, such as Kerrygold, softened at room temperature

½ teaspoon Texas Pete hot sauce

3 scant cups unbleached all-purpose flour

Directions

1. In a mixer, cream the cheese, butter, and hot sauce until smooth and thoroughly incorporated.
2. Add the flour 1 cup at a time, mixing as you add. You will need to periodically stop the mixer and scrape down on the sides of the bowl.
3. After all the flour is added, the mixture will be coarse and crumbly. With your hands, press and shape it into a large oval log. Wrap the cylinder in cling wrap and refrigerate until chilled, about half an hour.
4. Remove log from refrigerator. Cut into 4 equal parts.
5. Preheat oven to 375 degrees.
6. Roll one part on a smooth surface until ¼-inch thick. Cut wafers out with a 2-inch cookie cutter (or smaller if you'd prefer) and place on a lightly greased cookie sheet. Roll the other parts out until finished.
7. Bake for 12 to 15 minutes, until the sides turn a rich golden color.
8. Remove from wafers from the pans with a spatula and cool on a wire rack. Let the wafers cool completely before storing in an airtight container.

Makes 4 dozen 2-inch wafers

Chapter 9

Amazing Grace on Mobile Bay

There are many people you meet in life with a certain style that makes them exquisitely unique. However, it isn't often you encounter someone so sure of who they are, and so distinctive, that they are an especial tour de force. Beverly Smith is such a wonder, and to be drawn into her circle of light, laughter, and energy is a blessing. Affectionately called "Jingles" by her grandchildren due to her signature bangle bracelets and statement-making earrings—and I would guess as well because of her sparkling eyes that seem to sing when they light upon you—Beverly embraces life with joy, particularly through her love of friends, and food. When she combines those two loves together it is like watching a culinary fairy godmother at work. She can, absolutely, turn a pumpkin into a golden carriage.

I asked Jingles if she had any advice for new hosts and hostesses. Her sage answer: "Do not get stressed and ENJOY your party!" She matter-of-factly tells me that she "stopped entertaining to impress years ago!" and now simply wants to make her guests feel at home and be able to bond in friendship. "People just want to get together and ENJOY one another!"

Complementing this more-than-accomplished hostess is her husband, Prentiss. They both grew up in rural Lincoln County, Mississippi, in the small, unincorporated hamlets of Red Lick and Caseyville, respectively, located about fifty miles southwest of the state capital of Jackson. Beverly happily tells me that Prentiss was the only boy she ever dated. They married after college graduation; Jingles majored in art and home economics. And Prentiss, a retired radiologist, is as charming as Beverly vivacious; with his distinguished looks and wonderfully soft Southern accent, Hallmark could easily cast him in the role of the town's local favorite physician or learned barrister.

When speaking to Beverly about her attitudes on food and entertaining, I asked her what role Prentiss played in the plans and execution of one of their famous gatherings. She promptly replied "He PAYS for the party without ever complaining!! Plus, he always has a GREAT bar and WONDERFUL music. "And," she went on with a laugh, "he makes me look good!"

This delightful couple have a magnificent home perched on the historic wharf in Fairhope, Alabama, overlooking Mobile Bay. Walking into their abode—on the bay you enter on the "street side" of the house—you find high ceilings and open spaces designed for comfort and entertaining. Passing through the large expanse that includes a dining table that can seat twelve, along with some fine examples of Southern paintings and sculpture, you come to a large, enclosed piazza with sweeping, almost 180-degree views of Mobile Bay. Doors from the piazza open out into the front yard facing the water. A walkway leads to a dock with an entrance arch of large, intertwined driftwood logs; it is structurally stunning. The end of the dock is punctuated with a space designed specifically for parties: the open-air pavilion has exposed crossed timbers, ceiling fans, and modern amenities; it is rustically crowned with a gabled, tin roof. The area can easily accommodate fifty guests for one of the Smiths' famous sunset cocktail parties, where Judy Collins's rendition of "Amazing Grace" is played over the custom-made sound system—as old Sol slowly slips down through the bay's horizon. This touching tradition is one Jingles and Prentiss started years ago as a way to say, "thank you, Lord, for many, many blessings."

Now before I get to some of Jingles's wonderful recipes, let me tell you how we met. That is a story in itself—one in which I can find it easy to laugh at myself.

While Savannah is a city, it is still a small town, and even in a large historic neighborhood like ours, Ardsley Park, everyone knows everyone else. Or so I thought. Several years ago, I was at the home of my friends Barbara and Carter (you read about them in the Easter chapter) for a small gathering. Standing in the kitchen with Barbara, sipping my bourbon, I noticed an invitation pinned to the Hubbards' refrigerator. As one who is constantly seeking knowledge and information, I read it from top to bottom. The invitation was for the next night: "Join the Wallaces for libations and hors d'oeuvres," it read. The address was on the next block over,

Beverly "Jingles" Smith and Prentiss Smith

Washington Avenue. I was a bit taken aback. No such invitation was on *my* refrigerator.

"Barbara, hon, when did you get this invitation to the Wallaces'?" I asked, hoping that it was a last-minute delivery. "Oh, I can't remember. Maybe a couple of weeks ago," she answered, looking at me. "Why do you ask?"

"Well, I was just wondering. Apparently, Tom and I weren't included. I certainly don't understand that."

Barbara looked at me a bit innocently and said, "I didn't realize that you knew the Wallaces."

I rolled my eyes, just barely. "Barbara. Honey. You *know* that I know Susan and Dick! I mean, you were at my fiftieth birthday party with them last year. Y'all sat at the same table. You all have been out our house at the same time for all sorts of gatherings! Of course, I *know* the Wallaces. I just can't understand why we weren't asked." I was disappointed and wondering to myself what in the world had I done—or more likely what *Tom* had said, as he often doesn't have a filter—to irritate them.

Barbara laughed a little and made an exit. "Let me go check on my guests. See you in a bit."

Sulking, I thought to myself, "Go on, run off and leave me. You got invited, so what do you care?"

A few minutes later, at the bar to top off my glass, Barbara came walking toward me with a man and woman in tow. She was grinning like the Cheshire cat. "Johnathon, I want you to meet our new neighbors. They bought Mrs. McIntosh's house on Washington Avenue." A small light sparked somewhere in my little brain reminding me that Mrs. McIntosh lived next door to Susan and Dick Wallace. "I wonder if they were invited to the Wallaces' party?" I asked myself.

Ever the gentlemen, even in the midst of social disappointment, I extended my hand. "Welcome to Savannah and Ardsley Park. I'm Johnathon Barrett, and I live just two doors up at 102 East 45th."

The husband reached out for the shake and gave a warm greeting back. "Pleased to meet you. I'm Bill." The wife then gave me a well-manicured hand and smiled, looking at me with a bit of a gleam in her eye.

"Well, hello there. I have heard a lot about you already tonight. I'm Dale." She paused for a moment. "Dale Wallace."

Now, while I'm not always the brightest bulb in the chandelier and had a couple of Woodford Reserves under my belt, it didn't take but a skinny second to realize I had the *wrong* Wallaces in mind—same last name, almost the same exact street address.

Giving Barbara what I hoped she knew was an "I'll get you for this" look, Dale went on ever so smoothly say, "And I understand that I forgot to invite you to our party tomorrow night."

With that Barbara, Bill, and Dale all burst out laughing. I had taken a sip of my drink right at that moment, and almost spewed the contents. I was choking and laughing at the same time. The little minx Miss Barbara had gone and set me up for this exchange—and I guess I totally deserved it.

When Dick and Susan heard the tale, they got a good laugh, too. I now refer to them as "the original Wallaces" and Bill and Dale the "new Wallaces" when I'm talking about one or the other couple.

Anyway, the "new Wallaces" knew the Smiths from their home state of Mississippi; Bill and Prentiss went to college together. As we became friends (their party the next night was lovely, by the way!) and my first book was published, Dale told me about Beverly and her fame as a hostess. Dale said she was someone that "you absolutely *have* to meet." I did—and the rest is history.

On my first visit to see the Smiths, they rolled out the proverbial red carpet for me upon arrival, which included drinks in their wonderful home and a stroll through the grounds, a lovely lunch at the Grand Hotel, and a personal tour of one of the most incredible towns in the USA: Fairhope. As Jingles and Prentiss are thankful for many blessings, so am I. And those two wonderful folks are now two of mine.

Here are some of Jingles's favorite casual, summer-supper recipes that can be served on a dock, in the kitchen, or beachside. Hers is a long list ranging from cool adult libations to a sweet but admittedly "sad" pound cake. All of Jingles's selections are full of great flavors, are easy to prepare, and include tastes that marry so well. Put these together for your next hot-weather social and let the magic of Jingles spread amongst your gathering.

Cucumber Gin Martini

Ingredients
6 very thin slices of peeled and seeded cucumber
2 sprigs of mint
½ cup gin
2 tablespoons agave juice
1 tablespoon freshly squeezed lime juice
2 ribbons of cucumber peel, for garnish

Directions
1. In a bowl, muddle together the cucumber slices and mint; place the mixture in a martini shaker. Add the gin, agave juice, fresh lime, and a cup of ice to the shaker.
2. Shake vigorously and strain into chilled martini glasses.
Makes 2

Grapefruit and Tequila Martini

Ingredients
6 ounces tequila
1 cup ruby red grapefruit juice
Splash of With Co Bouquet mixer (if not available, use agave juice instead)
2 slices of lime, each speared with a sprig of rosemary, for garnish

Directions
1. Add a cup of ice, tequila, juice, and mixer to a martini shaker and shake vigorously.
2. Pour into 2 chilled martini glasses and garnish.
Makes 2

Sparkling Flowering Hibiscus Cocktail

Wild hibiscus flowers in syrup can be purchased at specialty markets or online. Each preserved hibiscus blooms before your eyes when placed in the bubbling cocktail!

Ingredients
1 wild hibiscus flower (jarred)
½ ounce St. Germain liqueur

4 ounces Champagne or prosecco

Directions
1. Gently place a wild hibiscus flower in the bottom of a champagne flute.
2. Pour in the St. Germain liqueur, then the bubbly, and serve immediately.
Makes 1

The following recipe is a party favorite on the dock at Beverly and Prentiss's and so easy to prepare. The sauce is Beverly's daddy's creation and can be used on seafood, fish, French fries—you name it!

For the recipe, get the fried chicken fingers from your favorite restaurant; you will have to gauge the number you need by how big the fingers are and how many Bird Dogs you want to serve. For the hot dog buns, I would suggest using the smaller varieties that are now available. However, regular bun-length will work as well.

Bird Dogs

Ingredients
Fried chicken fingers
Hot dog buns
WANT-MORE! Sauce (recipe follows)
Mack's by the Tracks coleslaw (recipe follows)

Directions
1. Add the number of fingers needed to fill each bun and top with the WANT-MORE! Sauce using an old-school style ketchup/mustard squeeze bottle.
2. Serve these with Mack's by the Tracks coleslaw.

WANT-MORE! Sauce

Ingredients
½ cup cooking oil
1 cup real mayonnaise
½ cup ketchup
Dash (or 2) garlic powder
1 teaspoon yellow mustard
1 teaspoon Worcestershire sauce
1 teaspoon black pepper
Dash hot sauce

Dash paprika

Directions
1. Mix all ingredients together, cover tightly, and refrigerate until ready to use.
Makes 2 cups (enough for 16 or so Bird Dogs)

This slaw was inspired by the dish made in a Jackson, Mississippi, bar called Mack's by the Tracks.

Mack's by the Tracks Coleslaw

Ingredients
2 bags angel-hair shredded cabbage
½ cup (or more) mayonnaise
1 medium yellow onion, chopped
Salt, pepper, and sugar to taste

Directions
1. In a large bowl, combine all ingredients—add more mayonnaise if you like a creamy slaw.
2. Cover tightly and chill 4 to 6 hours before serving.
Serves 8 to 12

Gulf shrimp are delicious cooked in so many ways, and this is a classic Mobile Bay recipe that Jingles likes to use. Serve these buttery shrimp with hot, crusty bread and cocktail sauce—plus with lots of napkins 'cause it is messy!

Sweet Bay Shrimp

Ingredients
5 pounds headed shrimp, unpeeled
3 tablespoons kosher or sea salt
3 tablespoons ground black pepper
3 tablespoons dried oregano
2 pounds butter
2 cups freshly squeezed lemon juice (about 8 medium lemons; reserve the lemon halves)
1 ounce garlic juice, or 4 large cloves, minced
1 teaspoon hot sauce

5 to 10 dried bay leaves
2 loaves crusty bread
Ginned-up Cocktail Sauce (see index)

Directions
1. Preheat oven to 350 degrees.
2. In a large bowl, toss the shrimp with the salt, black pepper, and oregano; coat well.
3. Place the spiced shrimp in a large (4-quart or bigger) baking dish.
4. Melt the butter in a saucepan over medium heat. Add in the lemon juice, garlic juice, and hot sauce.
5. Nestle the bay leaves and lemon halves with the shrimp.
6. Pour the butter sauce over the shrimp and coat evenly.
7. Cover and bake 40 to 50 minutes, stirring every 10 minutes. Serve immediately with warmed crusty bread and Ginned-Up Cocktail Sauce.

Serves 6 to 8 for a main course, 20 or more for a cocktail party appetizer

The following salad pairs excellently with the spicy sweet bay shrimp.

Arugula Salad with Lemon Dressing

Ingredients
2 (5-ounce) containers of baby arugula
kosher or sea salt to taste
2 Meyer lemons, finely zested and juiced (keep the zest and juice separate)
4 tablespoons olive oil
½ cup freshly shaved Parmesan cheese

Directions
1. Place arugula in a large salad bowl and toss with a bit of salt and the lemon zest; drizzle the lemon juice over the greens, and then follow with the olive oil.
2. Add the Parmesan cheese, toss, and serve immediately.

Serves 8

This fabulous jam is excellent spread over cream cheese and served on toast points or your favorite cracker.

Beverly's Tomato Jam

Ingredients
2½ pounds ripe tomatoes (about 3½ cups), peeled, seeded, and diced
¼ cup fresh lemon juice
¼ cup basil, chopped and loosely packed
3 cups sugar, divided
1 (1¾-ounce) package powdered fruit pectin for lower sugar recipes

Directions
1. Place the prepared tomatoes into an 8-quart stock pot and bring to a boil; stir.
2. Reduce heat to low and simmer, covered, for 10 minutes. Stir often.
3. Add lemon juice and basil, stir.
4. In a small bowl, mix ¼ cup of sugar and the fruit pectin; stir the mixture into the tomatoes.
5. Turn the heat to high, and bring to a full rolling boil, stirring often.
6. Stir in the remaining sugar. Return to a full rolling boil; boil for 1 minute, stirring constantly.
7. Remove from heat and quickly skim off any foam with a spoon. Discard foam.
8. Ladle hot jam into hot sterilized half-pint jars, leaving ¼ inch of space at the top of jar. Wipe the rim of the jars clean and add lids, screwing them on tightly (use a towel as the jars will be hot).
9. Process jars in boiling water for 5 minutes. Start the timer when water comes back to a boil.
10. Remove jars and cool. (Beverly says she loves to hear the popping sound as the jars seal!)
Makes 5 half-pint jars

This next hors d'oeuvre is another example of how Beverly serves up food with incredible taste but at the same time incredible ease. It is prepared in advance and garnished just before serving.

Mediterranean Hummus

Ingredients
2 large containers hummus (regular flavored)
3 tablespoons olive oil, divided
1 pint grape tomatoes, sliced lengthwise into quarters
½ (2.25-ounce) can pitted black olives
4 ounces feta cheese crumbles
¼ cup fresh parsley, chopped
Pita chips

Directions
1. Spread hummus evenly across the bottom of a serving dish with at least 1-inch-deep sides.
2. On 1 diagonal half of the hummus, use the back of a spoon to create swirls. Drizzle this side with a generous amount of olive oil to taste.
3. Top the plain side of the hummus with tomatoes, olives and feta crumbles. Drizzle this half with a little more olive oil and then sprinkle with fresh chopped parsley.
4. Cover and chill for 2 to 3 hours. Serve with pita chips.
Serves 16 to 20

Beverly told me about these extremely easy to make but amazing-tasting pickles before my visit to Fairhope. Upon arrival, she brought out a big jar from her pantry and gave me a few slices to sample. They were tremendous—and so good served on a Ritz cracker with a sliver of sharp cheddar cheese. The pickles are also great in chicken or tuna salad, or on a charcuterie platter with pâté, smoked meats, and cheeses. These spiced and sweet slices of green are the best B&B pickles ever!

Bread & Butter Pickles

Ingredients
1 gallon whole dill pickles
1 fist of garlic (about 8 cloves), thinly sliced
3 tablespoons whole allspice berries
11 cups sugar

Directions
1. Drain pickles and slice into ½-inch rounds. (Keep the juice if you like pickle juice!)
2. Make 4 layers in the jar starting with the pickles, followed by garlic, all-spice, and sugar. End with sugar as the final layer. The sugar will draw the pickle juice from the pickles and make a simple syrup.
3. Cover tightly and store in a cool, dark spot in your pantry. Gently shake well several times as they "cure" for one week, allowing all the sugar to melt.

Makes 1 gallon

Beverly, who writes in capital letters and speaks with exclamation points, has a life-affirming adage that "TOO MUCH IS NOT ENOUGH!"—as witnessed in the "let's make a gallon of pickles!" recipe. The same can be said with her recipes for party sandwiches—which produce two hundred each! I've trimmed down the ingredients to serve a party of twenty. If, though, you're hosting a Jingles-sized soiree, just do the math and make more if needed.

Tomato Sandwiches

Ingredients
10 ripe tomatoes, approximately the same width as a wine glass
salt and black pepper
4 king-sized loaves of thinly sliced white bread, such as Sunbeam
1 pint or more mayonnaise
Fresh basil or crumbled fried bacon, optional

Directions
1. Bring a large pot of water to a boil; working in batches, dip tomatoes in boiling water for 30 to 45 seconds and remove from the water. They should peel easily. Discard the peels.
2. Slice the tomatoes. You should get 5 slices out of each tomato. Drain the slices on 2 layers of paper towel. Blot the tops of the tomatoes then sprinkle with salt and pepper; set aside.
3. Use a cookie cutter or wine glass to cut out bread rounds from the loaves.
4. Spread a bit of mayonnaise on each of the bread rounds. Place a seasoned slice of tomato slice atop half the rounds, then top with the other halves of bread. If you'd like, you can also sprinkle on each tomato slice a bit of basil or some crisp, crumbled bacon.

5. Place the sandwiches in an airtight container with wax paper between each layer. Put a damp paper towel on the top layer, seal the container, and refrigerate until ready to use. May be made 3 to 4 hours in advance.

Serves 20

Next, let's substitute four twenty-ounce cans of pineapple rings for the sliced tomatoes—and leave off the salt and pepper. Prepare them in the same manner, cutting out rounds the size of a pineapple ring and then spreading each slice of bread with mayonnaise. I *love these* during summer; they've been favorite of mine since being a tow-headed three-year-old beach bum on St. Simons Island.

Pineapple Sandwiches

Ingredients
4 (20-ounce) cans sliced pineapple in sweetened juice, drained
4 king-sized loaves of thinly sliced white bread, such as Sunbeam King Thin White Bread
1 pint or more mayonnaise

Directions
1. Place the pineapple slices on 2 layers of paper towels. Blot the tops with another paper towel.
2. Cut the slices of bread into rounds using a cutter or wine glass the size of a pineapple ring.
3. Spread mayonnaise on each slice and make your sandwiches.
4. Place in an airtight container with wax paper between each layer, ending with wax paper. Put a damp paper towel on the top layer of the wax paper, seal the container, and refrigerate until ready to use. May be made 3 to 4 hours in advance.

Serves 20

This next recipe doesn't come from our friend in Fairhope—though I'm betting dollars to donuts she'll love them and will serve them on the dock someday soon. Rather, this creation came about as a result of a birthday party given for Tom. I wanted to have friends by the house for a small get-together and asked what food he wanted. In a particularly irritable mood that day (pick a day, haha!) he replied, "It doesn't matter. I would be happy with a bologna sandwich."

Well, not letting his disposition get in the way of a party, invitations went out to a crowd of about twenty. When guests arrived, in place was our requisite open bar and a multi-dish supper buffet. The pièce de résistance, however, was the specially hand-created bologna canapés lining four sterling silver Tiffany platters! People devoured them—many saying that a bologna sandwich took them right back to childhood. I ran out of the Oscar Meyer jewels that night; each and every one was eaten! Serve these and see what your friends think. I call them, with just a trace of sarcasm, my "Canapés à la Thomas Eugene."

Canapés à la Thomas Eugene

Ingredients
½ cup mayonnaise
2 tablespoons yellow mustard
1 (16-ounce) package regular-sliced Oscar Meyer bologna
1 king-sized loaf of thinly sliced white bread, such as Sunbeam King Thin
    White Bread
12 slices of dill pickles, cut into thin strips
Parsley sprigs for garnish

Directions
1. Mix the mayonnaise and mustard in a small bowl. Set aside.
2. Using a champagne flute, cut the bologna into rounds. Set aside.
3. Cut out rounds of bread with a champagne flute and set aside. You should get about 3 or 4 per slice.
4. Spread each bread round with a bit of the mayo-mustard mixture, followed by a bologna round. Top with a strip of dill pickle. Serve on a platter with parsley for garnish.
Serves 10 to 12 as an hors d'oeuvre

Moving finally to dessert, we have Beverly's favorite cake—one labeled "sad" because it falls, purposefully. She says it is "sooo very moist" and perfect for making strawberry shortcake. She adds, "The wish for my last meal would be fried chicken, sliced fresh tomatoes, biscuits, and my 'sad' pound cake, vanilla ice cream, and strawberries with heavy cream poured on top."

Jingles's Sad Pound Cake

Ingredients

1 cup butter, at room temperature
½ cup butter-flavored Crisco
3 cups sugar
5 eggs, at room temperature
3 cups cake flour, such as Swans Down
1 cup whole-milk buttermilk
¼ teaspoon baking soda
1 tablespoon vanilla extract
1 teaspoon almond extract
Fresh strawberries, vanilla ice cream, and heavy whipping cream to accompany

Directions

1. Cream butter and Crisco in a mixer.
2. Add sugar and continue to cream at medium speed for 10 minutes.
3. Add eggs one at a time, beating until well blended.
4. Add cake flour a ½ cup at a time.
5. In a small bowl, combine the buttermilk and baking soda; drizzle this into the batter mixture while beating.
6. Add the vanilla and almond extracts; mix until just incorporated.
7. Grease and flour a large tube pan; spread in the batter.
8. Place into a COLD oven.
9. Turn the oven to 325 degrees. Cook for 1 hour for a "sad" cake, or 1 hour and 10 minutes if you do not want it to fall.
10. Allow the cake to cool for 15 minutes before carefully removing from the pan. Serve with the strawberries, ice cream, and/or whipping cream.

Serves 12 to 14

Chapter 10

Julie & Julia

*"The only time to eat diet food is while you are waiting
for the steak to cook."—Julia Child*

One of my absolute favorite parties resulted from the movie *Julie & Julia*,
which starred Meryl Streep as Julia Child and told the story of a blogger
who prepared, in a year's time, all the dishes found in Julia's *Mastering the
Art of French Cooking*. This celebration described in the following pages is
a great example of how easy it is to find a reason to make merry and enjoy
life.

Tom and I asked thirty of our nearest and dearest to meet at a local
theater for a Friday matinee. Afterward, guests joined us at our house for
drinks and dinner. The invitation to the guests came with a request to
bring along a bottle of their favorite French wine; as hosts we provided
the bar and a Julia-inspired French dinner buffet.

All of our friends are extremely entertaining—life is too short to surround yourself with grumps—and everyone, as expected, brought their
best festive spirits to the movie and to the house afterward, all inspired by
seeing such a great interpretation of the French chef by the sublime Ms.
Streep. Drinks and wine flowed for hours, as did laughter and lively conversation.

That night my menu included a platter of gourmet cheeses, crackers,
and a country pâté de maison, followed by my Southern take on vichyssoise, a filet of beef, poached salmon, salad, and a large tray of Godiva
chocolates.

Everything on the menu was prepared in advance, including the beef,
which I served at room temperature. All to do at the last minute was place
the items in the serving dishes—and v*oilà*—dinner was served.

I used Julia's recipe for pâté de maison, a coarsely ground loaf of liver, chicken, sausage, and spices, made two days in advance to let the flavors develop properly. The recipe can be found in *The Way to Cook* or online. If you do not want to make the pâté, which, in all honesty, is *not* a pretty task as it requires grinding raw liver and chicken, there are gourmet brands that can be purchased by the pound at Fresh Market or Whole Foods. To serve, line a platter with lettuce leaves and sprigs of parsley; place the pâté in the center. Serve alongside a crock of whole grain mustard, tart lingonberry or plum jam, cornichons, and a thinly sliced baguette.

Vidaliassoise is my take on the French classic vichyssoise. The sweetness of the Vidalia onions makes the soup comparable to the traditional version, plus you don't have to worry about the burdensome task of cleaning the inside of gritty leeks. This course was served in gold-rimmed demitasse cups—no need for spoons; guests just sipped away.

Vidaliassoise

Ingredients
2 tablespoons butter
5 cups Vidalia onions, thinly sliced
5 cups russet baking potatoes, peeled and cut into 2-inch cubes (don't use a waxy variety of potato)
8 cups water (approximate)
1 tablespoon kosher salt
1 cup heavy cream
½ teaspoon finely ground white pepper
¼ cup chives, minced

Directions
1. Melt butter in large stock pot over medium-high heat; add onions, stir, and cook for about 5 minutes until onions are just becoming tender. *Do not let the onions or butter brown; turn down the temperature if needed.*
2. Add potatoes, salt, and enough water to just cover the onion and potatoes.
3. Bring to a boil; reduce heat and cook uncovered, stirring occasionally, until the potatoes are tender, about 25 minutes.
4. Remove from heat and allow to cool for half an hour.
5. In batches, purée the mixture in a blender until smooth. Pour the batches into a container that can be covered tightly and refrigerated.
6. When finished puréeing, add the cream and white pepper. Adjust salt if needed. Stir well. Chill for at least 6 hours or overnight.

7. To serve, garnish with minced chives.
Serves 16 as an appetizer, or 8 as a first course

The beef is an easily prepared, but expensive, roast. Some people do not dress the meat before cooking it; however, I highly recommend doing so. By removing the excess fat, silver skin, flat tail end, and the loose side muscle (called "the chain") that runs the length of the roast, you will have a uniform piece of meat that can be carved into slices of equal size. An important reason of removing the silver skin is that, left unpeeled, this membrane will constrict the roast while cooking, making it curl. Save the tail end and chain, which you can freeze and use later for a stir fry or other dish.

If you attempt to remove the membrane yourself, the main thing to remember is to take your time. Using a sharp paring or boning knife, make an inch-long cut into the skin at the top of the meat. Keeping your knife pointed upward, away from the roast, slowly and carefully slice the membrane until you can remove it. Continue until all the roast is unpeeled. I suggest asking your butcher, an expert, to complete these steps for you, though; it saves time and you'll be assured of getting exactly what you need.

You'll note that the recipe is for a six-pound tenderloin for eight people, which at first reading may sound like an overabundance of meat. However, after trimming, removing the chain, and shaping up the tail end, you will lose a good bit of the weight from the roast. The following recipe is a *foolproof* way of preparing a perfectly cooked beef tenderloin. It is simple, but you have to follow the recipe *exactly*.

Roast Tenderloin of Beef

Ingredients
1 (6-pound) beef tenderloin, trimmed and dressed
2 tablespoons Worcestershire sauce
2 tablespoons olive oil
2 teaspoons kosher salt
2 teaspoons freshly ground black pepper
2 teaspoons garlic powder
2 teaspoons onion powder

Directions
1. Preheat the oven to 500 degrees.
2. Brush the tenderloin with the Worcestershire sauce, and then with the olive oil.
3. In a small bowl, mix together the salt, pepper, garlic powder, and onion powder. Rub this mixture into the meat, covering the entire roast.
4. Set the roast in a shallow baking sheet and place in the oven. For a medium-rare roast, keep the oven turned on for *exactly* 5 minutes per pound of tenderloin; for the 6-pound roast, that would be 30 minutes. If you are using a smaller or larger roast, adjust the cooking time. After the allotted cooking time, turn off the oven and keep the roast in the oven for 1 hour. Do not open the door to the oven.
5. Remove the beef from the oven, loosely cover with aluminum foil, and allow to rest for 20 minutes. The resting time is important, so don't shortcut it. To serve, slice the roast into ½- to ¾-inch filets. The following aioli recipe can be drizzled on top of the beef or served on the side. The roast may be served hot or at room temperature.

Serves 8

The aioli (fancy name for flavored mayonnaise) is one that I use with roasted beef, lamb, pork tenderloin, or grilled chicken. It is simple.

Garlic and Rosemary Aioli

Ingredients
1 cup Hellman's, Duke's, or Sauer's mayonnaise
2 teaspoons fresh garlic, minced
1 tablespoon fresh rosemary, minced (do not use dried)
½ teaspoon coarsely ground black pepper

Directions
1. Mix all ingredients.
2. Cover and refrigerate at least 4 hours or overnight.

Makes 1+ cup

Julia adored fish, so it was appropriate to include a selection for the party. Her favorite, as any Juliaphile knows, was sole meunière. However, there was no way for me to prepare sautéed fish for thirty people. For this menu,

I chose a make-ahead salmon that created an attractive, as well as delicious, platter for our buffet.

JSB's Oven-Poached Salmon

Ingredients
⅓ cup olive oil, divided
1 whole side of salmon (4 to 5 pounds), boned
2 tablespoons fresh lemon juice
2 tablespoons dry vermouth
2 teaspoons kosher salt
1½ teaspoons black pepper
3 lemons, ends removed, cut crosswise into 12 thin slices
1 cup Vidalia onion, sliced crosswise very thinly
6 large sprigs of fresh dill
Lettuce leaves and parsley for garnish
Sour cream, diced red onion, capers, water crackers

Directions
1. Preheat oven to 350 degrees.
2. Cut off a piece of aluminum foil large enough to hold the salmon; place the foil on a large baking sheet. Brush the foil liberally with some of the olive oil. Place the fish skin side down on the oiled foil.
3. Mix together the lemon juice and vermouth; pour the contents over the salmon.
4. Sprinkle the salt and black pepper evenly over the filet.
5. Decoratively place the lemon slices flat against the salmon, then top with the onion rings, and finally with the dill.
6. Drizzle the remaining olive oil over the fish. Fold the foil over the sides of the fish to partially tent. Don't let the foil, though, touch the lemons, onions, or dill. Place the tray in the oven and cook for 20 minutes, or until done (timing will vary some depending on thickness of the filet).
7. Remove from oven; allow to cool for 10 minutes. Cover; refrigerate at least 4 to 6 hours or overnight.
8. Carefully transfer the salmon, in one piece, from the baking sheet to a large tray lined with lettuce leaves and parsley. Serve with sour cream, diced red onion, capers, and water crackers.

Serves 20 to 25 for a party, 8 for a main course

This uncomplicated salad is tossed with one of Julia's lemon-based dressings. Note that she used regular vegetable oil, not olive oil. A mixture of green and Bibb lettuces, arugula, and watercress, each with its own unique texture and flavor, are my favored greens for this dish.

Salad of Mixed Greens & Lemon Herb Dressing

Ingredients

2 teaspoons lemon zest
2 tablespoons lemon juice
1 teaspoon fresh thyme, minced
1 teaspoon shallots, minced
½ teaspoon Dijon mustard
⅛ teaspoon sugar
½ cup vegetable oil
12 cups fresh greens, such as baby arugula, watercress, Bibb, and green leaf lettuces
¼ teaspoon salt
Several grinds black pepper

Directions

1. Whisk together the zest, juice, thyme, garlic, mustard and sugar. Slowly drizzle in the oil, whisking constantly.
2. Sprinkle the greens with the salt and black pepper, tossing to coat.
3. Drizzle dressing over the seasoned greens and toss again. Serve immediately.

Serves 8

Chapter 11

Supper Clubs

These days the term "supper club" in the South means a group of friends with common interests who gather regularly for culinary camaraderie. Apparently, we feel like there aren't enough holidays, or birthdays, weddings, or other celebrations to allow us to get together and libate, nosh, talk college football, and share the latest town gossip. So, being uber social, we create supper clubs to provide additional dining, convivial, and companionable opportunities.

One impressive example is the Madeira Club in Savannah, whose history goes back more than seventy years. Created by a group of distinguished Savannah gentlemen, there are no written rules, minutes, or officers, but the traditions are definitive and include a formal, seated dinner where a paper is presented by a member. Madeira, which has been of importance to Savannah since Colonial times, is consumed with at least one course of the meal. (Apologies to the fine fellows in the Madeira Club if you take offense at me labeling your esteemed coterie as a "supper club," but, as they say, if it walks like a duck....)

These supper clubs are found throughout the South, and some are closely regulated with rules and decorum while others are much more relaxed. Most do have at least a few things in common in terms of structure, such as how often they meet and where, how the meal is planned, and who can be a part of the group.

I'll share here two supper clubs that are near and dear to my heart and highlight their framework and some of their stories and recipes. The first, Girls on the Grill (GOTG), prompted me to pen my first book, *Rise and Shine!: A Southern Son's Treasury of Food, Family and Friends*. GOTG has been in existence since 1997, when friends Monica McGoldrick and Debbie Keeney dreamed up the concept over glasses (or was it a bottle?)

of good vino and Italian food at a neighborhood restaurant. Their ponderings led to the formation of a group of Savannah ladies all known for their style, good taste, and the marvelous items created in their kitchens. This club numbers anywhere from twenty-five to thirty, with thirty being the cap. Charter member Elizabeth Skeadas (who is one of the most gracious and lovely ladies I have ever met!) shares that while there are rules, such as the membership number, the biggest parameters are that each participant has "a love of cooking and good food, and that they find joy in sharing with friends." Members rarely leave, and there isn't any admission committee or secret handshake, Elizabeth confides. She says that "there is just enough structure to keep the group going, and that everyone shares the responsibilities." But with as many as thirty guests and monthly meetings, certain items are written in stone, such as the hostesses' responsibilities. Each member is teamed with another to host once every eighteen months. These lead ladies are required, among other things, to secure the meeting place (usually one of their homes); set a theme; send invitations; provide all beverages, adult and otherwise; and have available the plates, glasses, napkins, utensils, etc., needed for the night.

Other members are listed in pre-assigned recipe categories (so that there aren't ten cakes at dinner and no vegetables). Five rotating members aren't required to bring food but instead are asked to arrive early to help set up and stay late to assist with cleaning. And all members must bring copies of their recipes to share.

This club is a tight-knit group, and the monthly gatherings are something that they keep in ink on their calendars. A sample of themes from prior years include "breakfast for supper" where the girls wore pajamas, a party honoring the talents of Ina Garten, and a celebration of the Augusta National's Masters Golf Tournament. Christmas meetings are always special in that the yuletide festivity includes spouses, and, in most cases, the dress is black-tie.

In winter 2013, Monica, whom I call Monique (not sure why, but it has stuck) was supposed to host at her home, but due to renovation work that hadn't been completed by the contractors—we've all been there, haven't we?—asked if she could entertain the group at mine and Tom's home on 45th Street. I gladly agreed; Monique is one of my best friends in the Hostess City, and I was happy to help out. We had met years before at a downtown cocktail party, finding ourselves outside on a townhouse veranda, bonding over vodka tonics, tomato sandwiches, and a love of Southern literature and food. The request came at a time, too, when I was absolutely in need of some distraction. My sport of a mama had just passed away in October, after being intubated for two months in the ICU, and I was still reeling from the loss. "Johnathon, darlin', if you don't mind," Monique had asked me sweetly, "we'd love for you to talk to us that evening about some of your favorite recipes, and maybe why they are special to you." And that request gave me a purpose.

As I pondered what dishes and tales to impart, memories flooded back to me: the warmth of my family's kitchen, the great dishes my mama, Carrie, and all my aunts would make, the camaraderie we shared in the kitchen eating a sandwich, or with the family and friends gathered round the dining table. The more I thought, the more I wrote, and those first stories and recipes turned into a book, and then there was a second—and here we are today. I have Monique, and the fabulous ladies with Girls on the Grill, to thank for giving me the initiative.

We had a wonderful time that night with a capacity crowd filling our living room, bar, library, dining room, and kitchen. The culinary selections were incredible. One effort was particularly memorable because I so love fried shrimp. My buddy Val Bowers brought her own FryDaddy, set it up on the kitchen counter, and served up dozens and dozens of perfectly cooked prawns worthy of any seafood house on the coast. Val is a great conversationalist and has a wonderful Middle Georgia accent; she is from Cobbtown, Georgia, which, she will tell you, is "about the size of a big living room." Because it's a small world, she and my dear buddy Nelda (see the Christmas chapter, divinity recipe) are first cousins.

Here are several recipes from the GOTG, all ones that are tried and true. And to all of you in the club reading this book, I send out big hugs and lots and lots of love from JSB!

The first selection is from Monique, who *loves* crab. I've never been to her house for a cocktail or dinner party when she didn't serve something made with this Low Country delicacy. This main dish wonder is easy to make, and excellent with a simple tossed salad.

Crab Pie

Ingredients
1 (9-inch) deep-dish pie shell, unbaked
½ cup mayonnaise
½ cup whole milk
¼ cup green onion, white and green parts, diced
2 eggs, beaten
2 tablespoons flour
½ teaspoon kosher salt
Pinch cayenne pepper
1 pound crab, picked for shells, and flaked to separate, but careful not to break the larger pieces
6 ounces Swiss cheese, finely shredded

Directions
1. Preheat oven to 350 degrees.
2. Place a piece of foil over the pie shell; fill with beans or pie weights. Bake for 10 minutes until just done. Remove from the oven, take off the foil and weights, set aside.
3. In a large bowl, whisk together the mayonnaise, milk, onions, eggs, flour, salt, and cayenne. Fold in the crab and cheese, being careful not to break the pieces of crab.
4. Gently spoon the mixture into the pie shell. Bake for 40 to 50 minutes until the top begins to brown and the middle sets. Place on a rack and allow to cool at room temperature for 10 to 15 minutes before serving.
Serves 6

A second entrée feature here comes from Debbie. Mrs. Keeney, from what I'm told, ensures that things run smoothly for GOTG—which is natural for her, given her thirty-year career as an educator. Debbie also has the sweetest disposition of anyone, anywhere; she is a complete joy to be around. I know when she makes certain the gang stays within their parameters that her encouragement is easily received by the other members.

In one of those small-world stories, her husband, Smokey, a native of Cordele, Georgia, went to high school with my first cousin, Bucky. I had an entire chapter about Bucky's dad and mom, my Uncle Telford and Aunt Martha, in *Rise and Shine!* Uncle Telford owned the Cordele Recreation Parlor, home of the world's best chili and slaw dogs—and one heck of a house on Lake Blackshear where I caught some of the most incredible white perch, ever. Anyway, I know I'm on a tangent, but bear with me. I love nicknames, and Smokey's is one of the best. His given name is Floyd—and no, he did not come by his moniker because of a penchant for cigars. When he was growing up, his favorite sandwich was one his mama made, one called a "Smokey Joe." He loved those juicy lunchtime treats so much that folks started calling him "Smokey" in kindergarten, and the nickname has followed him through the decades. Smokey is tremendous fellow, and I'm lucky to have the Keeneys as friends.

Back to this next entrée: if you're running short on time, you can purchase pre-made pesto and packaged grilled chicken at the grocery store. Not as good as homemade, but it is an option.

Grilled Chicken & Tortellini with Pesto Cream Sauce

Ingredients
1 cup fresh basil leaves, tightly packed
1 large clove of garlic, minced
1 tablespoon olive oil
4 to 5 walnut halves
1 tablespoon freshly grated Parmesan cheese
¼ scant teaspoon kosher or sea salt
2 sticks (½ pound) butter
2 cups heavy cream
1 tablespoons olive oil
12 julienned strips each red and yellow bell peppers
2 chicken breasts (about 12 ounces total), seasoned, grilled, and julienned
1 (10-ounce) container refrigerated cheese tortellini, cooked to the directions on the package

Directions
1. Make the pesto by placing the basil leaves, garlic, 1 tablespoon olive oil, walnut halves, Parmesan cheese, and salt into a food processor; process until smooth. Set aside.
2. In a boiler with a heavy bottom, melt the butter over medium heat. Add in the cream, whisking. Bring it just to a boil; pour in the pesto and stir to mix well. Allow the mixture to come just to a boil again, reduce the heat, and cook for 25 minutes. Stir occasionally to keep the sauce from sticking.
3. Just before the sauce is done, heat the remaining 1 tablespoon olive oil in a sauté pan over high heat; add the bell peppers and quickly cook until just tender, stirring constantly, about 1 minute.

4. Add the chicken and tortellini to the boiler with the pesto cream sauce; toss to mix being careful not to break the pasta. To serve, ladle the dish in bowls and garnish the top with crisscrossed strips of the sautéed peppers.
Serves 4

This next recipe is a terrific summer salad that pairs well with a piece of roasted lamb or beef. Or, if you'd like, make it a main course by adding a pound of cooked shrimp. It comes from the lovely Cindy Edwards, who grew up in the charming town of Claxton and now lives in Savannah. She adapted this dish from the late Emyl Jenkins, a renowned entertainment lecturer. In the 90s, I arranged for Emyl to come to Savannah on two occasions to speak to the Georgia Historical Society and Historic Savannah on the subject of Southern hospitality. She is so missed.

Artichoke, Rice & Pepper Salad

Ingredients
2 (6-ounce) jars artichoke hearts, drained, quartered, reserving the liquid from one jar
1 (6-ounce) box chicken vermicelli rice, cooked to instructions and cooled to room temperature
¼ cup mayonnaise
½ teaspoon curry powder
¼ cup green onions, white and green parts, chopped
¼ cup pimento-stuffed olives, sliced thinly crosswise
¼ cup bell peppers, preferably a mix of red, green, and yellow, diced (hint: whatever parts of the peppers you don't use, slice thinly into rings and use as a garnish)

Directions
1. In a large bowl, whisk together the reserved artichoke liquid, mayonnaise, and curry.
2. Fold in the remaining ingredients, cover, and chill 3 to 4 hours before serving.
Serves 6

Next is a classic holiday recipe provided by Elizabeth, one that comes from her mother, Martha Turnow. I have a whole chapter on Mrs. Turnow in *Cook & Tell* where Elizabeth shared a number of her mother's wonderful recipes. This congealed salad was an absolute staple at every family holiday gathering, bar none, in Laurinburg, North Carolina. It was loved so much by Elizabeth and her brother, Mac, that Mrs. Turnow would make two servings for each of them. Savoring a bite of this dish takes Elizabeth right back to childhood and the wonderful memories of home. It is because of such warm, delicious, and indelible stories that I reached for pen and paper to write this third book.

Mrs. Turnow's Cranberry Salad

Ingredients
Vegetable oil
2 envelopes unflavored gelatin
⅓ cup cold water
3 small boxes cherry-flavored Jell-O
3 cups boiling water
3 cups sugar
Pinch of salt
1 (18-ounce) can crushed pineapple, drained (don't use fresh; the salad won't congeal)
1 cup orange juice
Juice of 1 lemon
3 cups pecans, chopped
2 cups celery, chopped
3 cups fresh cranberries, chopped
Iceberg lettuce leave and mayonnaise, for garnish

Directions
1. Lightly oil a 2-quart mold or 10 individual ½-cup molds. Set aside.
2. In a large mixing bowl, whisk together the gelatin with ⅓ cup cold water.
3. Add the cherry Jell-O to the bowl and pour the boiling water over the gelatins. Add in the sugar and salt; whisk until the gelatin, Jell-O, and sugar are dissolved. Place in the refrigerator and chill for 30 minutes.
4. When the chilling gelatins start to set, add in the pineapple, juices, pecans, celery, and cranberries. Stir well. Refrigerate again for 15 to 20 minutes.
5. When the mixture starts to set again, pour into one large mold, or the smaller individual molds. Chill 4 to 6 hours, or overnight, until firm.

6. To serve, unmold onto lettuce leaves and serve with a dollop of mayonnaise.
Serves 8 to 10

Another GOTG *amie* is the unparalleled Anne Rockwell. Gracious beyond measure, she is always excellent company. I like to tell the story of the night the two of us went to the Heart Ball together back in the early 90s. It was a black-tie affair at the Hyatt Regency in Savannah. When the fundraiser was over, we strolled outside with Tom and our friend Mary Ann Smith (see the St. Patrick's Day chapter) to wait for our car. Anne and I spied a large line of partygoers across the street waiting to get into Hip Huggers dance club. Not ready to retire home yet, we waved Tom and Mary Ann on their way, assured them we'd get a taxi later (this was years before Uber and cell phones were still a bit of a novelty), and traipsed across Bay Street, me in my tuxedo and Anne in her little black dress. The bouncers working the door let us right in past that long line, and we commenced to the dance floor where we tripped the light fantastic and enjoyed several more drinks until closing time. When the lights came up to clear out, we walked outside—shoes in hand because our toes were throbbing from all those deft dance moves—and went to reach into our pockets to get money to hail a taxi. Well, taxis back in those days in Savannah didn't take credit cards, and we had spent, literally, our last dimes on the cocktails that allowed us to disco so well. It was 3 a.m., and we sat down on the curb and wondered what in the name of sweet Jesus were we going to do. Our feet ached too much to walk the dozen or so blocks to Anne's house on Houston Street. Fortunately, we spied a lone bellman at the Hyatt; I limped (I really did limp, folks, I swear my feet were throbbing) and explained our situation. He took pity on us, saying he had just gotten off his shift and would drive us home. Bless that man's heart. I did have a blank check in my wallet, which I took out and clumsily signed over to him for twenty-five bucks in gratitude when he dropped us off at Anne's door. What a night and what a wonderful gal is our Anne!

Her recipe here from a GOTG meeting comes from *Mrs. Wilkes' Boarding House Cookbook*. It is a very light—like a mist—but very flavorful cake; the subtle taste of Southern pecans is at the heart of this dessert. It's also excellent at breakfast with a cup of coffee.

Left to right Monica (Monique) McGoldrick, Debbie Keeney, and Elizabeth Skeadas of Savannah's famed Girls on the Grill having lunch at my late Uncle Telford's Cordele Recreation Parlor

With my dancing buddy, Girls on the Grill and
Ardsley Park Supper Club member, Anne Rockwell,
celebrating my 50th birthday, Savannah, Georgia

Mrs. Wilkes' Georgia Pecan Mist Cake

Ingredients
12 large eggs, separated
½ teaspoon salt
3½ cups confectioner's sugar
3 cups finely ground pecans (6 cups shelled pecans = approximately 3 cups ground)
Whipped cream for garnish

Directions
1. Preheat oven to 350 degrees. Prepare a 10-inch tube pan by lightly greasing and flouring. Add a lightly greased and floured piece of parchment or wax paper to the bottom.
2. In a large bowl, over medium-high speed, whisk the egg yolks until thick and lemon-colored, about 2 minutes. Set aside.
3. In another large bowl, beat the egg whites and salt until they are frothy, about 2 minutes. Over medium speed, gradually sift in the sugar. When all the sugar is used, turn speed up to high and whisk another 2 to 3 minutes until the mixture is stiff.
4. Gently fold in the beaten egg yolks to the egg white/sugar mixture, and then fold in the ground pecans until just mixed. Ladle the batter into the prepared tube pan. Bake 40 to 50 minutes, checking on the cake at the 40-minute mark. A toothpick or cake tester should come out clean, and the top should be a caramel brown color. Place the cooked cake on a rack and cool completely, at least 1 hour, before removing from the pan.

Serves 16 to 20

The second supper club I want to highlight is the one that I helped start with Tom and a handful of friends back in the mid-90s. We all gathered periodically anyway and decided to formalize just a bit our get-togethers, calling ourselves the Ardsley Park Supper Club after the neighborhood in which most of us lived. What delightful times we had over the years! Our group was structured so that membership was limited to the number of folks we could fit around one of our dining tables, and that was ten. The host/hostess would set the theme, provide the bar, and make the main course. Other members were assigned to hors d'oeuvres, soup, appetizer, and dessert, each with appropriately paired wines. We'd each talk about our course and how it was prepared, and something about the vino as well. Not that we always had fancy dinners; it was rare that we'd do "dress up";

sometimes the dinner might be a Southern barbeque or a comfort-food theme featuring a fat pot roast (recipe following). We had aprons, cocktail napkins, and other items monogrammed with our club's name.

It was at one of the first of these gatherings that I met Mary Kay Andrews, the bestselling author and magnificent cook/hostess. She joined us one night as a guest of one of our members, Anne Landers (see the Iron in the Fire chapter). We all had a grand time, and as a lovely gesture, Mary Kay included our supper club and the menu we had that night in her runaway hit novel *Savannah Blues*. When the book was released, our group hosted a cocktail buffet supper for Mary Kay and invited more than seventy-five folks to attend, and, of course, buy a book! We made her an honorary member, and any time she was in town, and we had a dinner, MKA was invited. (On a side note, Mary Kay and her tremendous cook of a husband, Tom, returned the party gesture at their stylish Avondale Estate home with a fabulous gathering for me and *Rise and Shine!* in 2015 just after the book's release.)

Our group lasted together for more than two decades; one member moved to Atlanta, one passed away, and Tom and I moved to Athens when my career took me to the University of Georgia. We still get together, just not monthly as we did in the past, and talk about the fun we had, and the friendships we enjoyed, and all that good, good food.

One entrée from our supper club days was a fat, fine pot roast with a rich, savory gravy. This version comes from my long-time friend Cathy Cullum Belford, of Savannah. More than fork tender, it is the dish I always hope to have when invited to her home. Cathy was nicknamed "Big Cath" as a child by her younger brother, John. Now Cathy was not then, nor is now, a big girl. No, as I explained in *Cook & Tell*, the adjective "big" in front of a name does not necessarily refer to physical size but rather to an expansive and strong personality. Cathy took her role of being the eldest seriously, and we good-naturedly remind her sometimes that the trait has stayed intact after these passing decades. BC is married to Lee, whom we all refer to as "Lee Boy" because of his ever-present jovial and congenial personality. They are two of mine and Tom's dearest friends, and we've had many, many good times together. Besides being a former

Miss Savannah, the lovely Cathy also is an extremely talented floral designer. The morning after my mom passed away, BC had put together and placed an enormous and beautiful wreath, in which black ribbons and bows were intertwined on my front door. I'll always remember that loving gesture. Anyway, for the pot roast, Cath shares, and I agree, that dried herbs work better here than fresh; seems that the taste of the dried is a bit heartier and imparts more sustaining flavor. Enjoy!

Big Cath's Beef Pot Roast

Ingredients
3 tablespoons vegetable oil, divided
1 (5-pound) chuck roast
2 teaspoons kosher or sea salt
1 teaspoon black pepper
3 cups onion, cut lengthwise into 2-inch-wide slices
1 cup celery, chopped
1 tablespoon garlic, minced
1 teaspoon dried rosemary*
1 teaspoon dried thyme*
½ teaspoon dried marjoram*
¼ teaspoon allspice*
2 dried bay leaves*
3 cups carrots, thickly sliced
1½ tablespoons butter, at room temperature
1½ tablespoon all-purpose flour
* *You can substitute 3 teaspoons of herbs de Provence instead of these five
    herbs.*

Directions
1. Lightly grease the bottom and sides of a crock pot with 1 tablespoon of oil and turn on low heat. Set aside.
2. Rub the salt and black pepper into the roast, covering all surfaces.
3. In a large skillet with a heavy bottom, heat 2 tablespoons of oil until smoking over medium-high heat. Brown the roast well, about 3 to 4 minutes per side. Place the roast in the crock pot/slow cooker. Add the onions, celery, garlic, thyme, marjoram, rosemary, allspice, and bay leaves (or herbs de Provence).
4. Cook the roast 6 to 7 hours or until fork tender. About 2 hours before the roast is done, add the carrots to the pot.

5. When fully cooked, remove the roast, place on a cutting board or platter, and allow to cool for about 10 minutes.
6. While the roast cools, melt the butter in a saucepan over medium-high heat; whisk in the flour and cook for 2 minutes. Whisking, stream in 3 cups of the liquid that accumulated in the crock pot; cook 4 to 5 minutes until thickened. Taste, and add additional seasonings, such as black pepper, or a bit of red wine, if needed.
7. Slice the beef and place on a platter; surround it with the carrots and other vegetables from the pot. Pour a bit of the gravy over the sliced meat and serve the remainder on the side.

Serves 8 to 10

This dessert dish is a go-to for me to prepare for a dinner party, and it was one of the courses we had when May Kay Andrews joined us for dinner. She then included the pie in *Savannah Blues*. The tartness of the pie, which is brought about with a good portion of grated lime zest, along with the delicious sweetness of the coulis, makes this dessert a standout. My recipe has a different crust than what you normally find with key lime pies—instead of graham crackers, butter-rich shortbread cookies are used along with ground pecans.

Key Lime Pie with Blueberry Coulis

Ingredients
2 cups shortbread cookie crumbs (I use Keebler Sandies shortbread cookies and crumble in the food processor)
¼ cup finely ground pecans
¼ cup light brown sugar
¼ cup unsalted butter, melted
⅛ teaspoon cinnamon
1 cup freshly squeezed lime juice (if you can't get fresh, use a reliable, not-from-concentrate brand, such as Santa Cruz)
6 teaspoons very finely grated lime zest
4 large egg yolks
2 (14-ounce) cans sweetened condensed milk
Blueberry coulis (recipe follows)
Whipped cream and fresh sprigs of mint

Directions
1. Preheat oven to 350 degrees.
2. In a large bowl, mix together the cookie crumbs, nuts, sugar, butter, and cinnamon. Put the mixture into a deep-dish, nonstick pie pan; using your hands, press evenly over bottom and up the sides, making certain it adheres to the pan.
3. In another bowl, beat the lime juice, zest, egg yolks, and milk until thoroughly incorporated.
4. Add the filling to the crust and bake 18 to 20 minutes. Remove and refrigerate overnight.
5. To serve, place slices of the pie on individual plates. Drizzle with the coulis, top with a bit of whipped cream, and garnish with a sprig of fresh mint.

Serves 8

Blueberry Coulis

Ingredients
2 cups fresh or frozen blueberries
½ cup sugar
1 tablespoon fresh squeezed lime juice

Directions
1. Add all ingredients to saucepan. Stir well and bring to a steady simmer.
2. Allow to cook, stirring occasionally, for 5 to 6 minutes until the sugar melts and the blueberries begin to cook slightly.
3. Remove from heat, and place in an airtight container. Chill 2 hours or overnight.

Makes 2 cups

I mentioned earlier that Mary Kay is an outstanding cook, and the following is one of her stellar dishes that is always in demand at her parties, particularly her New Year's Day celebration. The gourmet spread at Mary Kay and Tom's beach house on Tybee Island January 1 rivals any brunch buffet you'd find in Savannah, Atlanta, or New Orleans. While the original intent of this dish is to be served as a side, I like to serve it as an appetizer with crunchy tortilla chips; it makes an excellent dip. Either way, you'll bat a thousand by serving this delicious and totally Southern creation.

Grits & Greens Casserole

Ingredients
8 cups low-sodium chicken broth, divided
2 cups half-and-half
2 cups real or stone-ground grits, not instant or quick
2½ cups freshly grated Parmesan cheese, divided
1 cup (2 sticks) butter
½ teaspoon black pepper
1 pound collard greens, washed, trimmed, shredded, and chopped
8 slices bacon, cooked and crumbled
Tostitos Scoops or Fritos (if serving as an appetizer)

Directions
1. In a large pot, combine 6 cups of the stock and the half-and-half; bring to a boil. Slowly stir in the grits. Bring back to a boil, stir, and reduce heat to a steady simmer, stirring often, and cook until the grits are soft (follow the instructions on the grits container for timing).
2. When the grits are done, stir in 2 cups of the cheese, the butter, and black pepper. Set aside.
3. Preheat oven to 350 degrees and grease a 3-quart baking dish. Set the dish aside.
4. In another large pot, add the remaining 2 cups of stock and the collards. Bring to boil, reduce heat to a steady simmer, and cover. Cook for 10 minutes. Drain the collards in a colander. When cool to the touch, squeeze out the excess liquid.
5. Stir the collards into the grits mixture and mix well. Pour the contents into the greased baking dish and sprinkle the top with the rest of the cheese and the crumbled bacon. Cook in the preheated oven 30 to 35 minutes until bubbly. Serve as a side dish or with Tostitos Scoops or Fritos as an hors d'oeuvre.

Serves 6 to 8 as a side dish, 16 to 20 as a dip

Chapter 12

An Iron in the Fire

One of the best dinners we ever put together came about not because of a special occasion, but due in part to a scary incident. Fortunately, in the end, we all had something to celebrate, and were able to do so with some good laughs along the way.

On a Sunday night in late spring, Tom and I received a frantic phone call from one of our close friends and neighbors, Anne Landers. (Not the late advice column author, this Anne at the time owned the four-star Gastonian Inn, a Relais & Châteaux property, which Tom decorated. *Architectural Digest* featured the hotel, Anne, and Tom in an issue back in the 90s).

"Oh my God! My house is on fire!" she yelled in the phone. Tom and I rushed down the street to find our friend wrapped in a blanket in her front yard. While we waited for the firemen, we asked her what happened. Anne said she was ironing some linens in her bedroom when the cord on the iron sparked, catching the drapes on fire, and soon the whole room was engulfed.

Now Anne had just recently moved to our neighborhood, which is a historic suburb in Savannah. She was still getting to know people and had admitted to being a little intimidated by some of the old guard who lived here. To add a little lightness to the situation, I decided to tease her a bit and get her mind off the situation. I put my arm around her shoulder and said in a voice of deep concern, "Anne, hon, you really need to be careful how you tell people this fire actually started."

"What do you mean?" she asked. "Do you think I'll be blamed for causing it? One minute I'm ironing and the next there's a fire spreading across the room. I didn't even have the iron sitting down unattended! There had to be a short in the wire or something."

"No, Anne, don't worry about blame," I told her. "I'm sure it was something in the cord or the electric circuit. But you don't want to go around telling people about how it happened, that's all. Just keep it between you, the firemen, and your insurance people."

"But what do I tell people? I was just standing there in my bedroom ironing!" She was a little exasperated, and, of course, confused.

"That's just it, Anne," I said. "You were *ironing*. You don't want anyone in *this* neighborhood to know that you press your own linens. You'll never get into the Garden Club if all those dowagers find out you don't have a maid."

"Oh my God, are you serious?" she asked, incredulous and saucer-eyed. "I put my application in to join weeks ago and haven't heard a word. I bet they already know!"

Anne, though sweet and a shrewd businesswoman, was also sometimes gullible.

Tom and I laughed, and I told her that I was just pulling her leg. She punched me in the shoulder, and it became a standing joke—our scandalous friend, the one who throws convention to the wind by daring to iron her own dinner napkins. Fortunately, the house was not a complete loss, but it took several months for the renovations to be completed. During that time Anne moved from our neighborhood and lived downtown at the Gastonian.

We were ready to welcome her back home after such a long time away, and Tom and I decided to do so with a dinner party of twenty-four guests. At the time we were living in a circa-1926 English Tudor house with a commodious living room, which we used solely for large parties; the only piece of furniture in the space was a baby grand piano. Tom had decorated the large windows with rich, chocolate-colored damask draperies bordered by hand-stitched fringe bought on a trip to Spain. With the coved ceiling and rich, Jacobean-stained oak floors, it was a lovely backdrop for the festivities. We set up six portable tables for dinner and hired a piano player to entertain with background music.

To invite the guests, I came up with a cute limerick that fit perfectly onto an invitation that featured a firefighter theme, with illustrations of

Dalmatian puppies, fire-hats, and fire hoses printed around the border. It read:

> There was a girl who had an Inn
> Who needed the help of firemen
> She said "It's no joke—"
> (As she fanned away smoke)
> *"I'll never do ironing again!"*

The party was a huge success, with lots of laughter, jokes, and the warm camaraderie of close friends. (Epilogue: Anne did get an invitation to join the Ardsley Park Garden Club right after moving back into her home.)

The timing of Anne's return was late autumn, just after Tom and I had returned from a two-week trip to Germany, where I fell in love with the food and the country.

Five days of the trip were spent on a riverboat traveling the Rhine. We stopped in such renowned cities as Cologne, where we visited the magnificent and imposing Gothic cathedral, and Heidelberg, which fascinated us with the towering, illuminated ruins of the castle set aglow against the night sky. There were also visits to the small villages alongside the river, and it was in those spots where I came to find the incredible open food markets in the town squares, overflowing with an assortment of fresh vegetables, fruits, cheeses, cured meats, and fish—and the mouthwatering *bäckereis* filled with sweet pastries the likes of I'd never seen. Our cruise also coincided with the grape harvest. Sailing down the river, we could watch the pickers with large, oversized baskets set upon their backs, making their way along the vines which scaled the mountainsides bordering the Rhine.

After an overnight stop in the ancient city of Basel, where Switzerland, France and Germany meet, we took the train to Munich for a few days, and then continued on to visit the castles of "Mad" King Ludwig. While in Bavaria, we also visited the charming village of Oberammergau, famous for its Passion play, which started in 1643 in hopes that God would spare the village of the bubonic plague. The town is also full of artisan woodcarvers who specialize in religious figurines. Tom and I bought an exquisite twenty-piece crèche created from olive wood, and besides my family Bible and a handful of heirlooms, it is probably my most treasured possession.

This incredible trip through Germany exposed me to some of the finest food I ever tasted. The variety of sausages and cheeses alone could take several chapters to write about, and the pastries, known as Gebäcks or Kleingebäcks, were fabulous confections filled with fruits, nuts, marzipan, and a variety of creams. What a dream it was sitting at a Gasthaus, sipping one of the region's marvelous white wines, and enjoying a luncheon of local fare. The trip certainly inspired me to create more Deutschland cuisine at home, and the timing to do so was perfect with the upcoming party for Anne.

Because we were going to have a number of guests, my menu was planned with dishes that could be made in quantity and then easily served, such as sauerbraten—which is better cooked in advance and then reheated, as is the braised red cabbage I chose to go along with it. Also featured was a German-inspired soup and dessert, both which could be made before the guests arrived.

For hors d'oeuvres, I bought smoked German sausages; you would need about two pounds for eight people. I grilled the meats, sliced crosswise into two-inch circles, arranged on short skewers and refrigerated until the party was to begin. When ready to serve, I placed the skewers on a platter with a bowl of sweet, hot mustard for dipping.

Another platter was done with Tilsiter and Cambozola cheeses, along with small wedges of brown rye bread. Germany is one of, if not the, largest producers of cheese in Europe, and these two are selections that you should find easily enough here at home. Tilsiter is a semi-hard cheese, similar to Havarti, and is named for the town of Tilsit, which was at one time in East Prussia. Oftentimes it is laced with caraway seeds, giving it an even more German taste. Cambozola is one of my favorite cheeses; it blends the creaminess of a camembert with flavorful blue veins of gorgonzola, thus the name. Cambozola is patented and made in the Allgou region of Bavaria.

For the first seated course, I decided on a special soup. Most soups can be made in advance of a gathering, which is advantageous if time is an

With Anne Landers, Christmas 1997; the photo was taken at our home where we hosted her "welcome back to the neighborhood" party.

issue. For this party, I decided on making one of white beans. My variation is "dressed up" by puréeing the soup and adding fresh thyme and cream; the result is a hearty, but also elegant, dish. It is *gut, ya*.

Cream of White Bean Suppe (Soup)

Ingredients
1 pound cannellini beans
4 tablespoons olive oil
2 cups Vidalia or other sweet onions, chopped
2 cups celery, chopped
1 cup carrots, peeled and sliced into ¼-inch rounds
3 tablespoons fresh thyme, minced
1 teaspoon finely ground white pepper
1 large ham bone, or 2 cups cubed ham
6 quarts+ homemade chicken stock, or a good quality commercial brand, such as Better than Bouillon
1 quart heavy cream
Garnish of chopped fresh chives or green parts of green onions

Directions
1. Rinse beans; place them in a large stock pot, cover with water by 2 inches, and bring to a rolling boil; cover and remove from heat. Allow to soak for an hour. Drain.
2. In a large stock pan or Dutch oven, sauté the onions, celery, and carrots in the oil over medium-high heat until they soften, about 10 minutes.
3. Add the thyme, white pepper, ham bone, beans, and stock. Bring to a boil, reduce to a simmer.
4. Cook uncovered for about 2 hours, stirring occasionally, until the beans are soft. Add additional stock or water if needed.
5. Allow the soup to cool, and strain off all but ½ cup or so of the liquid.
6. In batches, purée the beans, vegetables, any pieces of ham that have fallen from the bone, and the cream in a blender until smooth.
7. At this point, the soup can be covered and refrigerated until ready to serve; simply reheat over medium until hot.
8. If you find that the soup seems too thick, add in some additional stock or cream. To serve, ladle in bowls and garnish with fresh chopped chives or scallions.
Serves 8 to 10 as a first course

I love sauerbraten, and this dish was adapted following a recipe found in Craig Claiborne's *New York Times Cookbook*. The richness of the chuck roast and the tartness of the red vinegar, when paired with the smoothness of the gravy, creates a delicious experience. Note that this dish requires an overnight marinade.

Sauerbraten

Ingredients
1 (4- to 5-pound) chuck roast
1 teaspoon kosher salt
½ teaspoon freshly ground black pepper
2 cups red wine vinegar
1 cup red onion, thinly sliced
2 large cloves garlic, thinly sliced
2 cups low-sodium beef stock
6 crushed allspice berries
2 bay leaves
⅓ cup light brown sugar
4 tablespoons olive oil
½ cup flour
1 cup sour cream

Directions
1. Sprinkle the beef on all sides with the salt and pepper. Set aside.
2. In a saucepan, bring the vinegar, onion, garlic, stock, allspice berries, bay leaves, and sugar to a boil. Remove from heat.
3. Place the roast inside a pot or container that can be covered tightly and pour the vinegar mixture over the beef. Cover and refrigerate overnight. If possible, turn the beef over a couple of times while it marinates.
4. Heat oven to 350 degrees.
5. Take meat from marinade and dry thoroughly with paper towels.
6. Heat oil on medium-high in a large Dutch oven. Dredge the beef in flour, place in the pan, and cook for 4 to 5 minutes per side, until dark brown on both sides.
7. Add the marinade to the Dutch oven. Cover and place in the oven. Cook for about 3 to 4 hours, until fork tender, but not falling apart.
8. Take beef from pot and slice on a cutting board into serving-size pieces. Place the slices on a serving platter or individual plates.

9. Remove the bay leaves from the liquid; whisk in the sour cream to make the creamed gravy. Pour gravy on top of beef and serve immediately, or cover, refrigerate, and reheat, uncovered, in a 350-degree oven.
Serves 8

While spätzle might be an obvious choice with sauerbraten, it is not easy to replicate at home for a large number of guests. A good substitute here are German egg noodles, such as Black Forest Girl brand.

German Noodles with Brown Butter and Parsley

Ingredients
2 (8-ounce) bags Black Forest Girl Extra Broad Original German Noodles
8 tablespoons (1 stick) butter
⅛ teaspoon freshly grated nutmeg
⅓ cup fresh parsley, chopped

Directions
1. Cook the noodles according to the instructions on the bag. Drain thoroughly, then add back to the pot you prepared them in.
2. In separate saucepan, whisk butter constantly over medium-high heat; after it foams, look for small particles of brown to start showing up in the bottom of the pan—immediately remove from heat. Be careful not to overcook.
3. Pour the butter over noodles, add nutmeg and parsley, toss, and serve immediately.
Serves 8

With this menu, I am going against one of my personal edicts—which is to not replicate flavors within the same course of a meal. I'm giving myself a mulligan, however, in pairing these two German classics, sauerbraten and braised red cabbage. You'll often find these two items side by side when dining at a German restaurant—and as the saying goes, when in Germany do as the Germans do. This red cabbage dish is one that I've developed over the years, adding in brown sugar, balsamic vinegar, and dried cherries.

Braised Red Cabbage

Ingredients
½ cup balsamic or sherry vinegar
½ cup dark brown sugar
1 cup red currant, lingonberry, or tart red plum jelly
½ teaspoon salt
2 bay leaves
4 allspice berries, crushed
1 large head of red cabbage, cored and thinly shredded (about 8 cups)
1½ cup dried tart cherries (frozen or fresh will work as well)

Directions
1. In large stockpot or Dutch oven, add the vinegar, sugar, jelly salt, bay leaves, and allspice berries; heat over medium-high heat until fully melted and hot.
2. Add the cabbage, stir, cover, and reduce to heat to medium-low.
3. Continue cooking for about 10 minutes, stirring occasionally. Add cherries, stir again.
4. Cook until the cabbage is soft and fully wilted, about 20 more minutes, stirring occasionally.
5. Remove from heat, discard bay leaves. Strain the juice from the pot. Serve immediately. If making in advance, cover and refrigerate. The cabbage can be reheated in a microwave oven, or stovetop.
Serves 8

The dessert, a dense and flavorful apple cake, finishes out the menu. The recipe is one received from my good 4-H friend Alice Yurke, originally from Rome, Georgia, and now of New York City. She lives on Park Avenue, and I tease her that every time I mail her something, *Green Acres* comes into my mind where Eva Gabor/Lisa Douglas sings, "Darling, I love you, but give me Park Avenue!" Alice is an attorney and also serves as the chancellor for the Episcopal Diocese of New York—besides being a great cook. Alice says the recipe is a legacy one from a friend's aunt from many decades ago.

I've changed the recipe a wee bit by not putting the walnuts in the cake but serving them on the side; that way I'm safeguarded from folks with a nut allergy when serving a large crowd—plus the arrangement provides for a nice crunchy texture against the moist cake. I also use brown sugar instead of regular, but either works.

Special Apple Cake

Ingredients
2 eggs
1 cup dark brown sugar
1 cup sugar
1¼ cup vegetable oil
3 cups all-purpose flour
½ teaspoon salt
1 teaspoon baking soda
1 teaspoon cinnamon
2 teaspoons vanilla extract
3 cups apples, peeled, cored, and diced
Sweet & Spiced Roasted Walnuts (recipe follows)
Whipped cream or vanilla ice cream
Pansies or fresh spearmint for garnish

Directions
1. Preheat oven to 350 degrees.
2. Over medium speed, beat eggs; add sugar and oil; beat this mixture 3 minutes.
3. Sift together dry ingredients; add to the beaten mixture. Mix well.
4. Add vanilla and apples and fold together to mix.
5. Place the batter in a greased and floured tube or Bundt pan; bake for 1 hour. Remove from oven and cool for 15 to 20 minutes. Invert onto cake plate.
6. To serve, place a large dollop of whipped cream on each slice of cake, scatter the plate with some of the walnuts, and garnish with the mint or flower.

Serves 8 to 10

Sweet & Spiced Roasted Walnuts

Ingredients
2 cups walnuts
3 tablespoons butter
3 tablespoons sugar
½ teaspoon cinnamon
¼ teaspoon freshly grated nutmeg
¼ teaspoon kosher salt

Directions
1. Preheat oven to 350 degrees.
2. Place walnuts in a large strainer and shake to sift off excess skins from the nuts and discard (the loose skins burn during baking and become bitter).
3. Melt butter; toss together with nuts and remaining ingredients. Place nuts in a single layer on a nonstick baking sheet; cook for 5 minutes; stir and toss well.
4. Cook another 7 to 8 minutes until lightly browned and cooked through. Store in an air-tight container after the nuts have cooled completely.

Makes 2 cups

Chapter 13

Fish Fries, Oyster Roasts, Low Country Boils, and Wild Game Dinners

One of the many attractions about living in the American South is our weather, which allows being outdoors in most regions a year-round option. And of the many ways we like to spend that time communing with Mother Nature—whether on the back porch, sitting under the canopy of a shady oak tree, or perched on a dock overlooking an expanse of water— is eating and entertaining. And four of the most popular venues to celebrate food and friendship outdoors in the sunny South include fish fries, oyster roasts, Low Country boils, and wild game dinners. Like many of you, I have some incredibly fond memories of these outdoor feasts, as well as the trips to the lake or out on a peanut field to bring the game home.

Fishing and hunting were a big part of my life growing up. My mother and father were known in three counties for their fishing abilities. I was given a cane pole and a rod and reel by the time I was three years old, so I learned how to fill a basket of fish at the knees of two fresh-water experts. Those times with Mama and Daddy are incredibly special to me; they taught me how to bait a hook and clean a fish as well as many life lessons the outdoors impart: the importance of patience—some things can't be rushed, and we have to wait for the right moments; the value of being a good steward—not only of my own possessions, such as our tackle, rods, and reels—but also of Mother Nature and the world around us; and how to enjoy the company of loved ones and friends—even in silence and stillness.

I know many ladies who are wonderful hunters, but my mom did not enjoy that sport, so the hunting times were just me and my dad. While I enjoyed being out in a peanut field with him in dove season or in the wetlands of Middle Georgia hunting for ducks, I think my favorite part was the ritual of cleaning the guns. I like structure and planning, so the predictable rituals, with the smell of the oil and feel of the well-used cloths, were especially appealing to me.

It was during those fishing and hunting trips—as I grew into my late teens and early twenties—that my mom and dad went from being my parents to becoming my friends. I say this often, but, oh, how I miss them both. I don't hunt any longer and have given my shotguns to my nephew and his son, but I still fish—just not as often as I'd like. I'll without shame tell you that there are many times I'm sitting on the dock, or out in the boat, line in the water, with tears streaming down my cheeks. It is there, during those quiet moments, that the memories of Mama and Daddy come back so clearly.

As I blow my nose and move along, let me say that an entire book could be written about just cooking fish, seafood, and wild game—and here I am limited in space and pages—so I'll try to hit the high points in each area. I'm not including any recipes for venison. While I shot and ate fowl, I was never a fan of deer hunting. Frankly, I'm not that crazy about the taste, so I've not mastered how to cook the meat.

FISH FRIES

Let's start with the fish fries. This was one of my parent's favorite ways to entertain, and my mother could turn these fish out in a hurry—using two deep, cast iron skillets simultaneously. In cold weather, we'd eat inside (unlike the oyster roast, but more on that later), but during the summer the favored spot was our picnic table in the side yard under the shade of an ancient live oak tree. The only variation in the menu would be the type of fish we'd be eating: catfish? bluegill? white perch? mullet with fresh roe? The side dishes usually served would be coleslaw, hush puppies, grits, or fried potatoes, and some griddle-cooked hoecakes with cane syrup. Mama could feed twelve folks out of those two frying pans in record time and without breaking a sweat.

Now a lot of fish-frying enthusiasts, such as my buddy Mike Giles, have turned to mega-cookers that you can use at home. I've known Mike since we were young'uns back in Middle Georgia—his uncle Bill Giles was married to my first cousin, Joyce Owens, the daughter of my Aunt Lil you've read so much about in my books. Mike is one of the finest fellows you'd ever meet, and I have the pleasure of working with him in his role as president of the Georgia Poultry Federation. Mike and I are both Rotarians as well, and he recently purchased two new cookers—each which can fry enough fish to feed thirty-five to forty folks at one time—so he could be host chef for the Rotary Club of Gainesville's annual fish fry. He includes a grits bar at the feast, where guests have their choices of a dozen or so toppings such as shredded cheese, milk gravy, green onions, and—the pièce de resistance—sautéed shrimp.

Another fish-frying enthusiast friend is my buddy Janis Owens, who provided the strawberry pretzel salad recipe (see index). She has an entire chapter in her native Florida cookbook treasury, *The Cracker Kitchen*, on fish fries. In it she tells, with great humor and much affection, about her husband, daddy, and brothers, and their love of fishing in the beautiful panhandle of the Sunshine State. In the chapter she also shares a side-splitting story of her scruffy ten-year-old brother who had an adventure with nail polish. Now what in the world do nail polish and fish fries have to do with one another? Nothing at all, but that is the way we Southerners tell a story—which usually includes a series of tales that make up the sum total.

Now going around my ass to get to my elbow in relating this chapter, nail polish did have something to do with fishing and hunting growing up for me—and it wasn't in a decorative sense. How many of you all got red-bugs—also called chiggers—from a trip to the creek or woods? And where would those damn little pests end up? Yep, down there behind the zipper line and latched into the skin that was held in place by your Fruit of the Looms. Daddy's solution to killing those itchy little bastards was clear nail polish dotted on each red blotch. He said it would suffocate them. Too much information? Hey, if you grew up in the South and ever spent any time outside, you got chiggers. And you probably got the nail polish treatment as well!

So now finally arriving at my elbow, let me share my simple fried fish recipe. This way of cooking fish is one my great-grandmother, grandmother, and mother all followed. I've jazzed it up some by including Old Bay seasoning, but that is the only change I made. And I still have and use my grandmother's deep-dish cast iron skillet she got when she married…in 1916. It cooks a helluva cobbler, too, which I shared in the Summer Holidays chapter.

Southern Fried Pan Fish
(also can be used for shrimp or oysters)

Ingredients
3 cups self-rising White Lily or Martha White cornbread mix, either yellow or white*
1 teaspoon salt
½ teaspoon black pepper
6 large or 12 small fresh pan fish, such as channel cats, bream, or perch
2 teaspoons Old Bay seasoning
3 cups or so peanut oil
* *You can also use commercial fish-fry or seafood mixes from such brands as Louisiana; just be careful of the sodium content. If you choose to use a packaged mix, skip the salt and Old Bay in the recipe here.*

Directions
1. In a shallow bowl, mix the cornbread mix, salt, and black pepper. Set aside.
2. Rinse the fish under cold water and drain well. Do not pat dry. Sprinkle the fish, whether whole or in filets, evenly with the Old Bay.
3. Dredge each piece of fish in the cornmeal mix; shake off excess flour. Set aside on a rack. This can be done in advance; just refrigerate until ready to cook.
4. Place a large cast iron or other heavy-bottomed skillet appropriate for frying over medium-high heat. Pour in oil to a depth of 2 inches and heat until hot.
5. Place fish in the oil, being careful not to crowd the pan. Brown evenly, turning once; the cooking time should be 2 to 3 minutes per side, depending on thickness of the fish.
6. Place the fried fish on a wire rack or a pan lined with paper towels; if cooking the fish in batches, place the fish in a warm oven as you take them out of the oil. Serve immediately.
Serves 6

To go along with the fried fish, there are two sauces I like to serve: cocktail sauce and tartar sauce. You can find my recipe for cocktail sauce later in the next chapter on tailgating. In *Rise and Shine!* I shared my Aunt Hazel's tartar sauce recipe. To provide some variety for my readers, here is another stellar recipe for this tangy condiment. It comes from my friend Fran Ivey Lemmen; a 4-H friend from forty-plus years ago. Originally from the small town of Wrightsville, Georgia, Fran tells me that her mother, Miss Frances, loved to fish, and the following recipe for her tartar sauce was always on the table when the catfish came out of the pan.

Mrs. Ivey's Tartar Sauce

Ingredients
1½ cups Duke's mayonnaise
2 tablespoons white vinegar
¼ cup Vidalia onions, minced
¼ cup dill pickles, minced
2 teaspoons fresh dill, minced (or 1 teaspoon dried dill)

Directions
1. Mix all ingredients together in a bowl until well blended.
2. Cover tightly and refrigerate 4 to 6 hours or overnight.
Makes 2 cups (8 servings)

In all the households I knew growing up, a big pot of creamy grits always accompanied fried fish. Now sometimes Mama would cook home fries—sliced white potatoes that were tossed in a bit of oil, seasoned with salt, pepper, and garlic salt, and roasted—but on most occasions we had grits. We'd also have grits with fried and smothered doves and quail, which I'll get to later in this chapter.

You can dress grits up in a variety of ways by adding cheese, sautéed Vidalia onions, bits of crisp bacon—you can also add an egg or two and bake as a casserole. Here I'm providing just the basics on how to get a good pot of this Southern staple. I do have three rules, though: first, do not, under any condition, no matter what someone tells you, add sugar to your grits. Second, and this is just as important as the first rule, do *not* use instant grits. Sugar and instant grits are just plain blasphemous, period. Third, make certain to salt the liquid in which you cook your grits; the dish simply won't turn out properly if you try and season them after they are cooked. Trust me on all three of these rules. Seriously.

And while there are many gourmet small-batch stone-ground grits on the market, such as Nora Mills or Marsh Hen Mills (formerly known as Geechee Boy), you can turn to Jim Dandy, Martha White, or Quaker for fine results as well. Yellow or white you ask? Either works as well as the other. I also cook my grits in a double boiler; it takes a bit longer, but it keeps me from getting splattered by hot hominy—it is sometimes hard to get the right temperature to just barely simmer—and I believe it turns out a creamier result.

Creamy Grits

Ingredients
1½ cups water
1½ cups whole milk
1 teaspoon salt
1½ cups regular or stone-ground grits
2 tablespoons butter
¼ to ½ teaspoon black pepper

Directions
1. Place the water, milk, salt, and grits in the top of a double boiler; stir well and place it over boiling water.
2. Cook for 20 to 30 minutes until soft, stirring occasionally. If cooking stone-ground grits, the timing will be somewhat longer. Follow the instructions on the grits package. As you continue cooking, add additional milk a bit at a time if the grits become too thick.
3. When finished, stir in the butter until melted, and add the black pepper. Serve immediately.

Serves 6 to 8

Hush puppies are de rigueur as well as grits at any fish fry. There are many commercial brands that can save you time and dirty dishes—such as Savannah Classics out of Savannah, Tennessee, which is my favorite. But homemade are best, and if you are willing to fry more food after you finish with the fish, here is my mom's outstanding recipe. Make the hush puppy dough in advance and chill; once the fish are cooked, drop the puppies in the oil used with the fish and they will cook up quickly.

Joyce's Hush Puppies

Ingredients
1½ cups self-rising White Lily or Martha White cornmeal mix, either yellow or white
½ cup self-rising flour
½ teaspoon baking soda
1 large egg, beaten
1 cup whole-milk buttermilk
1 cup onion, minced
Peanut or vegetable oil

Directions
1. In a large bowl mix the corn meal, flour, and soda.
2. In another bowl, whisk together the egg and buttermilk; stir into the dry mixture until just mixed.
3. Stir in the onion.
4. Using a tablespoon, dip out the batter and with floured hands shape into a ball. Place each hush puppy on a nonstick cookie sheet or on a piece of wax paper. Chill for 1 hour.
5. Using the pan in which your fish were cooked, add oil (if needed) to a depth of 2 inches. Heat the oil over medium-high. When the oil is hot, drop the chilled dough into the grease; cook for 2 minutes or so on one side until browned. *Do not overcrowd the pan; the hush puppies should have a good inch of space between them.* Turn over and cook another 2 minutes or so until the second side is browned. Remove with a slotted spoon or spatula to a rack. Serve immediately.
Makes 16 hush puppies and serves 8 people

Along with the hush puppies and grits, coleslaw is another "must have" on this menu. And slaw, like other salads, can be made differently to complement whatever entrée is being served. The oniony slaw Beverly Smith offers up in her chapter is excellent with fried chicken. For a fish fry, I like a bit sweeter slaw with a finer grind of cabbage. When I was a child, Carrie would make this slaw by grating the cabbage by hand on a box shredder. Thank goodness for the modern kitchen amenities such as Cuisinart!

Fish Fry Coleslaw

Ingredients
8 cups cabbage, finely ground or shredded (about a 2-pound head)
¼ cup sweet pickles, diced
¾ cup mayonnaise
2 tablespoons sugar
¼ to ½ teaspoon salt (to taste)
¼ teaspoon black pepper

Directions
1. In a large mixing bowl, stir together well all ingredients.
2. Place in an airtight container and refrigerate 4 to 6 hours or overnight. Stir before serving.
Serves 6 to 8

Now the dessert offering here would not be seen anywhere outside of the Deep South: buttered hoecakes with cane syrup. For those not from this part of the country, hoecakes are basically flat biscuits cooked on top of the stove. And like the deep-dish cast iron fryer I use for my fish, I have as well Ninnie's iron griddle that has seen many a hoecake and fried lacy cornbread patty over the decades.

Ninnie's Hoecakes

Ingredients
2 cups self-rising flour, sifted with a ¼ teaspoon salt
2 tablespoons chilled butter, cut into ¼-inch cubes
3 tablespoons Crisco
⅔ cup whole-milk buttermilk
Additional butter for topping
Pure cane syrup

Directions
1. In a large mixing bowl, add in the flour, butter, and Crisco. With your hands, fork, or pastry cutter, blend the ingredients together until the consistency of pea gravel.
2. Add the buttermilk and stir gently with a fork until just mixed together.
3. Using a spatula, turn out the dough onto a floured surface. Gently roll the dough to ½-inch thickness, then cut with a small biscuit cutter, and set the discs aside.

4. Heat a seasoned griddle, nonstick pan or skillet, over medium heat. When hot, place the hoecakes in the pan; don't overcrowd so to allow room to flip them over. Cook for 3 to 4 minutes, enough time for them to turn a golden brown. Turn once and brown the second side. You may need to cook these in 2 batches depending on the size of your griddle.
5. When done, serve with butter and cane syrup. A glass of cold milk is good, too!

Serves 8 to 10

OYSTER ROASTS

Oyster roasts are an art form in the South, both in terms of culinary as well as social enjoyment. From the coast of Virginia down to Louisiana, and spreading inland, an invitation to an oyster roast is a much sought-after acknowledgment of friendship and a delicious way to spend a cold winter afternoon. I've been to many that were in celebration of a birthday or anniversary, to raise money for charity, or for no reason at all except that some gracious host wanted to treat friends to this bounty of the sea. Several years back, I recall that Tom and I were invited to five roasts over one December weekend alone. And in cities such as Savannah, the setting is often dressed up for the occasion. I attended one such roast just before Christmas in the gardens of the historic and elegant Alida Harper Fowlkes House. On the long, waist-high shucking tables, the hostess had placed red and green plaid wool runners topped with magnolia, cedar, pine, and citrus centerpieces. It was a memorable setting in all senses of the word.

While the setting—and guests—may be decked out in winter finery, the food at these gatherings is simple and straightforward: roasted oysters, saltines, slices of lemon, and a few dipping choices, including cocktail sauce, Tabasco, and melted butter. A conscientious party-giver will look after the few poor guests who either are allergic to the bivalves or just plain don't eat them (bless their hearts) and will include perhaps a charcuterie of savory meats and some stout cheeses, or even maybe a pot of chili that is left simmering on a side table. But the star of the show is the oyster, and I can stand and eat a few dozen without breaking stride—except to refill my cocktail glass upon occasion.

Some of the most memorable and wonderful roasts I've attended have been with Elizabeth Oxnard and her late husband, Ben, at their home in

McIntosh County just south of Savannah. The extensive property sits on a bend in the Sapelo River with a raised Low Country–style cottage as the centerpiece. With a tin roof and framed on three sides by an enormous covered porch—with a ceiling painted "haint blue"—the white clapboard house boasts a view of one of the most beautiful expanses of marsh in the Southeast.

The interior is comfortably and unpretentiously decorated (Tom was the designer, wink, wink) and includes spacious entertaining areas and multiple bedrooms for overnight company. I like to point out to first-time visitors, if I happen to be in their company, a unique piece of art, which is an antique hand-drawn map showing the main sugar cane plantations along the Mississippi River in Louisiana. Ben was the former president and CEO of Savannah Foods and Industries, which owned Dixie Crystals, and he had a rich history in that region of the South. Elizabeth is from an old Mobile family and together they were two of the most gracious people I've ever met. Ben literally would give you the sweater off his back, which he did for me once at one of their oyster roasts. It was a cold January day, and, being hot-natured (I can break into a sweat walking across the living room), I didn't account for the wet, cold breeze blowing off the river. Seeing me uncomfortable, Ben put down his big cigar, pulled off his thick cable-knit sweater, and said, "Here, Johnathon. Warm up, bud." *What* a gentleman.

On any trip down to the Oxnard compound you'll see a menagerie of dogs running the property. Elizabeth has a heart bigger than Savannah, and folks in her neck of the woods have learned that she cannot turn away a stray. One-eared, three-legged, and from mutts to thoroughbreds, she is Mama to many. One of my favorite scenes from visits with the Oxnards was seeing Donah, the bloodhound, and Ootie, the otter, at play. Ootie lived in a culvert on the river that fronted the property. She would come up into the yard, find Donah, who would allow the otter to clamp her jaws and front paws around the loose, drooping skin folds of her neck. All set in place, Donah would then drag the otter from one end of the yard to the other, howling in fun. Now *that* was a sight. Elizabeth treats these pups like children, too. Tom and I let ourselves into the house one afternoon for a weekend trip, and, walking into the kitchen, we could detect a wonderful smell wafting into the air. Making myself at home, I went to the stove and stirred a big pot of what looked like chicken stew. Elizabeth strolled into the room and gave us a hug. I said, "Hey, hon. I stirred the stew for you. It smells delicious. I thought we were going to take you out for dinner tonight, though. You didn't have to cook." Elizabeth raised an arched eyebrow—a look she is known for, and it can be good sign or a bad one—and pointed to the aromatic pot I was admiring. "That," she said, "is for the dogs." As my mama would've said, "Well, I guess those dogs rate, don't they?"

Oyster roasts at the Oxnards are done in the traditional way—with a shallow pit dug into the ground in which to build a fire of hardwoods. On each of the four corners of the pit are stacked cement blocks that hold up a heavy metal grate. Oysters are scooped into a wide metal oyster (or clam) basket shaped like a shovel, spread in one layer onto the grate, and then covered with damp burlap bags. The mollusks cook under the heat and steam; they are done when their shells *just* start to open. The oysters are then scooped back up and placed directly on the serving tables for the guests to line up and enjoy.

Building a fire pit isn't an option for everyone, so let me share a couple of other ways you might go about hosting your own oyster roast. First, there is always the option of having it catered, which I generally do. The professionals come in with their industrial sized wood-fire oyster roasters and heavy bushels of oysters, and then they take away all of those bulky shells: no set up, no clean up, easy-breezy. However, for those of you who would like to have several roasts throughout the season, there are any number of home-sized oyster roasters on the market. I've run across pro-pane-powered steamers that can cook a half bushel at a time for about three hundred dollars. From there the price can increase to larger pieces and include roasters designed to use wood as the heating source so that you get that wonderful smell and flavor, but they are upwards of several thousand dollars.

Other equipment you'll need includes thick cloth gloves—oyster shells are extremely sharp and can make a nasty cut—and an oyster-shucking knife for each guest. These knives have a short, sturdy blade and are made especially for the task of opening the oyster. Some people are very,

very serious about their shucking utensils and will bring their own to the party. I've seen custom-made knives selling for $250 or more. However, you can find inexpensive ones for about five bucks a pop.

Shucking an oyster isn't difficult—particularly if the oyster is cooked correctly—but it does take a bit of practice. The most common method is to hold the roasted oyster, cupped side up, in one gloved hand, and then pry the hinge of the oyster with the knife. Twist and turn until the shell pops open. Remove the top shell and discard, keeping the oyster resting in the bottom half. Wipe your blade if there is any grit or debris on it, and then look for the muscle that attaches the oyster to the shell. Carefully slice the muscle loose without cutting into the oyster. Top the oyster with some cocktail sauce, or drawn butter, and then plop that baby right into your mouth. Some people like to place theirs on a saltine cracker before eating; it's your choice.

What I have done, when not hosting a full-blown roast with a caterer, is roast oysters as an appetizer for a party. I fire up the gas grill, get some wood chips smoking well, place the oysters directly on the grate, and close the lid until done. The timing depends on the size of the oyster; again, you want them to cook until the shells open slightly, about 6 to 10 minutes. When you shuck the oyster, there needs to be just a bit of hot juice still inside the shell. And let me emphasize that if you overcook an oyster, there is no way to undo the damage.

In terms of the amount and type of oysters, usual estimates hold that one bushel will feed about five people. With my appetite I really, really skew that statistic, but for most folks that is a good number. If you are preparing them as an appetizer, I'd count out eight to ten oysters per person.

As far as what kind of oyster, my preference is the larger varieties simply because of the effort involved in shucking. Some of the fattest and tastiest that I've sampled—they were like taking a big, sweet gulp of the sea—were ones that came from Damariscotta, Maine. The others I've tried, from the Chesapeake Bay down to Bluffton, South Carolina, and then over to Apalachicola, Florida, and into the Louisiana estuaries, were delicious as well. My best advice is to follow what your local seafood purveyor recommends.

In summary, for an oyster roast, you will need

- a caterer; or
- a two-foot-deep fire pit, grate, aromatic hardwood, concrete blocks, flat-end shovel, and burlap bags; or
- an oyster roaster, either propane or made for wood;
- one bushel of fresh oysters—that have been thoroughly rinsed and cleaned—for every five guests;
- cloth gloves;
- oyster shucking knives;
- condiments of cocktail sauce (see index), drawn butter, Tabasco, and saltines;
- something for the non-oyster-eating guests to nosh on; and
- an open bar featuring the usual choices as well as a variety of pilsner beers and dry white wines.

Another recommendation for hosting an oyster roast is a waist-high table for your guests. It is much easier to stand, rather than be seated, as you leverage that stubby knife into the oyster shell.

LOW COUNTRY BOILS

While oyster roasts are prolific in the colder months, Low Country boils are an extremely popular way to entertain and celebrate with friends from spring through the fall when shrimp are usually in season. Named for the region of the South where they were started, the coastal areas of Georgia and South Carolina, these boils are a great and easy way to feed a crowd. Like a roast, you'll see these parties thrown for a variety of reasons; they are a favored way to celebrate a graduation, engagement, or anniversary. For those of you who aren't familiar with these one-pot seafood wonders, a Low Country boil is a combination of shrimp, fresh corn on the cob, spicy smoked sausage, and little red potatoes. Most always the shrimp are served without being shelled, so a good portion of the meal is eaten by hand; it can get messy, and I've seen a number of hosts provide guests with bibs to wear and wet cloths to wipe their hands. My friend Dale Thorpe in Savannah would put out bowls of soapy water and towels for her guests when giving an oyster roast or shrimp boil.

In Mama and Daddy's backyard, getting ready
to go cane-pole fishing, summer 1968

With my dear friend, the late Amy Swann,
at Pinewood Christian Academy's Prom, Claxton, 1981

The menu for a Low Country boil isn't extensive and can be kept simple. Start one off with platters of bite-sized pimento cheese and tomato sandwiches (see index) along with, yes, you guessed it, an open bar. Ice cold beer is a favorite for boiled shrimp, so make sure you have plenty on hand. Favorite side dishes include coleslaw and hush puppies—see my recipes earlier in this chapter—as well as a big dish of Savannah red rice, a dish that is baked with tomatoes, onions, and spices (recipe follows). Don't fuss too much with dessert; folks will have already "had a gracious plenty," as Carrie would say, when that last shrimp has been peeled. A tray of ice cream sandwiches or Eskimo pies fits the bill.

Note that for a small crowd, these boils can be cooked on a kitchen stove or burner of a gas grill. The amount you can fix depends on the size of your pot, or if you can get two pots going at the same time. *Or*, you can invest in an outdoor propane fryer and boiler, which can easily cook upwards of thirty-five pounds of shrimp, sausage, corn, and potatoes; there are dozens on the market for sale.

My multi-talented cooking and journalistic friend Amy Swann introduced me to a Low Country boil as a teenager. In Perry our shrimp were either fried—like you would a fish—or served chilled as an appetizer with cocktail sauce. Amy and I met through 4-H and began a lifetime friendship of fun, shenanigans, and adventure. We would dress up in our plaid madras and hit all the old hotspots in Savannah on the weekend. The night would start at Palmer's out on Wilmington Island; we'd then swing by the Rain Forest bar at the Pirates' House for a Tom Collins, and then scoot on down to Night Flight to listen to some visiting band, do a bit of disco dancing up at Malone's, and shag about with some Carolina beach music at W.G. Shucker's.

All of those places are gone now, as is Amy. She departed this life way too early, at the age of fifty-three, from a hereditary pulmonary disease. And while she started her college career in home economics, she ended up with a degree in journalism and was a renowned reporter, winning multiple UPI awards, as well as providing the popular gossip column for the *Savannah Morning News*, "City Beat." I dedicated my last book to Amy and wrote under the photo of the two of us, dressed to go out dancing in Myrtle Beach, "*Cook & Tell* is dedicated in loving memory to Amy Allyn

Swann (1963–2016). That girl could cook up a storm and straight tell a story. And while she was from the small town of Claxton, Georgia, it seemed as if the whole world loved her. She was a once-in-a-lifetime friend." With her gone, it is literally like a piece of me is missing. May God rest her soul and let light perpetual shine upon her.

Here is her stellar Low Country Boil recipe. Make sure to use pork sausage— no chicken or turkey, thank you, ma'am—and don't skimp on that butter at the end. Fattening? Yes. Delicious? Absodamnlutely.

Amy's Low Country Boil

Ingredients
8 tablespoons (1 stick) butter, melted and divided
1½ cups Vidalia onion, chopped coarsely
1 cup Old Bay Seasoning, divided
2 pounds pork smoked sausage, cut into 3-inch slices
8 small ears of corn, or 4 large ears cut in half, shucked and silked
24 small, red new potatoes of equal size, boiled and fully cooked in salted water
2½ pounds large, fresh, wild-caught USA shrimp, heads off

Directions
1. In a large stock pot or Dutch oven over medium-high heat add ½ cup of butter and the onion; stir, cooking for 2 to 3 minutes until the onions soften. Do not allow to brown.
2. Fill the pot half full with water; pour in ½ cup of the Old Bay. Bring to a boil.
3. Add the sausage and reduce heat to a slight, gentle boil and cook for 10 minutes.
4. Add in the corn and cook, again at a gentle boil, for 5 minutes.
5. Turn the heat back up to a full boil and drop in the potatoes and shrimp. Cook 4 to 6 minutes, depending on size of the shrimp. When done, the tail end of the shrimp has curled up to the head area and is pink.
6. Pour the stew into a colander and drain. Then place the all the ingredients back into the pot, or in a large serving tray/bowl. Pour in the remaining butter and Old Bay, toss well, and serve.

Serves 8

An excellent accompaniment with the Low Country boil is Savannah red rice; it also pairs well with fried fish, roasted or fried chicken, or a variety of other entrées. My recipe is a go-to adapted from *Savannah Style: A Cookbook by the Junior League of Savannah*.

Savannah Red Rice

Ingredients
¼ pound bacon
1 cup onion, diced
½ cup green bell pepper, diced
½ cup celery, diced
2 cups regular white rice, uncooked (*not* instant)
2 (16-ounce) cans chopped tomatoes
2 teaspoons salt
¼ teaspoon black pepper
¼ teaspoon Tabasco

Directions
1. Preheat oven to 350 degrees.
2. In a large frying pan or Dutch oven, fry the bacon until crisp. Set the bacon aside to cool.
3. Add the onion, bell pepper, and celery to the pan and cook over medium heat, stirring occasionally, for 3 minutes or so, until the vegetables start to become tender.
4. Add the rice, tomatoes along with the juice from the cans, bacon (which you have crumbled), and seasonings. Bring the temperature up to a steady simmer and cook for 10 minutes, stirring occasionally.
5. Pour the mixture into a large, greased casserole dish, cover tightly, and bake for 1 hour.
6. To serve, remove from the oven and allow to sit for 5 minutes. Remove lid, fluff the rice, and serve.

Serves 8

Another 4-H friend of mine that likes to cook is Amy Monroe Denty of Jesup, Georgia. I came to know this Amy, too, at Rock Eagle back when we were in our early teens. Amy met her husband at Camp Jekyll, another 4-H Center. She tells me that, after her introduction to him at the beach and speaking with him for about ten minutes, she remarked to a mutual friend, "I will probably end up married to Eric!" Three years later they tied the knot. Eric is the publisher of the local paper in Wayne County, and Amy has a stellar career as an educator, being named Georgia Teacher of the Year in 2000. She and Eric host oyster roasts—with a fire pit—and Low Country boils. She shared with me a scrumptious way to use any leftovers from a shrimp boil: you make it into a chowder! Served with hot, crusty bread it makes for a wonderful meal for the next day. Here is her recipe.

Low Country Boil Chowder

Ingredients
4 tablespoons (¼ cup) butter
2 tablespoons flour
1 quart chicken broth
1 teaspoon Old Bay Seasoning (or more to taste)
½ teaspoon black pepper
1 quart or more leftover Low Country boil; the corn should be cut from the cob, and the shrimp, sausage, and potatoes chopped into ½-inch pieces, with the shrimp separated out
1 cup heavy cream
Crusty bread or saltine crackers

Directions
1. In a large pot, melt the butter over medium-high heat; whisk in the flour. Cook 2 to 3 minutes, whisking continuously, to make a roux.
2. Slowly whisk in the chicken broth, stirring until well-mixed. Allow this to cook at a steady simmer for about 5 minutes, until thickened, stirring occasionally.
3. Add the Old Bay, black pepper, and country boil ingredients except the shrimp. Stir well, and allow to cook, over a low simmer, for about 5 minutes until heated through.
4. Stir in the cream and chopped shrimp. Allow the mixture to heat through and become hot, but do not bring to boil. Serve immediately in warm bowls and with crusty bread or saltines.

Serves 4 to 6

Wild Game Dinners

While the American South doesn't have the entire market on hunting, we do take our marksmanship seriously, particularly when it comes to a variety of fowl, deer, and boar. My father was an excellent shot, and his abilities to bring home his limit from a dove shoot or quail hunt is still remarked upon to this day. My childhood buddy back in Perry—the fishing and cooking guru Tim Swearinger—remarked to me just the other day that "your dad was an *awesome* shooter." And Daddy passed away more than a quarter of a century ago.

The bounty of these hunts is prepared in many kitchens and restaurants across the South. Quail and venison in particular are featured on the menus of any number of renowned establishments, both big and small, such as my favorites Daphne's Lodge at Lake Blackshear, Georgia, where you can still get quail (or catfish, or shrimp, or oysters) fried to perfection, or at Frank Stitt's outstanding Highlands Bar & Grill in Birmingham, where he presents a succulent grilled quail served with butternut squash and dried fig risotto.

Too, celebratory events and fundraisers have sprung up using the bounty of the South's fields, forests, and streams—and most famous that comes to mind for me is the wild game dinner held each year to benefit the Coastal Georgia Botanical Gardens at the Historic Bamboo Farm just outside of Savannah. A division of the University of Georgia's College of Agricultural and Environmental Sciences Cooperative Extension (which I proudly work for!) this fifty-two–acre site is open to the public and includes walking paths through a variety of display gardens and collections, as well a fishing pond and educational center. The lovely and talented Pat Hackney, a former 4-H agent and home economist—and good friend of mine—started the wild game event in 1996. Having seen many wild game dinners sell for big bucks—tongue in cheek—at several charity auctions, Pat felt that people would be more than willing to pay to come to such a public dinner, and she was correct. An incredible cook and fundraiser, Pat called on several of her fellow board members at the Friends of the Coastal Gardens and their friends to donate the game, and she and other volunteers cooked the meal. The first dinners were limited to fried quail, grits, biscuits, winter salad, and lime cooler pie. Over the years the menu has expanded to include venison, duck, pheasant, gator, wild boar, fried fish, and assorted sides. This major dining production has raised well over a million dollars since its inception and sells out every February when held. To say the event is popular is an understatement.

The following recipes are for fowl only; there are many cookbooks and websites that can assist you with venison or boar—or any other variety of wild game. On a note here: while many of you have access to wild dove, quail, duck, and pheasant, just as many or more probably do not. However, a number of grocers stock such birds these days, and you can easily order them from online purveyors, such as D'artagnan, Manchester Farms, or Texas Quail Farms. And the great thing about purchasing them is the birds can arrive already deboned or with just the breast portion—the meatiest part of the bird.

If your doves or quail don't come boned, I suggest you clip off their wings and spatchcock them—being careful not to tear the breast skin—so that they lie flat and cook more evenly. This method is simple, and there are many online videos that can guide you through the process more clearly than I can write it out.

For the recipes here, I'm going to the basics of a few dishes. Following what Pat made at the first of her fundraising dinners, and like my mom's favorite way to present quail and dove, I'll start with the pan-fried method. This dish is best served with a side of creamy grits (see recipe earlier in this chapter), or a bowl of rice, along with baby butter beans (recipe follows), and a homemade biscuit (see index). With the main recipe are two variations: smothering the birds with gravy or cooking them in a stew with rice.

Fried Quail and Doves Basic Recipe

Ingredients
8 fully dressed, spatchcocked or deboned quail or doves (or breast portions)
2 cups whole-milk buttermilk
4 teaspoons Lawry's Seasoning Salt (or kosher salt), divided
2 teaspoons black pepper, divided
2 cups flour
Peanut or vegetable oil

Directions
1. Place the birds and buttermilk in a zip-lock bag or large pan. Refrigerate 4 to 6 hours.
2. Remove the birds from the bag and drain each bird well. Season the birds on both sides evenly with 2 teaspoons of the Lawry's and 1 teaspoon black pepper.
3. In a bowl, mix together the flour and remaining Lawry's and black pepper. Dredge the birds in the flour mixture; shake off excess flour. Place the birds

on a cookie sheet or other flat pan and set aside. (Save the leftover flour if you plan on making gravy.)

3. In a large frying pan, or Dutch oven, pour in oil to a depth of 1 inch. Heat the oil over medium to medium-high until a bit of flour will sizzle when dropped into the pan. Fry the birds in batches, not crowding the pan, 3 to 4 minutes per side or until a rich, golden brown. Set the cooked birds on a wire rack over a baking pan and place the batches in a warm oven to keep until the last of the birds are finished. Serve immediately.

Serves 4 to 8, depending on size of the bird and how hungry your crowd is!

Smothered Quail or Dove

Ingredients
Cooked birds from the basic recipe above
2 tablespoons butter, at room temperature
¼ cup flour (leftover from dredging)
2 cups low-sodium chicken stock

Directions
1. Preheat oven to 350 degrees. Grease a 9x13 baking dish with the butter.
2. Keep 3 to 4 tablespoons of the oil from the pan you cooked the birds in with the basic recipe and return it to medium-high heat. Add in the flour, and stir, scraping all of the browned bits from the bottom of the pan.
3. Whisk in the chicken stock. Allow the gravy to thicken, whisking occasionally, 4 to 5 minutes.
4. Pour half the gravy into a large baking dish. Place the cooked birds, breast-side up, on top of the gravy, all in one layer if possible, and pour the remaining gravy on top, covering all the birds. (The dish can be made in advance to this point, covered, and refrigerated until ready to finish.)
5. Bake, covered, for an hour. Remove cover and continue to cook another 20 minutes. Remove from oven and serve.

Serve 4 to 8

The next way to cook up wild fowl comes from my friend Ann Freeman, who provided the Copper Pennies recipe in the Easter chapter. Ann's father, Cleve, an entomologist for the department of agriculture, was the official cook for his hunting club near their hometown of Claxton. Ann relayed that her father was an avid fisherman and hunter, and their freezers were always full of fresh fish and game. Her father was also in charge of family Sunday and holiday dinners, and his technique for dishes was to glance at a recipe, and then go by taste, smell, and consistency. I would have loved to have met Mr. Cleve!

Quail or Dove Baked with Rice

Ingredients
8 tablespoons (1 stick) butter, divided and at room temperature
1 cup regular white rice (not instant)
1¾ cups low-sodium chicken stock
¼ cup heavy cream
Cooked birds from the basic recipe

Directions
1. Preheat oven to 350 degrees.
2. Grease a 9x13 baking dish with 3 tablespoons of butter and set aside.
3. Drain all but 1 or 2 tablespoons of the oil from the frying pan you cooked the birds in and return to medium-high heat.
4. Add the rice and stir to coat the grains in the oil. Make sure to scrape up any of the browned bits of flour or bird from the pan.
5. Whisk in first the chicken stock and then the cream; bring to a full, steady simmer.
6. Ladle the rice and broth into the buttered baking dish and then place the fried birds on top, breast-side up. Place a slice of butter on each of the birds.
7. Cover the pan tightly and bake for 1 hour. Remove from the oven, carefully remove the covering, and fluff the rice with a fork before serving.
Serves 4 to 8

The following recipe is a bit more dressed-up than what Mama and Mr. Cleve would make, but it's not complicated. I found this gem in my copy of *Four Great Southern Cooks*—which is out of print, and if you look to find one for sale, be prepared to pay a pretty penny. But for a die-hard Southern host or hostess, this 1980 collection of recipes is a treasure. The book provides the background stories and favorite dishes of four extraordinary chefs; the one I'm writing of here is from Miss Ruth Jenkins, originally from the small town of Thomson, Georgia. Miss Ruth was a renowned cook for an Atlanta and Highlands, North Carolina, family—and apparently folks lined up to learn her culinary secrets. I did modify a few of the ingredients and steps to reflect a little bit of "how Mama would've done it."

Roasted Quail with Wine & Mushrooms

Ingredients
8 fully dressed, spatchcocked or deboned quail (or breast portions)
1 teaspoon kosher salt, divided
½ teaspoon black pepper, divided
4 tablespoons butter
2 cups fresh mushrooms, sliced
¼ cup Vidalia onions, diced
¼ cup celery, diced
2 tablespoons flour
½ cup dry vermouth or dry white wine
½ cup low-sodium chicken stock
1 teaspoon fresh thyme (or ½ teaspoon dried)

Directions
1. Preheat oven to 350 degrees. Lightly grease a large baking dish and set aside.
2. Pat the quail dry and season with half the salt and black pepper. Set aside.
3. Melt the butter in a skillet over medium heat. Add the mushrooms and sauté for about 2 minutes. Add the onions and celery and continue cooking, stirring occasionally, until the vegetables begin to soften, 2 to 3 minutes.
4. Add the flour to the pan and stir together well with the sautéed items. Cook for 1 minute.
5. Stir in the vermouth and stock and stir to mix well. Cook for 3 to 4 minutes until thickened. Stir in the thyme and remaining salt and black pepper. Remove from heat and set aside.
6. Place the quail flat into the prepared baking pan, breast side up. Pour the gravy from the skillet evenly over the quail. Wrap the pan tightly with aluminum foil. Pierce the foil 6 to 7 times with small air holes.
7. Bake for 1 hour. Remove from the oven and rest for 5 minutes before serving.
Serves 8 (one quail each person)

Just about anything is good cooked over an open flame, and quail and dove are no exception. This method is extremely easy; the small birds cook quickly and require little seasoning or prep work. Some people wrap theirs with bacon in order to keep them moist, and, while I find that is fine, you end up tasting grilled bacon instead of grilled bird in many cases. The secret here is to cook them until just done; don't allow them to dry out on the charcoal. My buddy Mike Giles does a simple overnight marinade and then cooks the birds with a brick on top or a heavy pan. The birds are excellent this way. Serve these with a Caesar salad and you will have a splendid meal.

Grilled Quail or Dove

Ingredients
8 fully dressed, spatchcocked or deboned quail or doves
1 cup of marinade (see recipes below)

Directions
1. Marinate the birds overnight, turning two or three times in the process. Remove from the marinade and drain. Discard leftover marinade.
2. Place the quail or doves over hot coals (or on your Green Egg, or whatever sort of outdoor grill you have). Set atop the birds a few bricks wrapped in aluminum foil, or a heavy bottomed pan or two. A bacon press works as well. Cook 2 to 3 minutes, turn, put the weights back on the birds, and cook another 2 to 3 minutes. Remove from heat and serve immediately.
Serves 4 as an entrée, 8 as an appetizer

With quails being white meat, a lemony dressing to me befits the dish.

Lemon Marinade—Quail

Ingredients
¼ cup lemon juice
2 teaspoons Dijon mustard
1½ teaspoons fresh thyme, minced
1 teaspoon garlic, minced
1 teaspoon lemon zest, minced
½ teaspoon kosher salt
¼ teaspoon white pepper
¾ cup olive oil

Directions
1. Whisk together all ingredients except for the olive oil.
2. When well blended, slowly drizzle in the olive oil, whisking the entire time, until all ingredients are fully incorporated.
Makes 1 cup

Doves are dark meat through and through, and they usually taste a bit gamier than quail. This robust marinade is excellent for grilling these lovely morsels.

Red Wine Marinade—Doves

Ingredients
¼ cup red wine vinegar, or balsamic vinegar
2 teaspoons Dijon mustard
1½ teaspoons fresh thyme, minced
1 teaspoon garlic, minced
1 teaspoon coarsely ground black pepper
½ teaspoon kosher salt
¾ cup peanut oil

Directions
1. Whisk together all ingredients except for the peanut oil until well blended.
2. Slowly drizzle in the peanut oil, making sure all items are fully incorporated.

Makes 1 cup

The late Tina Stoddard of Savannah was a fabulous cook and often catered private dinner parties. She made a marinade for birds using just peanut oil and soy sauce. I've added in a bit of garlic and black pepper to give it a bit more kick. This recipe is good to use for grilled dove, quail, Cornish hen, or chicken wings.

Simple Marinade—Quail or Doves

Ingredients
½ cup lower sodium soy sauce
2 teaspoons fresh garlic, minced
1 teaspoon coarsely ground black pepper
½ cup peanut oil

Directions
1. Place the ingredients in a plastic container with a top. Close tightly and shake vigorously. If making in advance, shake again before serving.
Makes 1 cup

One of the best pairings—which is arch Southern—for quail and dove, whether fried or otherwise, is a side of tiny baby butter beans. While having fresh ones is ideal, they aren't always growing during bird seasons. However, there are any number of good frozen choices at the grocery store if you don't "put up" your own. My favorite brand is McKenzie's petite deluxe; Pictsweets and Birdseye brands carry them as well. The texture and flavor go perfectly with the fowl and either rice or grits.

Baby Butter Beans

Ingredients
1 pound small baby butterbeans, shelled
2 cups low-sodium chicken broth
2 slices side meat (or a small ham hock, or 2 pieces thick-sliced bacon)
3 tablespoons melted butter

Directions
1. Place all the ingredients in a medium-sized pot and bring to a boil. Stir and reduce heat to a low simmer.
2. Cook, uncovered, for 25 to 30 minutes, stirring occasionally, until the beans are tender. Serve hot, using a slotted spoon to drain the pot liquor as you plate the beans.
Serves 6 to 8

The abundance of creeks, rivers, and low-lying swampy areas in Middle Georgia provided for great duck hunting in the wintertime. Ringnecks, teals, and wood ducks are in abundance. My dad and I would get up well before dawn to be in our spots waiting as the birds would come flying in as the sun rose—and those birds are fast! I became too anxious one morning taking a shot, and buckshot knocked my dad's hunting cap off his head. By God's good grace, he wasn't hurt, but he sure did tear up my twelve-year-old butt with his belt….

Mom would roast the duck in a way similar to a baked hen, stuffing the cavity with onions, celery, and carrots. The process included draining off a good bit of fat during the baking time and making sure that the skin crisped well without the bird drying out. I prefer cooking just the duck breast, one that has had the bones removed—which you can find at specialty grocery stores like Fresh Market and Whole Foods (or order online). The following recipe is my favorite for a dinner party or for just Tom and me as a winter supper. It is easy to prepare, and the blackberry sauce gives a sweet, rich finish to the bird. My favorite sides with this dish include nutty brown rice and sautéed asparagus.

Seared Duck Breast with Blackberry Sauce

Ingredients
6 (8-ounce) or 4 (12-ounce) boneless duck breasts, skin on
1½ teaspoons kosher or sea salt
1½ teaspoons black pepper
2 teaspoons olive oil
¼ cup shallots, minced
2 teaspoons fresh thyme, minced (or ½ teaspoon dried)
1 bay leaf
1 cup low-sodium chicken stock
½ cup blackberry jam (lingonberry, plum, and peach can be used as well)
2 tablespoons butter

Directions
1. If the duck breasts vary in thickness—some are meatier than others—flatten slightly (but *do not* beat them; the breasts are tender) with a mallet or rolling pin until about 2 inches thick, being careful not to pull off the skin.
2. With a sharp knife, score the fat side of the breast in diagonal lines 1 inch apart. Do not cut all the way to the meat, just leave visible cuts to help render the fat.
3. Pat the breasts completely dry with paper towels. Evenly sprinkle the breasts on both sides with the salt and pepper.
4. Heat a large cast iron or other heavy, seasoned skillet over medium-low. When fully heated, add the olive oil and allow to become fragrant, about 1 minute.
5. Add the breasts, skin side down. Do not overcrowd. You may have to cook these in 2 batches. Cook for 15 to 20 minutes, depending on the size of the breast—the smaller ones will cook more quickly than the larger ones. While the breasts are cooking, drain off the fat occasionally with a ladle or turkey baster. Allow 2 to 3 tablespoons to remain in the pan at all times.

Place the reserved fat in a container with a cover and refrigerate; it will keep for several months. The fat is excellent to use with roasted potatoes.

6. When browned and crisped, turn the breasts over. Continue to cook for 5 minutes.
7. Remove the breasts to a rack and set aside. Drain off all but 3 tablespoons of the fat.
8. Turn the heat up to medium-high and add the shallots. Sauté 2 minutes, stirring; don't allow them to brown. Add the thyme and bay leaf. Stir to mix.
9. Pour in the stock and stir. Continue cooking, and stirring, until the stock reduces to ¼ cup, about 3 to 4 minutes.
10. Add the jam and butter and whisk until melted. Remove from heat.
11. To serve, slice the breasts crosswise into ½-inch pieces. Fan the slices across each plate, and drizzle with the sauce.

Serves 8

To close the chapter, Pat Hackney provided two favorite recipes for dessert. The first, lime cooler pie, is one that she and her fellow volunteers served those first years at the wild game fundraiser dinner. The pies are light and wonderfully tart, perfect to end a big meal. Pat says that this dish is also a family favorite and something she prepares whenever they visit.

Lime Cooler Pie

Ingredients
6 ounces frozen limeade concentrate, thawed
1 can sweetened condensed milk
1 (12-ounce) container Cool Whip
2 to 3 drops green food coloring
2 (9-inch) graham cracker pie shells

Directions
1. In a large bowl, mix the limeade, milk, and whipped topping with electric mixer.
2. Add coloring to desired shade; mix again until the color is consistent.
3. Pour into pie shells. Cover and freeze until ready to serve.

Serves 12

One of Pat's most memorable community projects was the Great Savannah Square-Lift. This culinary dynamo was asked to create a way to honor the 20,000 troops from nearby Ft. Stewart's 24th Infantry deployed to Saudi Arabia during the first Gulf War. She quickly developed a recipe for what she called Savannah Squares (aptly named after the city's historic downtown parks). A thousand volunteers were recruited to bake and package five tons of these sweet squares in one day. Pat and nine other volunteers then traveled to Saudi Arabia to personally deliver the cookies to the troops. The $500,000-project was funded by local and national corporate sponsors. Our servicepeople were overwhelmed by the show of patriotic love through food.

Pat Hackney's Savannah Squares

Ingredients
8 tablespoons (1 stick) butter, at room temperature
1 cup firmly packed light brown sugar
¾ cup white granulated sugar
1 teaspoon vanilla extract
2 large eggs
2½ cups self-rising flour
6 ounces semisweet chocolate morsels
½ cup pecans, chopped

Directions
1. Preheat oven to 375 degrees.
2. Cream together butter, sugars, and vanilla until smooth.
3. Beat in the eggs one at a time.
4. Add the flour to the mixture ½ cup at a time, beating as you add. Scrape down the batter from the sides of the bowl during the process.
5. Stir in chocolate morsels and nuts.
6. Spread the dough in a greased 15½ x 10½ x 1 baking pan. Bake 20 to 25 minutes.
7. Remove from the oven and allow to cool 15 minutes. Cut into 2- or 3-inch squares.
Makes 15 to 20 squares

Mr. Cleve Freeman with a big catch, near Claxton, 1949

The talented Pat Hackney in her kitchen with a batch
of homemade Meyer lemon marmalade

Chapter 14

Touchdown Tailgates

Tailgating is an American tradition popular from coast to coast; however, in the South we take this pastime to a fevered level. Families pitch their folding tables in the same spots year after year, and there is always a friendly rivalry between neighbors on who will have the tastiest and most attractive spread for the big game day. In Dixie, we enjoy a longer season of sun and warmth, allowing us to enjoy our outdoor dining until the end of pigskin season. In the Deep South, it can be downright hot through the middle of October. The weather always sets the gauge on what I will be preparing for that particular weekend outing. For those Indian summer days of fall, I have some incredible recipes that can be served chilled or at room temperature. They are full of flavor, satisfying to both the men and women in your crowd, and will garner the envious attention of the next-tent-over tailgaters. My goal (no pun intended) here is to give readers new ideas for the pre-game meal—not that I don't love a platter of hot wings or a layered taco dip—but let's admit, those dishes can become a bit monotonous.

My lineup starts with a throwback from the 1970s, a French onion dip with chips. Most of us grew up with that standby coming out of a can or made with an envelope of dried onion soup mix and sour cream. This homemade version will bring rave reviews. It is great with potato chips, fresh vegetables, or pickled okra. Important note here: don't use Vidalia or other sweet onions in this recipe. The sugar content in those varieties makes the dip taste more like an onion-flavored frosting than a savory spread.

JSB's Caramelized Onion Dip

Ingredients
2 tablespoons vegetable or olive oil
4 tablespoons butter
3 cups white or yellow onions, chopped
½ teaspoon salt
⅛ teaspoon cayenne pepper
4 ounces cream cheese, at room temperature
8 ounces sour cream
Chopped chives for garnish
Potato chips, crudité, pickled okra for accompaniment

Directions
1. Place a large saucepan over medium heat; add the oil and butter and stir until the butter is melted.
2. Add the onions; sauté for about 3 minutes until the onions are soft and wilted. Turn the heat down between low and medium-low; cover the pan.
3. Let the onions cook and sweat, stirring every few minutes.
4. After the onions begin to brown lightly, remove the cover and continue cooking. You want the vegetables to finish with a nutty-brown color and reduce to less than half their original volume. This process will take 20 to 25 minutes.
5. Remove the onions from the stove and cool for 10 minutes. Add the onions and cream cheese to a mixer and mix until well blended, then add the sour cream, continuing to mix until thoroughly blended.
6. Transfer the dip to a bowl; cover tightly and refrigerate 4 hours or overnight.
7. To serve, place in a bowl and garnish with chopped chives.

Serves 10 to 12 as an appetizer

The next recipe is for grilled pork tenderloin sliders, one of the most popular dishes I make for tailgating. Served on soft buns with garlic and rosemary aioli (see index), a thin slice of tomato, and a bite of arugula, you'll have a hard time keeping them on your serving platter. While the look of this dish definitely says "gourmet," these jewels are a hearty and filling way to please your crowd. Trust me, the fellas love them.

Grilled Pork Tenderloin Sliders

Ingredients
2 pork tenderloins, about 3 pounds total
2 tablespoons Worcestershire sauce
1 tablespoon kosher salt
1 tablespoon onion powder
2 tablespoons olive oil
Garlic and rosemary aioli (see index)
3 ripe but firm Roma tomatoes, cut into thin, round slices
3 cups baby arugula
16 slider buns

Directions
1. Rinse the tenderloins and wipe dry with paper towels. In a large bowl, combine the meat along with the Worcestershire, salt, onion powder, and olive oil. Set aside and allow to come to room temperature.
2. Fire up your grill to the point it is ready for the meat. Cook the tenderloins, turning occasionally, for 15 to 20 minutes until the meat is medium to medium-well in temperature. Remove from heat and allow to cool for about 10 minutes. Place the meat in a covered container, and refrigerate until chilled, about 4 hours or overnight. (The meat is much easier to slice when cold).
3. When ready to serve, cut the tenderloin crosswise into ½-inch-thick slices and set aside.
4. To make the sandwiches, spread some of the aioli on each slice of the rolls, add one piece of pork along with a slice of tomato, and several arugula leaves. Place in airtight containers and keep refrigerated until ready to serve.

Serves 16 as an appetizer

My next dish is a coastal favorite, Peel 'n' Eeat Shrimp with Ginned-Up Cocktail Sauce. Let your neighbors get a good look at these beautiful prawns, served chilled on a big platter alongside an outstanding sauce taken to another level by adding in a good shot of dry gin. Talk about tailgate envy! Just make sure to include some wet napkins on your tables: people get into a feeding frenzy with this dish: peels start flying and sauce gets splattered!

There are two main directions for this easy coastal classic: First, use *only* wild-caught, fresh USA shrimp. Imported shrimp from Malaysia or other countries from across the Pacific just don't hold a candle to the taste or quality of our Atlantic or Gulf coast harvests; the differences are undeniably evident. Second, do *not* overcook. Once a shrimp is overcooked there is not a thing you can do with that rubbery texture except maybe put it into a food processor to make shrimp butter.

Peel 'n' Eat Shrimp with Ginned-Up Cocktail Sauce

Ingredients
3 quarts water
⅓ cup Old Bay seasoning
3 pounds large, fresh, wild-caught USA shrimp, unpeeled
Ginned-up cocktail sauce (recipe follows)

Directions
1. In a large pot, bring the water and Old Bay to a steady boil.
2. Add the shrimp, stir, and cook for 4 to 5 minutes. The shrimp are done when their tail portion curves inward, almost but not quite touching the head.
3. Drain the shrimp but do not rinse; allow to cool for 15 minutes. Place in container with a tight-fitting lid and refrigerate 4 to 6 hours, or overnight. Serve with the Ginned-Up Cocktail Sauce and plenty of napkins!
Serves 10 to 12 as an appetizer

I read somewhere years ago that the secret to a zesty and bright cocktail sauce was the addition of a little dry gin; try it and see how it will liven up (even more) this wonderful dish.

Ginned-Up Cocktail Sauce

Ingredients
1½ cups ketchup
4 tablespoons prepared horseradish
2 tablespoons lemon juice
2 tablespoons Worcestershire sauce
2 tablespoons dry gin, such as Beefeater or Boodles

Directions
1. Mix all ingredients together.
2. Cover and chill for 2 hours.
Serves 10 to 12 as an appetizer

My friend Corinne Reeves of Bluffton, South Carolina, gave me Lee Bailey's *Portable Food* cookbook for my birthday in 1997. Corinne is an excellent cook and hostess, and I have always admired her skills when it comes to food preparation. In *Portable Food* there is a pasta salad recipe that's especially appealing. I've tweaked it a bit (though the original was delicious as presented), and it is a big touchdown when it comes to popularity with guests and friends. You'll enjoy the great burst of flavor the fresh dill gives this salad, which is accentuated even more by the tartness of sour cream.

Dilled Bowtie Pasta & Pea Salad

Ingredients
1 pound bowtie (farfalle) pasta, cooked to package directions and thoroughly drained
1 cup dill pickles, diced
1½ cups frozen small English peas, defrosted, drained, and dried with paper towels
½ cup green onion, diced
1 cup sour cream
1 cup mayonnaise
½ cup fresh dill, minced
4 tablespoons red bell pepper, diced
½ teaspoon kosher salt
½ teaspoon black pepper

Directions
1. In a large bowl place all ingredients together and stir to mix well.
2. Cover and chill at least 4 hours or overnight. Toss before serving.
Serves 10 to 12 as an appetizer

For something sweet for this chapter, there needed to be a dish that would transport easily and have the tastes of fall—and a sweet potato pound cake fits the bill perfectly. This moist cake has the aromatic flavors of cinnamon, allspice, and brown sugar and holds together well when sliced. You can, if you'd like, make a simple powdered sugar glaze to dress the cake, but for ease I pull out a can of Redi-Whip and give each slice a fizzy squirt.

Sweet Potato Pound Cake

Ingredients
3 cups all-purpose flour
2 teaspoons baking powder
1 teaspoon baking soda
1 teaspoon salt
1 teaspoon cinnamon
½ teaspoon allspice
2 cups light brown sugar
1 cup butter, at room temperature
2 tablespoons Crisco
4 large eggs
1½ cups baked sweet potatoes, peeled and mashed (about 2 pounds)
8 ounces cream cheese, at room temperature
2 teaspoons vanilla
1 cup pecans, chopped
Sweetened whipped cream

Directions
1. Preheat the oven to 325 degrees. Grease and flour a Bundt pan. Grease and flour a piece of waxed paper for the bottom of the pan, and place inside.
2. In a bowl, sift together flour, baking powder, baking soda, salt, cinnamon, and allspice. Set aside.
3. In another large bowl, cream together on high speed the sugar, butter, and Crisco until smooth.
4. Into the creamed mixture beat the eggs, one at a time, alternating with the mashed sweet potatoes and cream cheese.
5. Add the vanilla and mix on low speed for about 10 seconds.
6. Complete the batter by adding the sifted ingredients into the bowl, 1 cup at a time, and beating on low speed until just mixed together. Scrape the dough from the sides of the mixing bowl after each addition of the sifted ingredients.
7. Using a spatula, spread the batter evenly into the prepared pan.
8. Sprinkle the pecans evenly on top and press down gently.
9. Bake for 1 hour or until done. An inserted toothpick should come out clean.
10. Place cooked cake on a wire rack and cool completely before removing from the pan.
11. Slice and serve with sweetened whipped cream.
Serves 16 to 20

Chapter 15

To Dottie, with Love

One of my dearest friends ever was Dottie Eisenberg Lynch of Savannah. Though tiny of stature, she was quietly strong of opinion. A graduate of Sarah Lawrence, she also attended the Sorbonne in Paris, received a doctorate in Irish studies, and was one of the brightest people I've met; her grasp of politics and world affairs was astounding. Her personal style was understated but of the best quality; she had a truly amazing collection of jewelry that would be the envy of a duchess—yet she'd only wear one or two pieces at a time because anything more would be ostentatious. Dottie was one of the first of Tom's friends I met when we began dating in 1989. She immediately took me under her wing and introduced me to her many friends in the city. Having her stamp of approval was a coveted gift, and over the years she and I cooked and entertained together in our kitchens hundreds of times, celebrating holidays, birthdays, and friendship. Dottie's food, like her personality, was elegant but simple: only the best ingredients, and not too many of them. A repast in her dining room, with the museum-quality paintings and silver, was always memorable. We lost Dottie in 2017 unexpectedly, and it took a piece of my heart, as it did the many others who loved her so dearly. To close out this book, I wanted to remember her—with you—through a few of her favorite recipes, ones that keep her close by when I prepare them. My hope is that each of you have your own friend such as Dottie Lynch, like I did, to enrich your life.

This first recipe, while a bit pricy to put together, could not be simpler or more delicious. Don't let the simplicity or minimum of ingredients fool you; it is an amazing and impressive dish to serve.

Dottie's Crab & Shrimp Supreme

Ingredients

2 quarts water
2½ teaspoons kosher salt, divided
2 pounds large, fresh, wild-caught USA shrimp, peeled and deveined
¼ teaspoon sweet paprika
¼ teaspoon black pepper
3 tablespoons white vinegar
3 tablespoons fresh lemon juice
⅔ cup vegetable oil (not olive oil)
2 pounds fresh, special lump crab meat
⅓ cup mayonnaise
Lettuce leaves for garnish

Directions

1. Bring the water and 2 tablespoons kosher salt to a boil; add the shrimp and stir. Cover and remove from heat. Steep for 5 to 7 minutes until just done; the shrimp should be curled with the tail almost touching the head. Drain.
2. In a mixing bowl, add the remaining salt, the paprika, pepper, vinegar, and lemon juice. Stir to mix, then slowly drizzle in the oil, whisking constantly until fully incorporated.
3. Place the shrimp and vinaigrette in a gallon-sized sealable plastic bag. Toss to coat and refrigerate. Chill 4 hours or so; shake to mix 2 or 3 times while refrigerated.
4. Add the lump crab to the bag and toss gently to coat. Refrigerate another hour.
5. In a mixing bowl, whisk the mayonnaise until creamy and smooth. Remove the crab and shrimp from the refrigerator and add the mayonnaise. Toss gently to coat. Refrigerate another hour. Serve the shrimp and crab with a slotted spoon, draining some of the dressing before placing it on a bed of lettuce leaves.

Serves 8 as a main course, 16 as an appetizer

Dottie dearly loved cucumber soup; it was her absolute favorite dish to have for a summer supper. I worked on a recipe just for her and came up with the one below. It is the gentle, almost indiscernible heat of the jalapeño that brings out the flavor of the lemon and the herbs. Not to brag, but Dottie and everyone else I have served this dish to says it is the best cucumber soup they've ever sampled.

Friends Carolyn Stillwell (left) and Dottie Lynch at mine and
Tom's wedding dinner, New York City, December 2013

Herbed Cucumber Soup

Ingredients
3 large cucumbers, peeled, seeded, and cut into chunks
1¼ teaspoon kosher salt, divided
2 cups Greek style plain whole-milk yogurt (do not use a nonfat variety)
3 tablespoons fresh lemon juice
¼ cup fresh chives, minced and divided
1 teaspoon garlic, minced
¼ cup lightly packed fresh dill, minced
1 tablespoon fresh tarragon, minced (or 1 teaspoon dried)
1 tablespoon fresh parsley, minced
¼ teaspoon fresh jalapeño pepper, minced
¼ teaspoon ground white pepper
Thinly sliced lemons and chives for garnish

Directions
1. Place the cucumber in a colander and toss with ¼ teaspoon of the salt; allow it to drain for about 20 minutes. Blot dry with paper towels.
2. Place the cucumbers, yogurt, lemon juice, 1 tablespoon of the chives, garlic, dill, tarragon, parsley, jalapeño, white pepper, and remaining salt in a blender. Purée until smooth.
3. Pour the soup into an airtight container and refrigerate 6 hours or overnight.
4. To serve, stir well, and ladle into chilled bowls, garnishing with the remaining chives and the lemon slices.

Serves 8

Dottie and Tom took cooking lessons with the late, great Anne Thornberry in Savannah. The following recipe was one of her masterpieces, and Dottie used it as a favorite appetizer and entrée for dinner parties. Our mimeographed copy of the recipe is dated from summer 1975.

Salmon Timbales with Hollandaise Sauce

Ingredients
½ pound skinless, boneless salmon filet (1½ cups when cooked and flaked)
1 teaspoon olive oil
½ teaspoon kosher salt
3 teaspoons fresh lemon juice, divided
3 tablespoons butter plus additional for cooking molds, at room temperature
⅓ cup panko breadcrumbs

1 cup heavy cream
Pinch of cayenne pepper
Pinch of salt and pepper
½ teaspoon Worcestershire sauce
1½ teaspoons fresh parsley, minced
2 eggs, separated
Hollandaise sauce (recipe follows)

Directions
1. Preheat oven to 350 degrees.
2. Butter four 6-ounce cooking molds. Set aside.
3. Brush the salmon filet on both sides with the olive oil, then sprinkle with salt. Place the filet on a piece of aluminum foil and pour 1½ teaspoons of the lemon juice on top. Wrap and seal the filet completely, crimping the sides and edges. Cook on a baking sheet for 15 minutes or until just done. Remove from oven, unwrap the filet and allow it to cool.
4. In a saucepan over medium heat melt the butter and add the crumbs. Stir in the cream, and the pinches of cayenne, salt, and pepper. Add the remaining lemon juice and the Worcestershire; cook, stirring until smooth.
5. Remove the cream sauce from the stove and add parsley. Stir.
6. In another bowl, whisk together the 2 egg yolks then slowly drizzle them into the sauce, whisking constantly. Return the pan to the stove and cook, stirring, for 2 to 3 minutes. Remove from heat and stir in the salmon, measured out to 1½ cups flaked fish.
7. Pour 1 quart of water into a pot over medium-high heat; bring to a steady simmer while working on step 8 below.
8. In a separate bowl, beat 2 egg whites in a mixer until stiff, about 3 minutes. Fold the egg whites into the salmon mixture. Spoon the mixture in the buttered molds. Place the molds in a baking dish with 3-inch sides. Pour the hot water into the baking dish halfway up the molds.
9. Bake for 30 minutes or until set. To serve, turn out on heated plates and drizzle with the hollandaise sauce.

Serves 4

Hollandaise Sauce

Ingredients
3 egg yolks
1 teaspoon water
½ pound (2 sticks) butter
Pinch of salt

To Dottie, with Love

⅛ teaspoon white pepper
1 teaspoon lemon juice

Directions
1. In the top of the boiler, which should sit over very hot but not boiling water, combine the egg yolks and 1 teaspoon of water. Whisk well until light and fluffy.
2. Add in 5½ tablespoons of butter, whisking constantly until the mixture thickens slightly. Repeat with three, 3½ tablespoon butter portions, one at a time.
3. When the mixture is thickened well, add the salt, white pepper, and lemon juice. Serve immediately.
Makes approximately 1 cup

I learned this quick but excellent béarnaise sauce from Dottie. Yes, there are raw eggs in it, but if your eggs are fresh, you need not worry. This version is so much easier, and just as flavorful, as one you make in a double boiler.

Dottie's Béarnaise Sauce

Ingredients
½ cup dry white wine or dry vermouth
1 tablespoon shallot, minced
½ teaspoon dried tarragon
4 egg yolks
½ cup butter, melted
1 teaspoon fresh parsley, chopped

Directions
1. In a saucepan, cook the wine, shallot, and tarragon over medium-high heat until it is reduced to a glaze, 2 tablespoons or so.
2. Place the yolks in a blender and add in the glaze. Pulse on high 3 times.
3. With the mixer running, slowly drizzle in the butter. Add the parsley, pulse again once or twice, and serve.
Makes ¾ cup

Those two boys—and that girl from Butler, having late-night fun
at a Columbus, Georgia, Waffle House, 2017

Acknowledgments

Sincere and heartfelt thanks go out to the folks who generously contributed recipes and stories so that *Cook & Celebrate!* could become a reality. You have my utmost appreciation!

Thanks, too, to the wonderful folks at Mercer University Press for believing in me a third time. Please know how much I appreciate each of you, both professionally and personally.

And in closing, thanks go out to my two best friends of almost fifty years: Melinda Kay Allen Choppa and Alphus Christopher Spears. These comrades have been steadfast in their love, as well as being equally determined to "keep me humble." Chris, an educator, "pre-edited" all three of my cookbooks before I sent them off to MUP; he and I met in seventh grade and have remained inseparable since. We met Mindy, who lived about thirty miles away in Taylor County, after being introduced in the old Canteen at Rock Eagle 4-H Center, circa 1978. The three of us became fast friends and still make quite the trio; we have always, always excelled at having a good time. My mother would exasperatingly refer to us sometimes as, with a roll of her eyes, "those two boys [sigh]…and that girl from Butler." Thanks, Mindy and Chris, for keeping it fun, and for keeping it real. Love you both.

Index of Recipes

Beverages
Chatham Artillery Punch 32
Cucumber Gin Martini 163
Grapefruit & Tequila Martini 163
Grasshopper 24
Irish Coffee 24-25
Merry Bloody Mary 96
Pops's Eggnog 95
Southern Wassail 140–o41
Sparkling Flower Hibiscus Cocktail 163-64

Breads
Buttermilk Biscuits 93
Cornbread 18
Garlic Toast Points 126
Gram's Italian Egg Bread 48-49
Irish Soda Bread 29-30
Joyce's Hush Puppies 209
Ninnie's Hoecakes 210-11
Richmond Spoon Bread 94
Southern Scones 153-54

Breakfast Items
Baked Virginia Ham 92
Breakfast Tater Tot Casserole 97
Buttermilk Biscuits 93
Creamy Grits 208
Spoon Bread 94

Desserts
Cakes
Coconut Cake 49-50
Devil's Food Cake 83-84
Jingles's Sad Pound Cake 172
Lynda Talmadge's Lemon Cheese Cake 52

Index

Index